Inflation, Stock Price and Housing Cost:
Empirical Studies

Kilman Shin

Western Carolina University

Center for Economic Analysis
George Mason University
Fairfax, Va. 22030

Inflation, Stock Price and Housing Cost:

Empirical Studies

Inflation, Stock Price and Housing Cost:
Empirical Studies

Library of Congress Card Catalog Number: 77-84026

Printed in the United States of America

Center for Economic Analysis
George Mason University
Fairfax, Va. 22030

In Honor of
   Dr. and Mrs. William P. Snavely

Preface

Some of the influential economics books include: Adam Smith, *An Inquiry into the Nature and Causes of the Wealth of Nations* (1776), Thomas Robert Malthus, *An Essay on the Principle of Population* (1798), Karl Marx, *Das Kapital* (1867, 1885, 1894), and John Maynard Keynes, *The General Theory of Employment, Interest, and Money* (1936).

It is quite clear that the economists have chosen the important topics of their times and societies as their book titles. In this fashion, a number of years ago, the following titles of economics were published: *The Affluent Society* (John K. Galbraith, 1958), *Is the Business Cycle Obsolete?* (ed. by Martin Bronfenner, 1969), and *The Political Economy of Prosperity* (Arthur Okun, 1970). However, in recent years, such an optimism is apparently gone. Recent titles of economic publications include: *The Limits to Growth: A Report for the Club of Rome's Project on the Predicament of Mankind* (D.H. Meadows et al., 1972, 1974), *The No-Growth Society* (M. Olson and H.H. Landsberg, eds., 1973), *The End of Affluence* (Paul and Anne Ehrlich, 1974), *The End of Progress* (E.F. Renshaw, 1976), *The Joyless Economy* (T. Scitovsky, 1976), and *The Age of Uncertainty* (John K. Galbraith, 1977).

It appears that people are alarmed by the sudden realization of shortages or the high cost of natural resources including petroleum, gas, and other raw materials. Under the threat of shortages of such raw materials, an economic pessimism is apparently spreading all over the world today...not only in the capitalistic economy but also in the socialistic economy as well.

Indeed, the current economic society does not have only one single economic problem, but a multiple of economic problems, including inflation, unemployment, the ever increasing burden of taxes, housing shortage, pollution, crime, and urban congestion.

This book deals with some of the above important current economic problems with the empirical data. The first six chapters of this book deal with inflation, unemployment, tax burden, stock market, and investment with reference to the effects of inflation.

Chapter 1, "The Causes of Inflation and Unemployment: An International Comparison," reviews inflation theories and examines the variables which can explain the international differences in the rates of inflation and unemployment.

Chapter 2, "The Stock Prices and Inflation: The Monetary Model vs the Income Model," shows the empirical evidence that the high rate of inflation tends to suppress the stock prices. Chapter 3, "The Rate of Interest and Inflation: An International Comparison," shows that the rate of inflation tends to push up the rate of interest. Chapter 4, "The Burden of Tax and Inflation: An International Comparison," shows that inflation tends to increase the burden of tax. Chapter 5, "The Investment Ratio and Inflation: An International Comparison," tests the effect of inflation on the investment ratio. Chapter 6, "The Causes of High Inflation in South Korea, 1945-60," is a case study of causes of high inflation.

The second part of the book, namely, chapters 7-12 deal with other currently important economic and financial topics. Chapter 7, "The Keynesian Model with the Changing Supply of Money," shows the relationship between the fiscal policy and the monetary policy for economic stabilization. Chapter 8, "The Tax Burden in the U.S. States," compares the tax burden of the U.S. states. Chapter 9, "The Housing Cost and Home Ownership Rate in the U.S. States and Cities," compares the housing cost and the home ownership rate in the U.S. states and cities.

Chapter 10, "Cumulative Voting Formula: Derivation and Extension," shows how the cumulative voting formula is derived and suggests that such a voting method could be considered for a democratic decision making. Chapter 11, "The Cost of Human Capital," reviews several definitions of personal saving, consumption, and investment, and measures the cost of rearing children up to labor force as a component of the newly defined personal saving.

Finally, Chapter 12, "Home Ownership and Apartment Renting: The Comparative Cost Advantage," calculates the cost advantage of home purchase relative to apartment renting, and presents some policy implications.

This book contains articles of more than 10 years of empirical research, and during the long period, I am indebted to many persons, including Dr. William P. Snavely, Dr. Valluru B. Rao, Dr. Eun J. Kim, and Dr. Jerral C. Raymond. They have read some chapters of earlier drafts and provided very useful comments, suggestions and encouragements. Many graduate and undergraduate students provided efficient typing, key-punching and other research assistance. They include S. Lee, K. Chang, E. Pernia, and J. Grossman. The final excellent typing was accomplished by Mrs. June B. Smith. However, neither the above-mentioned persons nor the Center for Economic Analysis is responsible for the author's views expressed in this book.

It is the hope of this author that this book will contribute to a deeper understanding of the current and future economic problems.

October 15, 1977

Kilman Shin

Contents

Chapter 1

The Causes of Inflation and Unemployment: An International Comparison

I. Introduction

The high rates of inflation and unemployment have become major economic problems in many countries. However, a statistical survey shows that there is a wide range of variations in the rate of inflation and the rate of unemployment. For instance, in 1974 data, the rate of inflation ranged from 513% in Chile, 39.78% in Israel, to 6.99% in Germany (West) and 9.40% in Norway. In the U.S., the rate of inflation was 11.01%, which was a record high since World War II. As for the rate of unemployment, it ranged from 15.3% in Trinidad, 13.3% in Puerto Rico, to 1.4% in Japan, and 1.5% in Austria, Norway and Sweden.[1]

---

*The paper was presented at the annual conference of the Western Economic Association, Anaheim, California, June 20, 1977.

[1]All the data are taken or calculated from U.N., *Monthly Bulletin of Statistics*, Jan. 1977. In 1975 data, the rate of inflation ranged from 359.66% in Chile, 39.26% in Israel, to 5.98% in West Germany and 8.47 in Austria. The rate of unemployment ranged from 18.2% in Puerto Rico, 15.0% in Chile, to 1.4% in Sweden and 1.9% in Japan.

The objective of this brief paper is to review some alternative theories of inflation and unemployment, and to test if such theories can explain the international differences in the rates of inflation and unemployment. In the following sections II and III, we will review two major current theories of inflation and unemployment, namely, the quantity theory of money and the Phillips curve hypothesis. In section IV, we will present a more generalized inflation and unemployment model, in which we will point out that the quantity theory or the monetarists' argument that the natural rate of unemployment is independent of the demand-generating policy is theoretically defective. In section V, the international regression results are presented, and in the final section VI, a summary and conclusions are provided.

II. The Quantity Theory of Money

In order to review some inflation and unemployment theories, we have to discuss, first of all, the classical quantity theory of money. Given the equilibrium condition for the supply and demand,

$$MV = P Q \tag{1}$$

$$P = MV/ Q \tag{2}$$

where

M = the supply of money
V = the velocity of money
P = the level of prices
Q = the real output

In terms of the percentage growth rates, if the above variables are not constants, by totally differentiating Equation (2), we obtain:

$$\Delta P/P = \Delta M/M + \Delta V/V - \Delta Q/Q \qquad (3)$$

However, the uniqueness of the quantity theory is that the velocity and real output are independent of the supply of money and constant. So from Equation 2, we obtain,

$$\Delta P/P = \Delta M/M \qquad (4)$$

In a functional form, we may rewrite Equation (4) as,

$$\Delta P/P = F\ (\Delta M/M,\ e) \qquad (5)$$

Equation (5) states the basic quantity theory hypothesis that the rate of inflation is largely determined by the rate of increase in the supply of money, if other conditions are the same. The expected size of the coefficient of $\Delta M/M$ should be close to one.

A major controversy is concerned with the quantity theory's argument that an increase in the supply of money increases demand, but an increase in demand does not increase the supply of real output. This is, of course, in a direct conflict with the Keynesian theory that demand creates supply. The quantity theory's justification for the independence of the supply of money and the supply of real output is as follows: The demand for and the supply of labor are both functions of the real wage rate. Thus unless the real wage rate falls, the demand for labor cannot increase. Now assume that the supply of money increases. Then the actual real money balance exceeds the desired equilibrium real money balance which people wish to hold. So spending and demand increase. According to the quantity theory, the demand for commodities increases first. So the price level of the commodities rises. As the money wage rate is constant for the time being, the real wage rate W/P falls. So the demand for labor increases and the rate of unemployment decreases. However, according to the quantity theory, this is true only for the short run. Since the labor has no money illusion, and the supply of labor depends upon the real wage rate, the labor demands a higher money wage rate to catch up the previous real wage rate. Now the firms have to pay a higher money wage rate until the real wage rate is restored to the previous level. As the real wage rate rises, the demand for labor is cut back to the initial level, and so is the real output. The rate of unemployment is increased to the initial level.

In effect, an increase in the supply of money increases the demand for labor and real output only for the short run. In the long run, what has increased is only the level of prices and the proportional increase in money wage rates, maintaining the real wage rate, the real demand for labor, and the real long run output constant.[2]

---

[2]In the quantity theory, the demand for real money balances is given by:

$$M/P = F (Q, i, \Delta P^*/P, W, \ldots e)$$

where

i = the nominal rate of interest
$\Delta P^*/P$ = the expected rate of inflation
Q = real income
W = real wealth
e = the error term

When the supply of money is increased, the actual real money balance will be greater than the desired real money balance: $\overline{M}/P > M/P$. People increase spending to get rid of the excess holding of money. In this process, the price level rises, and $\overline{M}/P$ falls such that a new equilibrium is established at $\overline{M}/P = M/P$. The real money balance function may take the form of $M/Y = F(P, i, \Delta P^*/P, W, \ldots e)$.

In the Keynesian theory, the demand for money function takes the form:

$$M = F (Y, i, \ldots e) \quad , \quad \text{or } M/P = F (Q, i, \ldots e)$$

Note that in the quantity theory, the supply of and the demand for money determine the level of prices, while in the Keynesian theory, the supply of and the demand for money determine the rate of interest. See Johnson (1972).

For a good review of the quantity theory, see Humphrey (1974). For the quantity theory's argument that demand or inflation does not affect the natural

Thus under the quantity theory, the following function should "not" be significant in the long run.

$$U=F \ (\Delta M/M, \ e) \tag{6}$$

where $U=$ the rate of unemployment. According to the quantity theory, the rate of unemployment is independent of the rate of increase in the supply of money.

The quantity theory's argument that demand does not create supply nor employment is represented in Figure 1.

First, assume that the supply of money is increased by the monetary authority. The demand curve shifts up from D to D' in the commodity market of panel (a). The real output increases from Q_1 to Q_2, and the price level rises from P_1 to P_2. In the labor market of panel (b), the money wage rate is fixed for the time being. So as the price level rises, the real wage rate falls, and the supply of labor curve shifts from S to S', and the level of employment increases from L_1 to L_2. In panel (c), given the production function, employment increases from L_1 to L_2, and the real output increases from Q_1 to Q_2. Because of the concave production function, the marginal product of labor is lower at A' than at A.

However, the above situation is only for the short run. Soon the workers demand a higher money wage rate and the supply of labor curve shifts back from S' to S where the initial equilibrium real wage rate is restored. So employment is reduced to the initial level L_1 in panels (b) and (c). The supply curve in panel (a) shifts up from S to S', and the new equilibrium price level is P_3. The Keynesian IS$=$LM diagram is added in panel (d).

---

rate of unemployment, see Phelps (1967) and Friedman (1968), 1977). The natural rate of unemployment is defined as the unemployment which is determined by real as opposed to monetary factors. It is not a constant. Also see footnote 3 on the Phillips curve hypothesis.

In this paper, for simplicity, the same F notation is used for all the different functions.

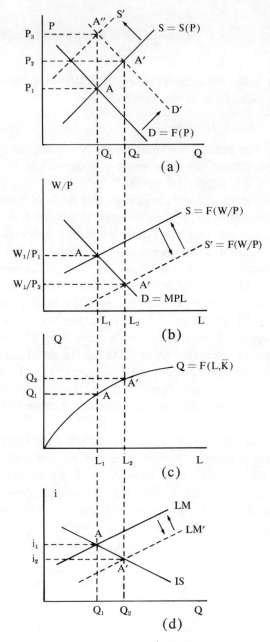

Figure 1   Classical Model

As the supply of money increases, LM curve shifts to LM'. As the rate of interest decreases, the amount of investment increases, and real output increases from Q_1 to Q_2. However, as the level of prices increases, the real money balance M/P decreases, and LM' curve shifts back to the initial LM curve, and the rate of interest is also restored to the initial rate.

The weakness of this classical quantity theory will be discussed in section V where we present a more generalized dynamic theory of inflation and unemployment.

III. The Excess Demand for Labor Theory

As a second theory of inflation and unemployment, we may list the excess demand for labor theory or the Phillips curve hypothesis. According to the theory, when the demand for labor increases, the level of employment increases and the job vacancy rate decreases. Now the workers are in a better position to demand a higher money wage rate. The firms are also willing to pay a higher money wage rate to keep the existing workers and to attract the new workers. The greater the excess demand for labor, the greater is the rate of increase in money wage rates. As the money wage rate rises, the firms will also increase the commodity prices to maintain or to increase the profit margin. In short, when the excess demand for labor increases, the rate of unemployment falls, and both the money wage rate and the rate of inflation increase. Conversely, if the excess demand for labor decreases, the rate of unemployment increases, the rate of increase in money wage rates and the rate of inflation fall.

The excess demand for labor theory may be summarized in the following equations:

$$U = F\left(\frac{S-D}{S}, e\right) \tag{7}$$

$$\Delta W/W = F(U, e) \tag{8}$$

$$\Delta P/P = F(\Delta W/W, e) \tag{9}$$

where

S = the supply of labor
D = demand for labor
U = the rate of unemployment
$\Delta W/W$ = the rate of increase in money wage rates

For the statistical test of the excess demand for labor theory various forms have been tested by many writers:

$$\Delta W/W = F (U, \Delta P^*/P, \ldots e) \tag{10}$$

$$\Delta P/P = F (U, \Delta W^*/W, \ldots e) \tag{11}$$

where

$\Delta P^*/P$ = the expcted rate of inflation, and
$\Delta W^*/W$ = the expected rate of increase in money wage rates.

When the labor anticipates a high rate of inflation during the year, then the labor will also demand a high rate of increase in money wage rates to maintain the real wage rate regardless of the current rate of unemployment. Similarly, the firm will increase the rate of inflation further if the expected rate of increase in money wage rates is higher.

Instead of the current rate of unemployment, some economists have used the reciprocal of the rate of unemployment, $1/U$. As additional independent variabls, some economists have included the lagged rate of unemployment, the weighted average rate of the past unemployment rates, the unemployment rate differential between the current and the preceding year's rates of unemployment, the difference between the overall rate of unemployment and the unemployment rate for the married males, the monopoly powers of firms and unions, social security tax, wage-price control, the profit rate, the change in the profit rate, the rate of change in the productivity of labor, income, sales, property, social security tax rates and other variables.[3]

A theoretical weakness of the excess demand for labor theory is that it is not concerned with how the excess demand for labor was generated at the beginning. In Figure 2, assume that the initial equilibrium employment level is at L_1. The excess demand for labor occurs when the demand for labor curve shifts from D to D', the excess demand for labor being L_1 L_2. The demand curve for labor can shift only when the

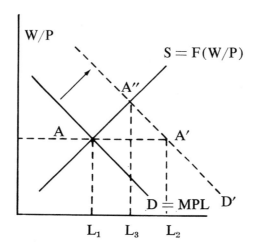

Figure 2

---

[3]The literature on the Phillips curve is too vast. Some of them are listed at the end of this paper including Phillips (1958), Lipsey (1960), Holt (1971), Kaldor (1959), Kuh (1967), Perry (1971) and Hicks (1976). A good review of the Phillips curve is summarized in Humphrey (1973, 1975, 1976).

marginal productivity of labor increases. Thus for the excess demand for labor to occur to push up the wage rate, the marginal productivity of labor must increase continuously. However, the excess demand for labor theory does not explain how the marginal productivity of labor rises continuously.

Alternatively, we may assume that the excess demand for labor was caused in the same way as in the quantity theory, i.e., by an increase in the supply of money. Then the quantity theory's argument that an increase in demand cannot increase the long run real output nor the level of employment may be applied.

IV. The Generalized Inflation Model
(Growth-Inflation Hypothesis)

As a third theory of inflation and unemployment, we present a more generalized model which can contain both the quantity theory and the Keynesian theory as special cases. We may call it a growth-inflation model or the generalized inflation model.

Given the equilibrium condition for demand and supply,

$$Y = P \ Q \tag{12}$$
$$P = Y/ \ Q \tag{13}$$
$$\text{Since } Q = A \ R \ K \tag{14}$$
$$P = Y \ / \ A \ R \ K \tag{15}$$

where

$Y =$ nominal demand
$P =$ the price level
$Q =$ the real output
$A =$ the average productivity of capital
$R =$ the capacity operation rate
$K =$ the production capacity or capital stock

Assuming that none of the above variables are constant, by the total differentiation or by the logarithmic differentiation, Equation (15) may be rewritten in the percentage growth rates:

$$\Delta P/P = \Delta Y/Y - \Delta A/A - \Delta R/R - \Delta K/K \qquad (16)$$

Equation (16) states that the rate of inflation depends upon the growth rates of demand, productivity, capacity operation, and the capital stock. It should be noted that the rate of capacity operation is not always constant. In times of energy shortage, resource bottlenecks, extremely cold or warm weather, strike, and labor shortage, the capacity operation rate will decrease, increasing the rate of inflation. Also, during the depression years, the capacity operation rate will further decrease.

On the other hand, during the period of recovery, the capital stock may not increase rapidly in the short run, but the rate of capacity operation will increase very rapidly. When the capacity operation rate reaches the maximum degree, the growth rate of capacity operation rate will become zero.

In effect, the uniqueness of Equation (16) or the generalized inflation equation is that the growth rates of productivity, the capacity operation and the capital stock are all related to the growth rate of demand. For instance, when demand increases, commodity price will tend to rise. But demand does not necessarily confine to the consumer goods, when the demand for capital goods increases and when the capital stock is expanded, the supply of real output will increase to partially offset the inflationary pressure.

For these reasons, we may assume that the growth rates of productivity, the capacity operation rate and, most of all, the capital stock, are functions of the rate of increase in demand within certain limits, and we may obtain Equation (17):

$$\Delta P/P = \Delta Y/Y \ (\ 1 - a - r - k \ ) \tag{17}$$

where

$$\Delta A/A = a\Delta Y/Y, \ \ \Delta R/R = r\Delta Y/Y, \ \text{and} \ \Delta K/K = k\Delta Y/Y.$$

In terms of the quantity equation of money, the growth rate of demand is equal to

$$\Delta Y/Y = \Delta M/M + \Delta V/V \tag{18}$$

Substituting Equation (18) into (17), we obtain

$$\Delta P/P = (\Delta M/M + \Delta V/V \ ) \ (\ 1 - a - r - k \ )$$

or

$$\Delta P/P = \Delta M/M \ (1 - a - r - k \ ) \tag{19}$$

when $\Delta V/V = 0.$[4]

---

[4]From Equation (13), by the total differentiation, we may obtain

$$\Delta P/P = \Delta Y/Y \ - \ \Delta Q/Q$$

Assuming $\Delta Q/Q = h\Delta Y/Y.$

$$\Delta P/P = \Delta Y/Y \ (\ 1 \ - \ h \ )$$

Comparing Equation (17) with the above, we notice that

$$h = a + r + k$$

We may also assume

$$\Delta Q/Q = h_0 + h\Delta M/M$$

But the growth rate of the real output should have a maximum rate beyond which it cannot increase. If the supply of money increases too rapidly, it will cause a hyperinflation or a too high rate of inflation, and the growth rate of real output will rather decrease. In such a case, both the rate of unemployment and the rate of inflation will increase. So, we may state

Equations (16) - (19) are the generalized inflation equations. They state that the rate of inflation should be less than the rate of increase in the supply of money in general cases.[5]

$$\Delta Q/Q = h_0 + h \Delta M/M \qquad \text{if } \Delta M/M < m_0$$
$$\leq q_0 \qquad\qquad\qquad \text{if } \Delta M/M \geq m_0$$

where m_0 may be regarded as the optimal rate of increase in the supply of money for the maximum economic growth rate. For another variation of Equation (16) see footnote 10.

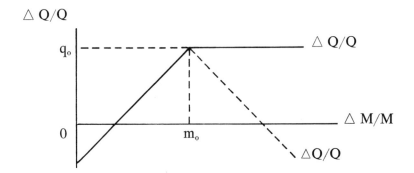

[5]In terms of the elasticity, J.M. Keynes presents "the generalized statement of the quantity theory of money":

$$e = e_d (1 - e_e e_0 + e_e e_0 e_w)$$

where

e = price elasticity of money supply,
e_d = liquidity demand for money elasticity with respect to the supply of money,
e_e = employment elasticity with respect to demand,
e_0 = output elasticity with respect to demand,
e_w = wage rate elasticity of demand.

(J.M. Keynes, *The General Theory of Employment, Interest, and Money*, 1936, Harbinger ed., 1964, p. 305. "And obviously there is a variety of other special cases in which $e = 1$. But in general e is not unity; and it is perhaps, safe to make the generalization that on plausible assumptions relating to the real world, and excluding the case of a 'flight from the currency' in which e_d and e_w become large, e is, as a rule, less than unity" (p. 306).

However, the classical quantity theory or the monetarists maintain that the rate of inflation should be equal to the rate of increase in the supply of money. That would be true only if $a+r+k=0$.

The implication of the generalized inflation equation may be summarized: As demand increases, whether as a result of an increase in the supply of money, or by an increase in autonomous expenditures, such as a tax cut, export increase, or an autonomous investment increase, the level of prices tends to rise on the one hand, but as a result of an increase in demand, the capital stock, the capacity operation rate, and the productivity will tend to rise to partially offset the inflationary pressure. Thus in this generalized inflation equation, not only the aggregate demand, but also the composition of the demand will make the rate of inflation different. The greater the portion of the consumption demand, the greater will be the inflationary pressure, and the greater the portion of investment demand the less will be the inflationary pressure in the long run.

For the statistical test of the generalized inflation model, Equation (19) may be tested in the following function:

$$\Delta P/P = F \ (\Delta M/M, \dots \ e \ ) \qquad\qquad (20)$$

where the coefficient of the rate of increase in the supply of money is expected to be less than one. Recall that Equation (20) is the same as Equation (6) of the quantity theory. But the difference is concerned with the size of the regression coefficient. For the quantity theory, the coefficient is expected to be close to one, and in Equation (20), the coefficient is expcted to be significantly less than one. In other words, the price elasticity of money supply $(\Delta P/P)/(\Delta M/M)$ should be about equal to one in the quantity theory, and it should be very much smaller than one in the generalized inflation model.

Furthermore, as demand increases, output will tend to rise on the one hand, and the price and the money wage rates will tend to rise on the other hand. As the rate of economic growth increases, the rate of unemployment will tend to decrease, if other conditions are the same. Thus according to the generalized inflation model, the following functional relationships should exist:

$$\Delta Q/Q = F \ (\Delta M/M, \dots \ e \ ) \qquad\qquad (21)$$
$$U = F \ (\Delta Q/Q, \dots \ e \ ) \qquad\qquad (22)$$
$$\Delta P/P = F \ (\Delta Q/Q, \dots \ e \ ) \qquad\qquad (23)$$
$$\Delta W/W = F \ (\Delta Q/Q, \dots \ e \ ) \qquad\qquad (24)$$

The generalized inflation model is represented in Figure 3. In panel (a), the demand curve shifts from D to D' as a result of an increase in the supply of money. In the short run, the real output increases from Q_1 to Q_2 and the level of prices rises from P_1 to P_2. In panel (b), the money wage rate is constant for the time being, so the real wage rate falls, and the supply of labor curve shifts down from S to S', and employment increases from L_1 to L_2. In panel (c), employment increases from L_1 to L_2 and output increases from Q_1 to Q_2. But in the long run, workers demand a higher money wage rate to catch up the previous real wage rate. So the labor supply curve shifts back to S from S'. Thus far, the process is the same as the quantity theory.

According to the quantity theory, in such a case, the level of employment will be reduced to the initial level L_1. However, in the generalized inflation model, that will not happen. When output increases from Q_1 to Q_2, some portion of the output increase is an increase in investment goods. As a result of an increase in the capital stock, in panel (c), production function shifts upward from Q to Q', and in panel (b), the marginal product of labor or the demand for labor curve shifts from D to D'. So the new equilibrium employment is L_3 and the new equilibrium real wage rate is W_2/P_3. This process is also illustrated in panel (d)

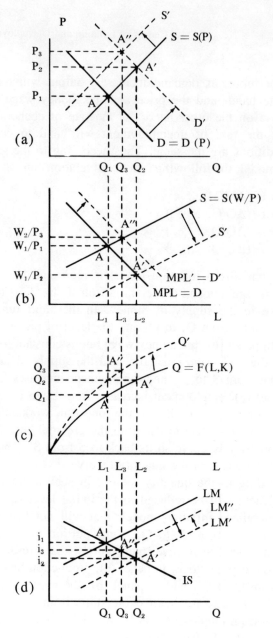

Figure 3   Growth – Inflation Model

16

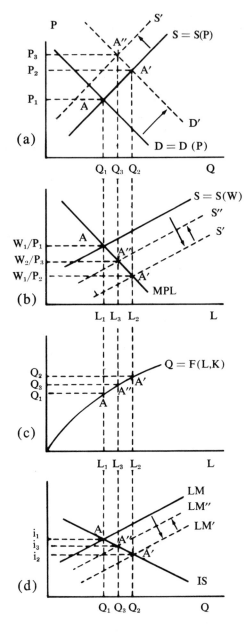

Figure 4   Keynesian Model

17

of the IS = LM diagram. When the supply of money increases LM curve shifts to LM', and the rate of interest falls. So investment increases and real output increases from Q_1 to Q_2. As the level of prices rises, the supply of real money balances falls, and LM' curve shifts up to LM'', where the new equilibrium rate of interest is i_3 and real output is Q_3.

Figure 4 depicts the effect of an increase in the supply of money in the conventional Keynesian model, which holds the capital stock and thus the demand for labor curve constant. As a result, in the Keynesian model, in panel (b), we note that employment and real output increase only as a result of a decrease in real wage rate. In summary, in the classical model, the new and the initial equilibrium real wage rates remain the same; in the conventional Keynesian model, the new equilibrium real wage rate is lower than the initial equilibrium real wage rate; and in the generalized growth-inflation model presented in this paper, the new equilibrium real wage rate should be higher than the initial equilibrium real wage rate.

V. The International Regression Results

In the preceding section, we have reviewed three theories of inflation and unemployment. In this section, we wish to test the empirical significance of the theories in explaining the international differences in the rate of inflation and the rate of unemployment. The basic data are collected for 21 countries and for the year 1974 for which the most recent data are available.[6] A total of 16 variables were calculated. All the basic data were taken from U.N., *Statistical Yearbook*, 1974-75, U.N., *Monthly*

---

[6]For 1975, the growth rate of GDP was not available for many countries, though all other data were available for the year. Table 1 provides the data for 23 countries. But we have excluded Chile and Cyprus from the regressions, considering the political and war disturbances during 1973-74 in those countries.

Bulletin of Statistics, January 1977, and International Labor Office, *Yearbook of Labor Statistics*, 1975. The variables are defined below:

$\Delta P/P$ = the rate of increase in consumer prices (%)

$\Delta M/M$ = the rate of increase in the supply of money, currency + demand deposits (%)

$\Delta N/N$ = the rate of increase in population (%)

A/Y = the agricultural income ratio, the income originating from the agricultural sector divided by GDP, gross domestic product (%)

F/Y = the foreign trade ratio, the sum of exports and imports in the absolute value divided by GDP (%)

Y = per capita national income in U.S. dollars

$\Delta W/W$ = the rate of change in money wage rates (%)

U = the rate of unemployment (%)

$\Delta Q/Q$ = the growth rate of GDP at constant prices (%)

$\Delta Q/Q(a)$ = the average annual growth rate of per capita domestic product at constant prices, 1970-74 average (%)

$\Delta Q/Q(b)$ = the average annual growth rate of total domestic product at constant prices, 1970-74 average (%)

U_{t-1} = the rate of unemployment with one year of time lag (%)

$1/U$ = the rate of unemployment, its reciprocal

$\Delta W/W_{t-1}$ = the rate of increase in money wage rates, with one year of time lag (%)

$\Delta P/P_{t-1}$ = the rate of inflation, with one year of time lag (%)

L/N = the labor force participation rate (%)

With the above variables, we have computed a large number of regression equations for a variety of combinations of the independent and dependent variables. As the ceteris paribus variables, we have included the following variables: the rate of increase in population, the agricultural income ratio as an index of industrial composition or the degree of industrialization, the foreign trade ratio as an index of openness of the economy, and per capita income which may represent the degree of economic development, capital stock, wealth or the level of economic technology. However, the per capita income was highly correlated with the agricultural income ratio. So we will present the regression results which did not include the per capita income.

Some other variables which may be significant but were not available may include the following: the size income distribution, the capital-output ratio, capital stock, social security and unemployment benefit system, the degree of political, economic and social freedom, the degree of labor unionization, the development of financial and banking systems, the index of working conditions including the work hours and fringe benefits, monopolistic market power, labor mobility, labor training programs, etc.

The international regression results were obtained by the method of ordinary least squares. Instead of presenting all the regression results in tables, for the purpose of easy reference, we will present only some selected regression results for each hypothesis:

(1) First, according to the Phillips hypothesis, a country which has a low rate of unemployment should tend to have a high rate of increase in money wage rates and a high rate of inflation. Some of the regression results are:

(R-1) $\Delta P/P = 15.6477 + 0.4359\ U_t$
        (0.81)

$$R = 0.1834 \quad \overline{R}^2 = -0.0172 \quad F = 0.6614$$

(R-2) $\Delta P/P = 0.5001 + 0.1737\ U_t + 7.2118 \Delta N/N + 0.1602 A/Y$
        (0.54)   (4.98)**   (1.00)

$\qquad -0.0402 F/Y + 0.6208\, \Delta W/W_{t-1}$
$\qquad (-0.88) \quad (3.03)$**

$$R = 0.8823 \quad \overline{R}^2 = 0.7047 \quad F = 10.5458$$

(R-3) $\Delta W/W = 20.9471 - 0.2371\,U_t$
                    (-0.46)

$\qquad\qquad\qquad R = 0.1045 \quad \overline{R}^2 = -0.0411 \quad F = 0.2098$

(R-4) $\Delta W/W = 5.9617 - 0.8135\,U_t + 1.6392\Delta N/N + 0.0821\,A/Y$
                    $(-1.56)\qquad (0.72)\qquad\qquad (0.33)$
                    $+ 0.0481\,F/Y + 1.2280\Delta P/P_{t-1}$
                    $(0.66)\qquad (2.90)^{**}$

$\qquad\qquad\qquad R = 0.6298 \quad \overline{R}^2 = 0.1956 \quad F = 1.9727$

We note that the rate of unemployment is not significant at the 5% level in any of the above regression equations. In Equation (R-4), the rate of unemployment has a negative sign as the Phillips hypothesis expects, but it is significant only at the 10% level. We have also tested the reciprocal of the rate of unemployment 1/U, but it was also not significant. However, when 1974-75 average data were used, the rate of unemployment was negative and significant at the 5% level only for the rate of increase in money wage rates $\Delta W/W$.

(R-2)′ $\Delta P/P = -3.6021 + 0.1157\,U_t + 5.8956\Delta N/N - 0.1108\,A/Y$
                    $(0.45)\qquad (4.28)^{**}\qquad (-0.64)$
                    $- 0.0308\,F/Y + 1.2323\Delta W/W_{t-1}$
                    $(-0.79)\qquad (4.46)^{**}$

$\qquad\qquad\qquad R = 0.7684 \quad \overline{R}^2 = 0.6913 \quad F = 9.9555$

(R-4)′ $\Delta W/W = 6.0252 - 0.7070\,U_t + 2.3759\Delta N/N - 0.2639\,A/Y$
                    $(-1.77)^*\qquad (1.10)\qquad\qquad (-0.96)$
                    $+ 0.0512\,F/Y + 1.5197\Delta P/P_{t-1}$
                    $(0.85)\qquad (3.15)^{**}$

$\qquad\qquad\qquad R = 0.6884 \quad \overline{R}^2 = 0.2985 \quad F = 2.7018$

---

[7]The numbers in parentheses are the t-ratios. **Significant at the 1% level, *significant at the 5% level. In order to examine the problem of multicollinearity we have added the independent variables one by one. Also we have calculated the regression equations including the per capita income. It had a high correlation with the agricultural income ratio, and the results were better without the per capita income. These procedures were taken for all other regression equations.

(2) Secondly, according to the quantity theory, a country which has a high rate of increase in the supply of money should tend to have a high rate of inflation, and the rate of increase in the supply of money should be independent of the "natural rate of unemployment," and of the real economic growth rate. Some of the regression results are:

(R-5) $\Delta P/P = 12.3923 + 0.4105 \Delta M/M$
$\qquad\qquad (2.14)^*$

$\qquad\qquad\qquad\qquad\qquad\qquad R = 0.4405 \quad \overline{R}^2 = 0.1516 \quad F = 4.574$

(R-6) $\Delta P/P = 0.5073 + 0.3101 \Delta M/M + 7.805 \Delta N/N - 0.0425 A/Y$
$\qquad\qquad\quad (2.98)^{**} \qquad\quad (6.89)^{**} \qquad\quad (-0.29)$

$\qquad\qquad\quad -0.0527 F/Y + 0.5391 \Delta W/W_{t-1}$
$\qquad\qquad\quad (-1.50) \qquad (3.27)^{**}$

$\qquad\qquad\qquad\qquad\qquad\qquad R = 0.9263 \quad \overline{R}^2 = 0.8107 \quad F = 18.132$

(R-7) $U_t = 3.6722 + 0.0806 \Delta M/M$
$\qquad\qquad (0.91)$

$\qquad\qquad\qquad\qquad\qquad R = 0.2054 \quad \overline{R}^2 = -0.0082 \quad F = 0.8370$

(R-8) $U_t = 0.1610 - 0.0522 \Delta M/M - 0.2011 \Delta N/N + 0.0602 A/Y$
$\qquad\qquad (-2.06)^* \qquad\quad (-0.73) \qquad\quad (1.76)^*$

$\qquad\qquad +0.0096 F/Y + 1.0178 U_{t-1}$
$\qquad\qquad (1.15) \qquad (16.04)^{**}$

$\qquad\qquad\qquad\qquad\qquad R = 0.9782 \quad \overline{R}^2 = 0.9426 \quad F = 66.6808$

In the above regression results, the first two equations are apparently consistent with the quantity theory in that the rate of increase in the supply of money is positively correlated with the rate of inflation and significant either at the 5% or 1% level. However, we note that in Equation (R-8), the rate of increase in the supply of money is negatively correlated with the rate of unemployment, and it is significant at the 5% level. This result does not support the quantity theory that the rate of increase in the supply of money is independent of the long-run rate of unemployment. It rather supports the generalized inflation model in which an increase in the rate of increase in the supply of money increases the growth rate of real output and the rate of inflation on the one hand, and decreases the rate of unemployment on the other.

(3) Thirdly, before we present the empirical evidence in support of the generalized inflation model or the growth rate hypothesis, we may see why the regression equations (R-5) and (R-6) are not strictly in accordance with the quantity theory hypothesis. As we have seen in sections I and III, according to the quantity theory, the coefficient of the rate of change in the supply of money or the price elasticity of the supply of money should be close to one, but it should be far below one according to the generalized inflation theory. Regression equations (R-5) and (R-6) indicate that the price elasticity of money supply is between 0.31 and 0.41. These low values of the price elasticity of money supply support the generalized inflation model rather than the quantity theory.

Next, for a more positive evidence, according to the generalized inflation model, as demand increases, the supply of real output will also increase. The regression results are:

(R-9) $\Delta Q/Q = -0.1585 + 0.2397 \Delta M/M$

$\qquad\qquad\quad$ (4.67)**

$\qquad\qquad\qquad\qquad\qquad$ R=0.7309 $\overline{R}^2$=0.5097   F=21.94

(R-10) $\Delta Q/Q = -0.3150 + 0.2352 \Delta M/M - 0.1296 \Delta N/N + 0.0149 A/Y$

$\qquad\qquad\quad$ (3.70)**   (−0.19)   (0.17)

$\qquad\qquad$ +0.0036F/Y

$\qquad\qquad$ (0.17)

$\qquad\qquad\qquad\qquad\qquad$ R=0.7320 $\overline{R}^2$=0.4198   F=4.6180

We note that the rate of increase in the supply of money is highly significant and has positive signs, as the generalized inflation model expects. Also as the real economic growth rate rises, the rate of unemployment should tend to decrease, if other conditions are the same. The regression results are:[8]

---

[8]Compare these results with the Okun's Law obtained for the U.S. economy during 1947 II-1960 IV:

(R-11) $U_t = 5.0780 - 0.1236 \Delta Q/Q$
                    (-0.45)

$$R = 0.1034 \quad \overline{R}^2 = -0.0414 \quad F = 0.2052$$

(R-12) $U_t = 0.0935 - 0.1853 \Delta Q/Q - 0.1619 \Delta N/N + 0.0558 A/Y$
                    $(-3.00)** \quad (-0.66) \quad\quad (1.95)*$

$\quad\quad\quad\quad + 0.0115 F/Y + 0.9740 U_{t-1}$
$\quad\quad\quad\quad\;\; (1.52) \quad\quad (18.17)**$

$$R = 0.9826 \quad \overline{R}^2 = 0.9540 \quad F = 83.8849$$

According to the generalized inflation model, as demand increases, output tends to increase, but the elasticity of supply is not perfectly elastic. So as demand increases, the level of prices also tends to increase, and so does the money wage rate.[9] The regression results are:

(R-13) $\Delta P/P = 14.8660 + 0.9640 \Delta Q/Q$
                            (1.57)

$$R = 0.3392 \quad \overline{R}^2 = 0.0685 \quad F = 2.4706$$

(R-14) $\Delta P/P = 9.7555 + 0.8264 \Delta Q/Q + 7.8077 \Delta N/N + 0.0070 A/Y$
                            $(2.02)* \quad\quad (5.02)** \quad\quad (0.04)$

$\quad\quad\quad\quad - 0.0608 \; F/Y$
$\quad\quad\quad\quad \;\; (-1.28)$

$$R = 0.8453 \quad \overline{R}^2 = 0.6432 \quad F = 10.0137$$

$\quad\quad\quad \Delta U = 0.30 - 0.30 \Delta Y/Y \quad\quad\quad r = 0.79$
or,
$\quad\quad\quad U_t = U_{t-1} + 0.30 - 0.30 \Delta Y/Y$

where U and $\Delta Y/Y$ are measured in percentage points. The equation implies that if the growth rate of real GNP is zero, the rate of unemployment will increase by 0.3 points from one quarter to the next due to increases in productivity and growth in labor force. If the growth rate of GNP increases by 1 percentage point, the rate of unemployment will decrease by 0.3 percentage points. Okun (1962). Also see Gordon (1977).

[9]For studies on the relationship between the economic growth and inflation, see Kaldor (1959), Kuh (1967) and Hicks (1976).

(R-15) $\Delta P/P = 5.2597 + 0.9296\,\Delta Q/Q - 1.2763\,\Delta Q/Q(a) + 8.4544\,\Delta N/N$
         (2.32)*   (−1.28)   (6.27)**

         $+\,0.0437\ A/Y\ -0.0524\ F/Y + 0.5480\,\Delta W/W_{t-1}$
         (0.29)   (1.34)   (2.95)*

                                   $R = 0.9157\quad \overline{R^2} = 0.7692\quad F = 12.107$

(R-16) $\Delta W/W = 15.7954 + 1.3711\,\Delta Q/Q$
         (2.55)**

                                   $R = 0.5055\quad \overline{R^2} = 0.2163\quad F = 6.5213$

(R-17) $\Delta W/W = 0.6540 + 1.1276\,\Delta Q/Q + 1.5966\,\Delta N/N - 0.1211\ A/Y$
         (1.83)*   (0.72)   (−0.45)

         $-\,0.0150\ F/Y + 0.7586\,\Delta P/P_{t-1}$
         (−0.24)   (1.77)*

                                   $R = 0.6540\quad \overline{R^2} = 0.2370\quad F = 2.2425$

(R-18) $\Delta W/W = -1.9499 + 0.1969\,\Delta Q/Q + 3.0939\,\Delta Q/Q(a) - 0.5061\,\Delta N/N$
         (0.31)   (2.52)*   (−0.24)

         $-\,0.0564\ A/Y + 0.0081\ F/Y + 0.9444\ \Delta P/P_{t-1}$
         (−0.24)   (0.14)   (2.52)*

                                   $R = 0.7790\quad \overline{R^2} = 0.4383\quad F = 3.601$

In the above regression equations, we note that either the short-run annual growth rate, $\Delta Q/Q$, or the long-run average annual growth rate, $\Delta Q/Q(a)$, is positive and significantly correlated with the rate of inflation or the rate of increase in money wage rates.

These results support the generalized inflation model or the growth-inflation hypothesis that when demand increases, production tends to increase on the one hand, and the rate of inflation and the rate of increase in money wage rates tend to rise on the other hand.

Table 1. The Basic International Data (1974, %)

	(1) U	(2) $\Delta P/P$	(3) $\Delta P/P$ (1973)	(4) $\Delta W/W$	(5) $\Delta W/W$ (1973)	(6) $\Delta Q/Q$	(7) $\Delta N/N$	(8) $\Delta M/M$
Australia	2.3	15.13	9.44	27.84	12.82	−0.92	1.60	−0.99
Austria	1.5	9.52	7.55	15.73	12.69	4.21	0.27	5.61
Belgium	4.0	12.66	7.00	25.49	13.99	4.02	0.31	8.84
Canada	5.4	10.96	7.51	13.51	8.76	3.16	1.58	−0.33
*Chile	8.3	513.62	353.99	530.00	201.74	4.26	1.82	272.00
*Cyprus	4.1	16.23	7.78	—	—	−17.96	1.59	9.84
Denmark	5.2	15.25	9.31	19.39	15.74	0.46	0.60	4.71
Finland	1.7	17.41	11.74	22.62	16.29	4.13	0.43	18.85
Germany (W)	2.6	6.99	6.93	11.33	10.91	0.69	0.11	12.03
Ireland	7.9	17.00	11.32	20.82	22.90	0.37	1.31	9.09
Israel	3.0	39.78	20.75	37.25	23.64	6.26	2.80	17.57
Italy	2.9	19.14	10.83	25.16	22.59	3.37	0.91	9.36
Japan	1.4	24.27	11.81	25.97	24.25	1.32	1.22	11.51
Korea (S)	4.1	24.31	3.15	35.28	11.07	8.71	2.66	29.59
Netherlands	3.3	9.66	7.93	16.67	13.99	2.43	0.74	11.43
Norway	1.5	9.40	7.46	17.30	10.64	5.27	0.76	11.63

Table 1. The Basic International Data (1974, %)—Continued Vertically

Philippines	4.8	40.51	7.08	5.32	9.45	4.88	2.94	23.29
Puerto Rico	13.3	19.83	7.34	8.92	6.50	-3.50	2.71	2.87b
Sweden	1.5	9.88	6.77	11.60	8.53	4.19	0.25	25.22
Trinidad	15.3	22.02	14.85	—	14.85a	5.10	0.95	32.82
U.K.	2.7	15.94	9.22	16.97	12.99	0.35	1.21	10.53
U.S.	5.6	11.01	6.22	8.09	7.09	-1.79	0.70	2.87
Yugoslavia	9.0	21.08	19.66	29.14	17.71	8.78	0.91	25.18

Note: All the data are calculated from U.N., *Monthly Bulletin of Statistics*, Jan. 1977 except for Y in column 14 and $\Delta Q/Q$ in column 13, which are taken from U.N., *Statistical Yearbook*, 1975. $\Delta Q/Q$ (a) in column 13 is the average annual growth rate of per capita real output for 1970-74, while $\Delta Q/Q$ (b) in column 16 is the average annual growth rate of total real output for 1970-74.

a. $\Delta W/W$ (1973), assumed to be equal to $\Delta P/P$ (1973). b $\Delta M/M$, assumed to be equal to U.S. $\Delta M/M$.

*Chile and Cyprus were excluded from the regressions whose results are presented in the text.

27

Table 1. The Basic International Data (1974, %)—Continued Horizontally

	(9) A/Y	(10) L/N	(11) U_{t-1}	(12) F/Y	(13) ΔQ/Q (a)	(14) Y (U.S.,$)	(15) 1/U (ratio)	(16) ΔQ/Q (b)
Australia	8.54	41.8	1.9	30.44	3.10	5448	0.2999	4.8
Austria	5.21	41.5	1.6	73.63	5.10	3916	0.571	5.6
Belgium	2.79	40.8	3.6	92.75	4.80	5029	0.187	5.2
Canada	4.72	40.9	5.6	49.11	4.20	5673	0.163	5.6
*Chile	6.88	29.5	4.8	34.20	-0.50	731	0.120	1.2
*Cypurs	16.75	42.3	1.2	93.65	0.80	1280	0.244	1.3
Denmark	7.68	49.0	2.4	68.59	2.50	6020	0.123	3.2
Finland	10.85	46.1	2.3	57.32	4.90	4706	0.513	5.3
Germany(W)	2.71	43.9	1.2	50.96	2.60	6198	0.274	3.2
Ireland	14.00	36.4	7.2	83.87	3.60	2176	0.100	4.5
Israel	4.69	32.9	2.6	74.52	5.50	4029	0.328	8.9
Italy	8.36	35.4	3.5	41.08	3.00	6214	0.323	3.8
Japan	5.27	48.1	1.3	20.35	5.50	4152	0.606	6.8
Korea (S)	25.10	36.1	4.0	68.45	9.10	504	0.244	10.9
Netherlands	5.47	40.8	2.7	103.13	3.00	5109	0.247	4.0
Norway	5.91	37.7	1.5	90.11	3.60	5825	0.526	4.4

Table 1. The Basic International Data (1974, %)—Continued Vertically

Philippines	28.31	33.6	4.8	44.47	3.30	359	0.227	6.3
Puerto Rico	3.37	28.3	11.7	119.57	3.70	2337	0.063	6.7
Sweden	4.71	42.3	1.9	58.75	2.40	6876	0.690	2.8
Trinidad	7.80	34.5	15.4	77.87	2.87	732	3.000	3.8
U.K.	26.17	46.3	0.1	53.67	3.20	3375	0.142	3.5
U.S.	4.47	44.1	4.9	13.66	4.10	5918	0.065	5.1
Yugoslavia	17.70	43.3	8.1	51.93	5.94	1300	0.103	5.9

VI. Summary and Conclusions

We have reviewed three inflation and unemployment models, namely, the Phillips hypothesis or the excess demand for labor theory, the quantity theory or the monetarists' argument, and the generalized inflation model or the Keynes-Harrod-Domar type growth rate inflation theory. First, according to the Phillips hypothesis, a country which has a low rate of unemployment should tend to have a high rate of inflation. However, the international empirical evidence suggests that the rate of unemployment is not always a significant factor in pushing up the rate of increase in money wage rates and the rate of inflation.

Second, according to the quantity theory, a country which has a high rate of increase in the supply of money should tend to have a high rate of inflation, independent of the rate of unemployment. In the international regression results, the rate of increase in the supply of money was indeed significantly correlated with the rate of inflation. This result is apparently consistent with the quantity theory that the major determinant of inflation is the rate of increase in the supply of money. However, the price elasticity of the supply of money was between 0.31 and 0.41, and these low values of elasticity does not fully support the quantity theory that expects the elasticity to be close to one.

Furthermore, the rate of increase in the supply of money was negatively correlated with the rate of unemployment. Also, the rate of increase in the money wage rates and the rate of unemployment were all significantly positively correlated with the growth rate of real output. These results support the generalized growth-inflation model rather than the quantity theory.

A policy implication of the above analysis is clear. A demand creating policy is indeed significant in increasing the rate of economic growth and in reducing the rate of unemployment.

The rate of inflation is a necessary evil for the above objectives. However, the necessary evil need not be greater. First, the rate of increase in the supply of money should not exceed a maximum rate beyond which the rate of increase in real output cannot be further increased. Second, the policy emphasis should be placed not only on the level and the growth rate of demand, but also on the composition of the aggregate demand. For instance, if the government expenditures are directed to increase the productivity and the capital stock the short-run demand-creating multiplier effect will be the same as the pure government consumption expenditures, but the long-run capacity-creating effect will lower the price elasticity of demand.[10]

Finally, it should be added that the regression results have only a limited value. The trouble with regression analysis is that the significance of the regression coefficients varies with many factors such as the number of observations, the number and the nature of the independent variables, and the period of observation, as well as the methods of regression in the forms of linear, non-linear, multiple-stage regression in the ordinary numbers or in the differenced values, with a variety of lag structures. Indeed the above regression results presented in this paper are entirely subject to the above general rule. Particularly, due to a relatively small sample size, elimination or addition of some countries will significantly affect the regression results. Furthermore, there is the im-

---

[10]Since $\Delta K/K = (Q/K)(I/Q)$, Equation (16) may be rewritten as

$$\Delta P/P = \Delta Y/Y - \Delta A/A - \Delta R/R - (Q/K) \cdot (I/Q) \qquad (16)'$$

where Q/K = output-capital ratio, I/Q = investment ratio. Equation $(16)'$ states that the greater the investment ratio, the less will be the rate of inflation.

We may introduce a time lag in Equation $(16)'$:

$$\Delta P/P = \Delta Y/Y - \Delta A/A - \Delta R/R - (Q/K) \cdot (I/Q)_{t-1} \qquad (16)''$$

portant question of the reliability of the international data. The international data are often not reliable or not consistent with each other due to the differences in the definition of a variable, the method and the period of sampling, the sample size, and often by political disturbances particularly in countries of political instability. Perhaps the rate of unemployment may be of the least reliable data. Even if the data may be complete and accurate, and yet there is no rule that economic relationships are fixed over the years. These and other reasons may justify the continuous need for the empirical studies to observe and establish dynamic economic relationships to help formulate economic policies.

Appendix Note:

The three models may be represented in the following equations:

Shin's growth-inflation model	Conventional Keynesian demand-pull inflation model	Classical-neoclassical-monetarists demand-pull inflation model

1. $Q = C + I$
2. $C = C(Q, i)$
3. $I = I(i)$
4. $S = S(Q, i)$
5. $I(i) = S(Q, i)$
6. $MP_L = F'(L, K_{t-1} + I)$ $\qquad$ $MP_L = F'(L, \overline{K})$ $\qquad$ $MP_L = F'(L, \overline{K})$
7. $S_L = S_L(W/P)$ $\qquad\qquad$ $S_L = S_L(W)$
8. $S_L(W/P) =$
   $\quad F'(L, K_{t-1} + I)$
9. $M/P = D_M(i, Q)$
10. $M = \overline{M}$
11. $\overline{M}/P = D_M(i, Q)$

where

Q = real output	K = capital stock
C = real consumption	W = money wage rate
I = real investment (net)	P = the level of prices
i = the rate of interest	M = the supply of money
S_L = the supply of labor	S = real saving

If we assume a Cobb-Douglas production function,

$$Q = A L^\alpha K^\beta$$
$$\partial Q/\partial L = A\alpha L^{\alpha-1}K^\beta$$
$$= A\alpha L^{\alpha-1}(K_{t-1} + I)^\beta$$

If $\alpha + \beta = 1$,

$$\partial Q/\partial L = A\alpha[(K_{t-1} + I)/L]^\beta$$

The investment function may take many other forms:

$$I = I(Q, i) \text{ or } I = I(\Delta Q, i) \text{ or } I = I(\Delta Q, K_{t-1}, i)$$

REFERENCES

Braun, A.R., "The Phillips Curves," *Finance and Development*, Nov./Dec., 1971, pp. 58-65.

Flanagan, R.J., "The U.S. Phillips Curve and International Unemployment Rate Differentials," *American Economic Review*, March 1973, pp. 114-131.

Friedman, M., "The Role of Monetary Policy," *American Economic Policy*, March, 1968, pp. 1-17.

Friedman, M., "Inflation and Unemployment," *Journal of Political Economy*, June 1977, pp. 451-472.

Gordon, R., "The Theory of Domestic Inflation," *American Economic Review, Papers and Proceedings*, Feb. 1977, pp. 128-134.

Hicks, J.R., "The Little that is Right with Monetarism," *Loyds Bank Review*, July, 1976, pp. 16-18.

Holt, C.C., MacRae, C.D., Schweitzer, S.O., and Smith, R.E., *The Unemployment-Inflation Dilemma: A Manpower Solution*, Washington, D.C., Urban Institute, 1971.

Humphrey, T.M., "Changing Views of the Phillips Curve," *Economic Review*, Federal Reserve Bank of Richmond, July, 1973, pp. 2-13.

Humphrey, T.M., "The Quantity Theory of Money: Its Historical Evolution and Role in Policy Debates," *Economic Review*, Federal Reserve Bank of Richmond, May/June, 1974, pp. 2-18.

Humphrey, T.M., "The Persistence of Inflation," *Sixty-First Annual Report*, Federal Reserve Bank of Richmond, 1975, pp. 4-16.

Humphrey, T.M., "Some Current Controversies in the Theory of Inflation," *Economic Review*, Federal Reserve Bank of Richmond, July/August, 1976, pp. 8-19.

Jacobson, L., and Lindbeck, A., "Labor Market Condition, Wages and Inflation—Swedish Experiences, 1955-67," *Swedish Journal of Economics*, June 1969, pp. 64-103.

Johnson, H.G., *Macroeconomics and Monetary Policy*, 1972, pp. 63-74, 148-163.

Kaldor, N., "Economic Growth and the Problem of Inflation," *Economica*, Nov. 1959.

Keynes, J.M., *The General Theory of Employment, Interest, and Money*, 1936, Ch. 21.

Kuh, E., "A Productivity Theory of Wage Levels: An Alternative to the Phillips Curve," *Review of Economic Studies*, Oct. 1967, pp. 333-365.

Lipsey, R.G., "The Relation between Unemployment and the Rate of Change of Money Wage Rates in the United Kingdom, 1862-1957: A Further Analysis," *Economica*, Feb. 1960, pp. 1-31.

Modigliani, F., "The Monetarist Controversy or, Should We Foresake Stabilization Policies?", *American Economic Review*, March 1977, pp. 1-19.

O'Brien, J.M., "Inflation and Unemployment: The Great Debate," *Business Review*, Federal Reserve Bank of Philadelphia, Jan. 1973, pp. 13-18.

Okun, A., "Potential GNP: Its Measurement and Significance," *Proceedings of the Business and Economics Statistics Section of the American Statistical Association*, 1962, reprinted in *The Political Economy of Prosperity*, 1970, pp. 132-145.

Perry, G., "Inflation versus Unemployment: The Worsening Trade-Off," *Monthly Labor Review*, Feb. 1971, pp. 68-71.

Phelps, E.S., "Phillips Curves, Expectations of Inflation and Optimal Unemployment Overtime," *Economica*, Aug. 1967, pp. 254-281.

Phillips, A.W., "The Relation between Unemployment and the Rate of Change in Money Wage Rates in the United Kingdom, 1961-1957," *Economica*, N.S., Nov. 1958, pp. 283-299.

Samuelson, P.A., and Solow, R.M., "Analytical Aspects of Anti-Inflation Policy," *American Economic Review*, May 1960, pp. 177-194.

Chapter 2

The Stock Price and Inflation: The Monetary Model versus the Income Model

I. Introduction
II. Monetary Model vs. Income Model
III. Regression Results
IV. Conclusions

I. Introduction

A large number of empirical monetary models have been published to predict the stock prices or the rate of return in the stock market. However, recently, unsatisfied with the poor performances of the monetary models or in defense of the efficient market hypothesis, several papers have appeared in criticism of the monetary models. Miller (1972), Pesando (1974), Rozeff (1974, 1975) and Auerbach (1976) reviewed some of the major monetary models, including Sprinkel (1964, 1971), Palmer (1970), Keran (1971), Reilly and Lewis (1971), Homa and Jaffee (1971), Hamburger and Kochin (1972) and Cooper (1972),[1] and main-

---

[1] Obviously not all these writers may be monetarists because they may not follow the quantity theory of money, classical or modern. In this paper, any model which finds the lagged or the current monetary variable statistically significant is regarded as a monetary model.

tained that the monetarists' findings that some monetary variables are statistically significant in predicting stock prices are based on methodological errors such as the imposition of the Almon lag, tenuous graphical analysis, inclusion of the non-independent variables in the regressors, and no consideration on the lead-lag relationship or the interdependent relationship between money and the stock prices, spurious regression on the trend and the cycles, etc., and concluded that the lag of stock price behind changes in the monetary policy is for all practical purposes non-existent in the regression test, and of no use in trading rules.

However, it should be noted that these critics agree to existence of some degree of correlation between the current monetary variables and the current stock prices or the stock return.

This brief paper is not intended to show another attack on the monetary models with regard to the "methodological errors" of the monetary models, but to consider the following question, whether or not there exist any other more important variables than the monetary variables in determining or in predicting the stock prices.

In the following section II, the monetary model and an alternative model, namely, the income model are formulated. In section III, the empirical tests are presented. In the final section IV, conclusions are summarized.

II. Monetary Model vs. the Income Model

The monetarists argument that the monetary variables are significant in determining or predicting the stock price or return is often called the monetary portfolio model. Under this theory, consumers maintain their wealth in several forms including the money balance, real estate, durable consumer goods, stocks and bonds. If the money stock is increased above the desired level, consumers increase their spending on the above items including the stocks. So the stock price rises. The greater the rate of increase in the stock of money, the greater will be an increase in the demand for stocks and thus the greater will be the increase in the stock price.

Although there is no simple unified or standard monetary model, we may call it a monetary model if it assumes that the supply of money and/or the rate of change in the supply of money affects the stock prices or returns. Such monetary models may include the simple lagged monetary variables or weighted lagged monetary variables. In this paper, we assume a very simple monetary model which may be divided into the nominal monetary model and the real monetary model:

$$S = F_1(M, \Delta M/M, e_1) \tag{1}$$

$$S = F_2(M/P, \Delta M/M - \Delta P/P, e_2) \tag{2}$$

where

S = the current stock price
M = the supply of money
$\Delta M/M$ = the rate of change in the supply of money
P = the level of prices
$\Delta P/P$ = the rate of change in prices
M/P = the real money balance
e_i = the error term

The assumption in the above equations is that the money stock variable determines the long run trend of the stock prices, and the rate of increase in the money stock influences the short run fluctuations in the stock prices. Both variables are expected to have positive signs. However, it should be noted that Equation 1 does not consider the effects of an increase in the money stock on price level. In Equation 2, if the price level rises in proportion to the money stock, as the classical rigid quantity theory of money would maintain, the real money balance will remain constant, and the real rate of increase in money stock will be zero. So the stock price will not be affected at all. However, if the money supply and the price level do not move in the same proportion, the stock price is expected to increase with the real money balance and the real rate of increase in the supply of money.

It is conceivable that an increase in the money stock may influence the rate of interest and thus the stock price. Indeed, according to the classical quantity theory, as the money stock rises, the level of prices rises, and the nominal rate of interest should rise in proportion to the rate of inflation which will in turn decrease the demand for stocks and thus the stock price. But the current monetarists ignore this negative side of the Fisher effect, and emphasize only the positive side of the real money balance effect or the liquidity effect.

As an alternative model, we may list what may be called the income model which may be derived from the familiar present value equation:

$$S_t = PV_t = \sum_{t=1}^{\infty} \frac{D^*_t}{(1+d)^t} = \frac{D^*_{t+1}}{d-g} \tag{3}$$

where

PV = the present value which is assumed to be equal to the current stock price, S_t

D^*_t = the expected dividend in year t

d = discount rate

g = growth rate of dividend or the stock price

The last term of Equation 3 is obtained based on the assumption of a constant rate of growth g, i.e.,

$$S_t = \frac{D_t(1 + g)}{(1 + d)} + \frac{D_t(1 + g)^2}{(1 + d)^2} + \ldots + \frac{D_t(1 + g)^n}{(1 + d)^n}$$

Assume that the next year's dividend depends upon this year's money GNP, which in turn depends upon this year's real income and the rate of inflation, then we may rewrite Equation 3 as:

$$S_t = PV_t = \frac{a \cdot GNP_t}{d-g} = \frac{a\ Y_t(1+\Delta P/P)}{d-g} \qquad (4)$$

where a is a constant, representing the portion of GNP which goes to dividend. Instead of Equation 3, we may start with the following present value equation for one year holding period:[2]

$$S_t = PV_t = \frac{D^*_t}{(1+d)} + \frac{S^*_{t+1}}{(1+d)}$$

$$= \frac{a \cdot GNP_t}{(1+d)} + \frac{S^*_{t+1}}{(1+d)} \qquad (5)$$

$$= \frac{a\ Y_t(1+\Delta P/P)}{(1+d)} + \frac{S^*_{t+1}}{(1+d)}$$

where

Y_t=real income in year t,

$\Delta P/P$=the expected rate of inflation during year t,

S^*_{t+1}=the expected stock price at the beginning of year t+1.

D^*_t=the expected dividend which will be received during year t

---

[2]The "after-tax" present value formula will take the following form:

$$PV_t = \frac{D^*_t\ (1-x_1)}{(1+d)} + \frac{S^*_{t+1} - (S^*_{t+1} - S_t)x_2}{(1+d)}$$

where x_1=dividend tax rate, x_2=capital gain tax rate. As the tax rates rise the present value and the stock price will fall.

Now the problem is the discount rate. According to the capital asset pricing theory,[3] the minimum required rate of return on the stock holding is the sum of riskless return on a riskless or safe asset and the risk premium for holding the risky stock:

$$E(R_i) = R_F + [E(R_m) - R_F] \cdot \frac{Cov\ (R_i,\ R_m)}{V\ (R_m)} \qquad (6)$$

where

$E(R_i)$ = expected minimum rate of return on security i
R_F = riskless rate of return on a riskless asset   .
$E(R_m)$ = expected rate of return on the market portfolio
$Cov(R_i, R_m)$ = covariance of the rate of return on security i and the rate of return on the market portfolio
$\dfrac{Cov\ (R_i,\ R_m)}{V(R_m)}$ = β coefficient or the slope of the regression line in R_i and R_m space, where R_i is the dependent variable
$E(R_m) - R_F$ = the slope of the security market line, i.e., the slope of the regression line in R_i and β space, where R_i is the dependent variable

β measures the systematic risk or the undiversifiable risk. The lower the β, the smaller is the risk of holding stock i. In the above equation, R_F is defined as the riskless rate of return on a safe asset, and inflation rate is assumed to be zero. Adding the risk premium for the purchasing power loss, or the rate of inflation, $\Delta P/P$, and substituting the β coefficient, we may rewrite Equation 6 as:

$$E(R_i) = R_F + \Delta P/P + [E(R_m) - R_F]\beta \qquad (7)$$

---

[3]For the capital asset pricing theory, see Sharpe, W.F., "Capital Asset Prices: A Theory of Market Equilibrium Under Conditions of Risk," *Journal of Finance*, Sept. 1964, pp. 425-442. H.A. Latane, et. al., *Security Analysis and Portfolio Management*, 2nd ed., 1975, pp. 270-299.

Equation 7 states that the expected minimum rate of return on security i depends upon the risk and infla free rate of return R_F, the rate of inflation $\Delta P/P$, the expected rate of return on the market portfolio $E(R_m)$, and the β coefficient.

Replacing the riskless rate of return R_F by, say, the short-term Treasury yield, or the rate of interest i, and the risk premium $(E(R_m)-R_F)\beta$ by m, and assuming that the expected minimum rate of return on security i is equal to the discount rate of the present value of a stock d, we have:

$$d=i+\Delta P/P+m \qquad\qquad (8)$$

Substituting Equation 8 into the present value equation 5, we have:

$$S_t= \frac{aY_t(1+\Delta P/P)+S^*_{t+1}}{(1+i+\Delta P/P+m)} \qquad\qquad (9)$$

where

$$\frac{\partial S_t}{\partial Y_t} = \frac{a(1+\Delta P/P)}{(1+i+\Delta P/P+m)} > 0 \qquad\qquad (10)$$

$$\frac{\partial S_t}{\partial i} = \frac{-[1+(\partial m/\partial i)]\cdot[aY_t(1+\Delta P/P)+S^*_{t+1}]}{(1+i+\Delta P/P+m)^2} < 0 \qquad\qquad (11)$$

$$\partial m/\partial i > 0$$

$$\frac{\partial S_t}{\partial(\Delta P/P)} = \frac{aY_t(i+m)-S^*_{t+1}}{(1+i+\Delta P/P+m)^2} < 0 \qquad\qquad (12)$$

$$\text{subject to } aY_t\,(i+m)<S^*_{t+1}$$

The last constraint should hold true in general since the expected stock price is usually greater than the dividend payment a Y_t and the sum of the riskless rate of return and the risk premium rate is smaller than one, i.e., $(i+m) < 1$.

In Equation 9, we further assume that the expected stock price in year $t+1$ depends upon the current stock price of year t and the actual tock price of the preceding year $t-1$.[4] As to the risk premium of the risky stocks, we do not have any satisfactory measure of it. However, when the rate of interest rises, the firm's financial risk will tend to increase, and pessimistic market and economic conditions will be forecast, and the risk premium will also rise. So we may assume that the risk premium is a function of the rate of interest. Under these simplifying assumptions for the purpose of the statistical test, Equation 9 may be stated as:

$$S_t = F_3(Y, \ i, \ \Delta P/P, \ S_{t-1}, \ e_3) \qquad (13)$$

Or combining the rate of interest and the rate of inflation,[5] we may write:

$$S_t = F_4(Y, \ i + \Delta P/P, \ S_{t-1}, \ e_4) \qquad (14)$$

---

[4]The expected stock price at the beginning of year $t+1$ is the sum of the current price at the beginning of year t and the expected increase in price during the year. Then,

$$S^*_{t+1} = S_t + \Delta S^*_t$$
$$= S_t + \alpha(S_t - S_{t-1})$$

We are assuming that the expected increase in the stock price in year t, ΔS^*_t, is a function of the actual increase in stock price in year t, $S_t - S_{t-1}$. The role of S_{t-1} may be interpreted by the habit-persistence assumption. That is, a stock seller is reluctant to sell stocks at prices lower than the prices they paid, just as a buyer of a home wishes to sell at a higher price than at which he purchased.

[5]In Equation 8, we have assumed that i is the risk and infla free rate of interest, and so i and $\Delta P/P$ are independent. However, as the Fisher effect maintains, when $\Delta P/P$ rises, i will tend to rise. In such a case, a simple sum of i and $\Delta P/P$ will overestimate the discount rate. Given the initial discount rate, omitting the risk premium,

$$d_0 = i_0 + (\Delta P/P)_0$$

Equation 14 is the income model we wish to test. The monetary model of Equation 2 may be also rewritten including the lagged stock price variable.[6]

$$S_t = F_5(M/P, \ \Delta M/M - \Delta P/P, \ S_{t-1}, \ e_5) \qquad (15)$$

However, according to the efficient market hypothesis, the lagged stock price will be statistically insignificant in predicting the current stock price.

III. The Regression Results

Before we discuss the regression results, it may be useful to explain the sources of the data and the definitions of the variables. The annual data are taken from the U.S. Council of

---

Assume that $(\Delta P/P)_0$ rises to $(\Delta P/P)_1$, and i_0 rises to i_1. Then the adjusted discount rate net of the double counting is

$$d_1 = i_1 + (\Delta P/P)_1 - \Delta i_1$$

If $\Delta i = k \ (\Delta P/P)$, then

$$d_1 = i_1 + (1-k) \ (\Delta P/P)_1$$

The above discussion does not imply that the risk and infla free rate of interest should remain constant. It may fluctuate with the demand and supply conditions in the financial market even if the rate of inflation is zero. In such a case, Δi should not be subtracted. It may be a difficult task to separate the increase in the rate of interest into the two components; one, due to the increase in the rate of inflation and another, due to changes in the financial market conditions.

The simple correlation coefficient between the rate of inflation (implicit GNP deflator) and the rate of interest (3 month new issue Treasury bill) was 0.1838 for the annual data, 1946-76; and the correlation coefficient was 0.7184 for the quarterly data, 1962 II-1976 IV. $r=0.1838$ is not significant, but $r=0.7184$ is significant at the 1% level.

[6]Since the demand for real money balances is

$$M/P = F(Q, \ i, \ \Delta P^*/P, \ W, \ldots e)$$

Equation 15 may be rewritten as

$$S_t = F(Q, \ i, \ \Delta P^*/P, \ \Delta M/M - \Delta P/P, \ S_{t-1}, \ e)$$

Economic Advisers, *Economic Report of the President*, 1976, and complemented by the U.S. Council of Economic Advisers, *Economic Indicators*, Jan. 1977, for 1975 and 1976. The quarterly data are taken from the various editions of the *Economic Report of the President*, and also complemented by the *Economic Indicators* for 1975 and 1976. The variables are defined below.

$S =$ Standard and Poor's stock price index for 500 stock prices,

$GNP/P = Y$, real income; money GNP in current prices divided by the implicit GNP price deflators $(1972 = 100)$. Money GNP is in billions of dollars.

$M_1/P =$ the supply of money, i.e., the currency + demand deposits, in billions of dollars divided by the implicit price index. Real money balance.

$M_2/P = M_2(M_1 +$ time deposits at commercial banks other than large certificates of deposit) divided by the GNP implicit price deflator. In billions of dollars.

$i + \Delta P/P =$ the 3-month Treasury bill rate on new issues (i) + the rate of change in the implicit price index.(%) Discount rate of the present value.

$\Delta P/P =$ the rate of change in prices, $P =$ the implicit GNP deflator, $1972 = 100.(\%)$

$\Delta M_1/M_1 - \Delta P/P =$ the real rate of change in the supply of money, M_1 (%)

$\Delta M_2/M_2 - \Delta P/P =$ the real rate of change in the supply of money, M_2 (%)

$S_{t-1} =$ the lagged stock price; one year of time lag for the annual data, and one quarter of time lag for the quarterly data.

With the above data, a large number of regression equations were computed. For instance, as for the income model, money income and real income, the rate of interest and the rate of inflation separately and combined, with and without time lagged variables were tested. As for the monetary model, for each of the M_1 and M_2 models, nominal and real money balances, the nominal and real rates of increase in the supply of money, with and without lagged variables were tested. Some of these regression results are summarized in Appendix Tables 1-8.

For the purpose of easy reference and comparison of the regression results of the monetary and income models, in the below we will represent some of the selected results. First, the best arithmetic regression results; second, the regression results with all the lagged independent variables; third, the first difference regression results; and fourth, the logarithmic regression results.

1. The best arithmetic regression results are presented below for the annual and quarterly data for the income model and the monetary model:[7]

Income Model (Annual Data, 1946-1976; Quarterly Data, 1962 II-1976 IV)

Annual Data

$$S = -14.2528 + 5.9714 \text{ GNP/P} - 1.1484 \ (i + \Delta P/P) + 0.5949 S_{t-1} \qquad (16)$$
$$ (3.76)^{**} \phantom{\text{GNP/P} -} (-3.55)^{**} (4.62)^{**}$$
$$\overline{R}^2 = 0.9623 \quad \text{D.W.} = 1.6742$$

---

[7]We have chosen the equation which has the largest $\overline{R}^2$, also the equation has the smallest standard error of estimate. The numbers in parentheses are the t-ratios. Also $d = i + \Delta P/P$ produced better results when i and $\Delta P/P$ were included as separate independent variables. So we pesent in the text only the results obtained for $i + \Delta P/P$. Also we have tested money GNP, nominal money balance, the consumer price index, and the long-term corporate bond yield.

Quarterly Data

$$S = 3.3564 + 2.8466 \ GNP/P - 2.2159 \ (i + \Delta P/P) + 0.7979 \ S_{t-1} \qquad (17)$$
$$\quad\;\; (3.44)** \qquad\qquad (-4.20)** \qquad\qquad (11.21)**$$

$$\overline{R}^2 = 0.8322 \quad D.W. = 1.9720$$

Monetary Model (Annual Data, 1946-1976; Quarterly Data, 1962 II-1976 IV)

Annual Data

$$S = -6.5318 + 6.3167 M_2/P + 1.6286(\Delta M_2/M_2 - \Delta P/P) + 0.7584 \ S_{t-1} \qquad (18)$$
$$\qquad\quad (2.00)** \qquad\qquad\quad (3.97)** \qquad\qquad (7.98)**$$

$$\overline{R}^2 = 0.9573 \quad D.W. = 2.0103$$

Quarterly Data

$$S = 3.8492 + 3.3642 M_2/P + 1.9248(\Delta M_2/M_2 - \Delta P/P) + 0.7763 S_{t-1} \qquad (19)$$
$$\quad\;\; (2.04)* \quad\; (3.55)** \qquad\qquad\qquad\quad (10.31)**$$

$$\overline{R}^2 = 0.8224 \quad D.W. = 1.8430$$

In the above regression results we note that all the regression coefficients are significant at the 1% level, and all have the expected signs. Comparing the annual results with the quarterly results, the annual regression equations have higher values of $\overline{R}^2$. Comparing the monetary model and the income model, the income model shows slightly higher values of $\overline{R}^2$. The above income and monetary models each explain about 96% of the annual variation and about 82-83% of the quarterly variation in the stock price. The D-W statistic indicates no serial correlation for the above 4 regression equations.

2. To see the effects of the lagged variables, we have lagged all the independent variables by one year or one quarter. First, the results of the income model are:

Income Model

Annual Data

$$S = -5.8050 + 3.7028 \ (GNP/P)_{t-1} - 0.6181 \ (i + \Delta P/P)_{t-1} + 0.7198 \ S_{t-1} \qquad (20)$$
$$\qquad\qquad (1.37) \qquad\qquad\quad (-1.39) \qquad\qquad\quad (3.70)**$$

$$\overline{R}^2 = 0.9358 \quad D.W. = 1.9246$$

Quarterly Data

$$S = 6.4341 + 2.6757\ (GNP/P)_{t-1} - 1.7843\ (i + \Delta P/P)_{t-1} + 0.7564\ S_{t-1} \qquad (21)$$
$$\quad\ \ (2.58)** \qquad\qquad\ \ (-2.79)** \qquad\qquad (9.45)**$$
$$\overline{R}^2 = 0.8052 \quad D.W. = 1.7789$$

For the annual and quarterly monetary models, we have obtained the following results:

Monetary Model

Annual Data

$$S = 4.7042 + 0.3774\ (M_2/P)_{t-1} + 0.2820\ (\Delta M_2/M_2 - \Delta P/P)_{t-1} + 0.9542 S_{t-1} \qquad (22)$$
$$\qquad\quad (0.09) \qquad\qquad\quad (0.46) \qquad\qquad\qquad\quad (7.12)**$$
$$\overline{R}^2 = 0.9305 \quad D.W. = 1.9282$$

Quarterly Data

$$S = 8.8910 + 1.8803(M_2/P)_{t-1} + 0.6347\ (\Delta M_2/M_2 - \Delta P/P)_{t-1} + 0.8088 S_{t-1} \qquad (23)$$
$$\qquad\quad (0.99) \qquad\qquad\quad (0.98) \qquad\qquad\qquad\quad (9.34)**$$
$$\overline{R}^2 = 0.7820 \quad D.W. = 1.6560$$

In the above lagged regression results, we note that the lagged stock price is significant at the 1% level for all the four equations. The other independent variables are significant only for the quarterly income regression equation. Comparing the two models, the annual monetary model has a slightly higher $\overline{R}^2$ than the income model, but the quarterly income model has a higher $\overline{R}^2$ than the monetary quarterly model. However, none of the monetary variables are significant in the annual and quarterly lagged models.

　　3. The regression results obtained by the first differences are presented below for the income and monetary models:

Income Model

Annual Data

$$\Delta S = -0.9597 + 14.9512 \Delta (GNP/P) - 0.4126 \Delta (i + \Delta P/P)$$
$$\qquad\quad (4.65)** \qquad\qquad\quad (-1.31) \qquad\qquad\qquad\qquad (24)$$
$$\overline{R}^2 = 0.4588 \quad D.W. = 2.2617$$

Quarterly Data

$$\Delta S = 0.5633 + 2.1562\Delta(GNP/P) - 2.3932\Delta(i + \Delta P/P) \tag{25}$$
$$(0.41)(-2.73)^{**}$$
$$\overline{R}^2 = 0.0866 \quad D.W. = 1.9761$$

Monetary Model:

Annual Data

$$\Delta S = 0.6709 + \ 25.8970 \ \Delta(M_2/P) + 0.4967\Delta(\Delta M_2/M_2 - \Delta P/P) \tag{26}$$
$$(2.53)^*(1.15)$$
$$\overline{R}^2 = 0.2874 \quad D.W. = 2.2873$$

Quarterly Data

$$\Delta S = -0.3918 + 29.3227\Delta(M_2/P) + 0.5673\Delta(\Delta M_2/M_2 - \Delta P/P) \tag{27}$$
$$(2.27)^*(1.04)$$
$$\overline{R}^2 = 0.1278 \quad D.W. = 1.9369$$

Although the $\overline{R}^2$ values are very low for both the income and monetary models, the income model is better than the monetary model for the annual data, but the monetary model is better than the income model for the quarterly data. The D-W statistic indicates no serial correlation for all the four equations.

4. The double log regression equations were calculated only for the income model since the monetary model contained zero and negative values in the regressors. The annual and quarterly regression results for the income model are presented below:[8]

Income Model

Annual data

$$\ln S = 0.0725 + 0.4484 \ln(GNP/P) - 0.0800 \ln(i + \Delta P/P) + 0.7960 \ln S_{t-1} \tag{28}$$
$$(1.93)^*(-2.09)^{**}(7.82)^{**}$$
$$\overline{R}^2 = 0.9727 \quad D.W. = 1.9275$$

---

[8]We have calculated also the semi-log regression equations. The results did not improve.

$$\ln S = 0.1939 + 0.3107 \ln (GNP/P)_{t-1} - 0.1019 \ln (i + \Delta P/P)_{t-1} + 0.8511 \ln S_{t-1}$$
$$(1.23) \qquad\qquad (-2.73)** \qquad\qquad (7.80)** \qquad (29)$$
$$\overline{R}^2 = 0.9735 \quad D.W. = 2.1939$$

Quarterly Data

$$\ln S = 0.3825 + 0.3104 \ln (GNP/P) - 0.1388 \ln (i + \Delta P/P) + 0.8112 \ln S_{t-1} \qquad (30)$$
$$(2.81)** \qquad\qquad (-3.08)** \qquad\qquad (10.56)**$$
$$\overline{R}^2 = 0.8109 \quad D.W. = 1.7454$$

$$\ln S = 0.5266 + 0.2662 \ln (GNP/P)_{t-1} - 0.1031 \ln (i + \Delta P/P)_{t-1} + 0.7881 \ln S_{t-1}$$
$$(2.06)* \qquad\qquad (-2.03)* \qquad\qquad (9.76)** \qquad (31)$$
$$\overline{R}^2 = 0.7931 \quad D.W. = 1.6455$$

In the above regression results, all the independent variables are significant at the 5% level or less, except for the real income variable in the annual lagged regression equation. These results are improvements compared with the arithmetic regression results where the real income and the discount rate were not significant. As for the $\overline{R}^2$ values, we note that the log annual results have slightly higher values, while the log quarterly results have slightly lower values than the arithmetic regression results. The D-W statistic indicates no serial correlation at the 5% level for Equations 28-30 and at the 2.5% level for Equation 31.

IV. Conclusions

In the preceding section, we have seen a number of regression equations for the monetary and income models, for the annual and quarterly data. Although the performances of the two models are very much alike, it may be said that the income model is slightly better than the monetary model. We note that out of the 6 comparable regression results, 5 income regression results have higher $\overline{R}^2$ values. The same conclusion is reached whether the criterion is the F ratio, the standard error of the estimate, the number of significant variabls, or the size of t ratio. What we have shown in this paper is that, given an identical methodology of regression, defective or not, the traditional present value approach produced better results than the monetary model.

However, the superiority of the income model may be a tentative one due to many reasons: First, more sophisticated monetary models may be developed than the simple model formulated in this paper. Such sophisticated models may include various lag structures and the other independent variables. Second, for the estimating technique we have used the ordinary least squares method which might have produced biased regression coefficients.[9] Though we have applied the same technique to test the two models, if the estimation technique is different, different results may be obtained. Alternative estimation techniques may include the two-stage least squares, and the cross spectral analysis. Third, the above regression results do not solve the question of lead-lag, the casual or the interdependent relationships between the stock price and the independent variables. As we have shown in the appendix tables, it is quite obvious that when the stock price regression equations are reversed, that is, when the stock price is the independent variable to predict the real income or the real money balance, the regression equations are as good as the regression equations to predict the stock prices.[10] Finally, in this paper, we were concerned with predicting the stock prices and not the total rate of return which consists of the capital gain and the dividend yield. These and other points suggest that there is need for a continuous research in the stock market behavior.

---

[9]The ordinary least squares estimation of the autoregression model produces biased regression coefficients. (See Hu, T., *Econometrics*, 1973, pp. 90-95.)

[10]The Sim's test did not provide any definite answer.

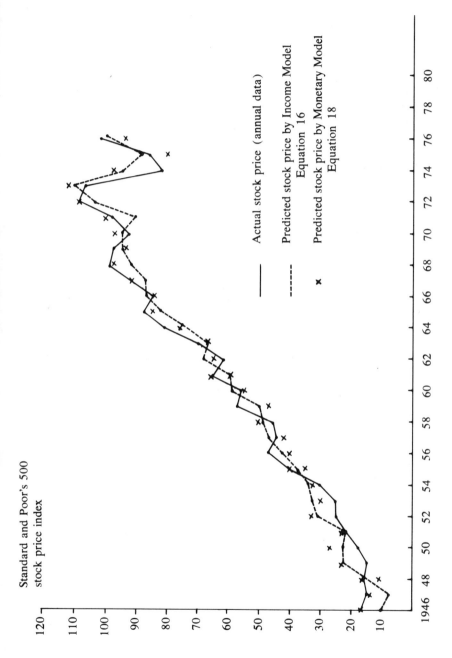

Standard and Poor's 500
stock price index

—————— Actual stock price (annual data)

- - - - - Predicted stock price by Income Model
Equation 16

✗ Predicted stock price by Monetary Model
Equation 18

Figure 1   Income Model vs. Monetary Model

53

Table 1. Stock Price Equation (Annual Data, 1946-76)

	Intercept	GNP/P	$i+\Delta P/P$	S_{t-1}	R	$\bar{R}^2$	S.E.	F	D.W.
S_t (1)	-39.4518	13.1819 (18.39)**	-1.0949 (-2.53)**		0.9679	0.9324	8.3624	207.7636	0.5433
(2)	-14.2528	5.9714 (3.76)**	-1.1484 (-3.55)**	0.5949 (4.62)**	0.9829	0.9623	6.2439	256.3050	1.6742
(3)	-5.8050	3.7028 (1.37)(t-1)	-0.6181 (-1.39)(t-1)	0.7198 (3.70)**	0.9707	0.9358	8.1518	146.6508	1.9246

	Intercept	M_1/P	$\Delta M_1/M_1 - \Delta P/P$	S_{t-1}	R	$\bar{R}^2$	S.E.	F	D.W.
S_t (4)	-251.5878	134.9188 (5.02)**	3.4995 (3.58)**		0.6364	0.6105	20.0726	24.5072	0.7900
(5)	- 9.7751	7.7430 (0.62)	1.4276 (4.01)**	0.8681 (14.87)**	0.9800	0.9560	6.7441	218.4094	2.2532
(6)	47.2602 -	-19.7068 (-1.52)(t-1)	0.4659 (1.03)(t-1)	0.9906 (15.28)**	0.9720	0.9386	7.9668	153.9636	2.0667

	Intercept	M_2/P	$\Delta M_2/M_2 - \Delta P/P$	S_{t-1}	R	$\bar{R}^2$	S.E.	F	D.W.
S_t (7)	-48.6221	29.2895 (12.65)**	2.5220 (3.55)**		0.9331	0.8615	11.9694	94.2945	0.7058
(8)	- 6.5318	6.3167 (2.00)*	1.6286 (3.97)**	0.7584 (7.98)**	0.9806	0.9573	6.6488	224.9772	2.0103
(9)	4.7042	0.3374 (0.09)(t-1)	0.2820 (0.46)(t-1)	0.9452 (7.12)**	0.9682	0.9305	8.4799	134.8383	1.9282

Note: The numbers in parentheses are the t-ratios. **Significant at the 1% level, *significant at the 5% level.
In Equations 3, 6 and 9, all the independent variables have one year of time lag. N (number of observations) = 31 years.

54

Table 2. Stock Price Equation (Quarterly Data, 1962 II-1976 IV)

	Intercept	GNP/P	$i+\Delta P/P$	S_{t-1}	R	$\bar{R}^2$	S.E.	F	D.W.
S_t (1)	26.0964	8.1286 (6.67)**	-3.0170 (-3.22)**		0.6909	0.4587	10.1606	25.5750	0.3730
(2)	3.5634	2.8466 (3.44)**	-2.2159 (-4.20)**	0.7970 (11.21)**	0.9170	0.8322	5.6565	96.9098	1.9720
(3)	6.4341	2.6757 (2.58)**(t-1)	-1.7843 (-2.79)**(t-1)	0.7564 (9.45)**	0.9029	0.8052	6.0952	80.9175	1.7789

	Intercept	M_1/P	$\Delta M_1/M_1 -\Delta P/P$	S_{t-1}	R	$\bar{R}^2$	S.E.	F	D.W.
S_t (4)	-44.4650	60.6338 (8.14)**	4.5234 (4.88)**		0.7111	0.5898	8.8451	42.6966	0.8389
(5)	-0.4877	10.8467 (1.37)	2.1710 (3.13)**	0.7395 (8.14)**	0.9057	0.8104	6.0129	83.6543	1.6138
(6)	19.9473	-6.6128 (-0.82)(t-1)	-0.7404 (-0.91)(t-1)	0.9485 (9.71)**	0.8899	0.7806	6.4684	69.7962	1.6948

	Intercept	M_2/P	$\Delta M_2/M_2 -\Delta P/P$	S_{t-1}	R	$\bar{R}^2$	S.E.	F	D.W.
S_t (7)	21.0856	15.0781 (7.44)**	2.6296 (2.85)**		0.7113	0.4882	9.8796	28.6660	0.4844
(8)	3.8492	3.3642 (2.04)*	1.9248 (3.55)**	0.7763 (10.31)**	0.9119	0.8224	5.8200	90.5267	1.8430
(9)	8.8910	1.8803 (0.99)(t-1)	0.6347 (0.98)(t-1)	0.8088 (9.34)**	0.8906	0.7820	6.4488	70.3314	1.6560

Note: The numbers in parentheses are the t-ratios. **Significant at the 1% level, *significant at the 5% level. In Equations 3, 6 and 9, all the independent variables have one quarter of time lag. N (number of observations) = 59 quarters.

55

Table 3. Stock Price Equation (First Order Difference Regression Results, Annual Data, 1946-76)

	Intercept	$\Delta(GNP/P)$	$\Delta(i+\Delta P/P)$	$\Delta(S_{t-1})$	R	$\bar{R}^2$	F	S.E.	D.W.
ΔS_t (1)	-0.9597	14.9512 (4.65)**	-0.4126 (-1.31)		0.7035	0.4588	6.0104	13.7151	2.2617
(2)	-0.8855	15.3880 (4.61)**	-0.3535 (-1.06)	-0.0875 (-0.58)	0.7078	0.4456	6.0832	9.0371	2.1873

	Intercept	$\Delta(M_1/P)$	$\Delta(\Delta M_1/M_1 -\Delta P/P)$	$\Delta(S_{t-1})$	R	$\bar{R}^2$	F	S.E.	D.W.
ΔS_t (3)	2.7870	51.1635 (2.47)**	0.3650 (1.01)		0.5275	0.2267	7.1845	5.3969	2.2592
(4)	3.1003	57.1210 (2.45)*	0.2553 (0.62)	-0.1162 (-0.59)	0.5360	0.2081	7.2701	3.6285	2.1283

	Intercept	$\Delta(M_2/P)$	$\Delta(\Delta M_2/M_2 -\Delta P/P)$	$\Delta(S_{t-1})$	R	$\bar{R}^2$	F	S.E.	D.W.
ΔS_t (5)	0.6709	25.8970 (2.53)**	0.4967 (1.15)		0.5787	0.2874	7.0486	6.8968	2.2873
(6)	0.7230	27.0276 (2.46)*	0.4429 (0.94)	-0.0566 (-0.32)	0.5808	0.2637	4.5819	7.0103	2.2025

Note: **Significant at the 1% level, *significant at the 5% level.

Table 4. Stock Price Equation (First Order Difference Regression Results, Quarterly Data, 1962 II-1976 IV)

	Intercept	Δ(GNP/P)	Δ(i+ΔP/P)	$\Delta(S_{t-1})$	R	$\bar{R}^2$	S.E.	F	D.W.
ΔS_t (1)	0.5633	2.1562 (0.41)	-2.3932 (-2.73)**		0.3437	0.0866	6.3070	3.7502	1.9761
(2)	0.6332	0.8099 (0.14)	-2.3252 (-2.62)**	0.0776 (0.56)	0.6332	0.0752	6.3462	2.5728	2.0870

	Intercept	Δ(M$_1$/P)	$\Delta(\Delta M_1/M_1 - \Delta P/P)$	$\Delta(S_{t-1})$	R	$\bar{R}^2$	S.E.	F	D.W.
ΔS_t (3)	0.4658	35.0232 (1.03)	1.2929 (2.02)*		0.3892	0.1212	6.1865	4.9995	1.8870
(4)	0.4673	27.5705 (0.72)	1.3583 (2.05)*	0.0587 (0.42)	0.3927	0.1081	6.2325	3.3426	1.9678

	Intercept	Δ(M$_2$/P)	$\Delta(\Delta M_2/M_2 - \Delta P/P)$	$\Delta(S_{t-1})$	R	$\bar{R}^2$	S.E.	F	D.W.
ΔS_t (5)	-0.3918	29.3227 (2.27)*	0.5673 (1.04)		0.3973	0.1278	6.1633	5.2478	1.9369
(6)	-0.3769	28.4728 (2.05)*	0.5843 (1.04)	0.0233 (0.18)	0.3979	0.1124	6.2173	3.4484	1.9724

Note: **Significant at the 1% level, *significant at the 5% level.

Table 5. Reversed Stock Price Equation (Dependent Variables are GNP/P, M₁/P and M₂/P, Annual Data, 1946-76)

	Intercept	S	$i+\Delta P/P$	$(GNP/P)_{t-1}$	R	$\bar{R}^2$	S.E.	F	D.W.
GNP/P (1)	3.2067	0.0701 (18.39)**	0.1017 (3.47)**		0.9725	0.9420	0.6098	244.4535	0.5715
(2)	0.7666	0.0175 (3.06)**	-0.0112 (-0.62)	0.8132 (9.75)**	0.9940	0.9867	0.2921	741.9999	2.1512
(3)	0.1728	0.0007 (0.08)(t-1)	-0.0157 (-0.80)(t-1)	1.0203 (8.56)**	0.9908	0.9817	0.3608	483.2960	2.4285

	Intercept	S	$\Delta M_1/M_1 -\Delta P/P$	$(M_1/P)_{t-1}$	R	$\bar{R}^2$	S.E.	F	D.W.
M₁/P (4)	2.0679	0.0035 (5.02)**	-0.0079 (-1.35)		0.7086	0.5021	0.1024	14.1200	0.5879
(5)	-0.0592	-0.0006 (-1.55)	0.0180 (6.46)**	1.0260 (13.92)**	0.9691	0.9324	0.0365	138.8196	1.5927
(6)	0.5472	0.0007 (1.40)(t-1)	0.0075 (2.31)*(t-1)	0.7353 (7.96)**	0.9229	0.8354	0.0569	51.7369	1.9437

	Intercept	S	$\Delta M_2/M_2 -\Delta P/P$	$(M_2/P)_{t-1}$	R	$\bar{R}^2$	S.E.	F	D.W.
M₂/P (7)	1.9736	0.0291 (12.65)**	-0.0670 (-2.81)**		0.9241	0.8435	0.3770	81.8406	0.5746
(9)	-0.0100	0.0015 (1.40)	0.0323 (5.79)**	1.0012 (28.52)**	0.9977	0.9948	0.0688	1908.536	1.5922
(9)	0.1384	0.0040 (2.00)*(t-1)	-0.0003 (-0.03)(t-1)	0.9197 (13.77)**	0.9918	0.9819	0.1284	541.9998	1.6961

Note: **Significant at the 1% level, *significant at the 5% level. Equations 3, 6 and 9 have independent variables of one year time lag.

Table 6. Reversed Stock Price Equation (Dependent Variables are GNP/P, M_1/P, and M_2/P, Quarterly Data, 1962 II-1976 IV)

	Intercept	S	$i+\Delta P/P$	$(GNP/P)_{t-1}$	R	$\overline{R}^2$	S.E.	F	D.W.
GNP/P (1)	2.2716	0.0544 (6.67)**	0.4829 (9.10)**		0.8662	0.7413	0.8314	84.0970	0.3401
(2)	−0.2086	0.0048 (2.84)**	−0.0406 (−2.89)**	1.0123 (46.54)**	0.9969	0.9935	0.1320	2945.7309	2.1449
(3)	−0.2072	0.0045(t−1) (2.70)**	−0.0467(t−1) (−3.48)**	1.0179 (46.75)**	0.9971	0.9939	0.1279	3138.3431	2.4379

	Intercept	S	$\Delta M_1/M_1 - \Delta P/P$	$(M_1/P)_{t-1}$	R	$\overline{R}^2$	S.E.	F	D.W.
M_1/P (4)	1.4049	0.0089 (8.14)**	−0.0439 (−3.64)**		0.7372	0.5272	0.1074	33.3317	0.5883
(5)	0.0178	0.0005 (2.32)*	0.0166 (8.88)**	0.9730 (57.82)**	0.9963	0.9922	0.0138	2462.4832	1.8139
(6)	0.1388	0.0015(t−1) (4.26)**	−0.0015(t−1) (−0.52)	0.8771 (29.64)**	0.9890	0.9769	0.0238	817.0985	1.6191

	Intercept	S	$\Delta M_2/M_2 - \Delta P/P$	$(M_2/P)_{t-1}$	R	$\overline{R}^2$	S.E.	F	D.W.
M_2/P (7)	1.5576	−0.0330 (7.44)**	−0.1314 (−3.08)**		0.7184	0.4988	0.4619	29.8569	0.3646
(8)	−0.1172	0.0011 (2.17)*	0.0383 (9.34)**	1.0026 (87.84)**	0.9983	0.9964	0.0392	5344.2464	1.9373
(9)	−0.0053	0.0013(t−1) (1.42)	0.0106(t−1) (1.56)	0.9804 (49.05)**	0.9948	0.9892	0.0679	1763.9235	1.6165

Note: **Significant at the 1% level, *significant at the 5% level.
In Equations 3, 6 and 9, all the independent variables have one quarter of time lag.

59

Table 7. Stock Price and Real Income Regression Results in Log (1946-76, Annual Data)

	Intercept	ln (GNP/P)	ln (i+ΔP/P)	ln S_{t-1}	R	$\bar{R}^2$	S.E.	F	D.W.
ln S (1)	−0.3364	2.1682 (16.09)**	−0.1136 (−1.68)	−0.1136	0.9590	0.9138	0.1985	160.0824	0.3387
(2)	0.0725	0.4484 (1.93)*	−0.0800 (−2.09)*	0.7960 (7.82)**	0.9876	0.9729	0.1118	356.5966	1.9275
(3)	0.1939	0.3107(t−1) (1.23)	−0.1019(t−1) (−2.73)**	0.8511 (7.80)**	0.9880	0.9735	0.1100	368.75	2.1939

	Intercept	ln S	ln (i+ΔP/P)	ln(GNP/P)$_{t-1}$	R	$\bar{R}^2$	S.E.	F	D.W.
ln(GNP/P) (4)	0.2942	0.4162 (16.09)**	0.0728 (2.62)**		0.9637	0.9237	0.0870	182.6298	0.4320
(5)	0.0546	0.0673 (2.28)*	−0.0010 (−0.08)	0.8595 (12.58)**	0.9948	0.9885	0.0338	858.8893	2.0086
(6)	0.0415	−0.0061(t−1) (−0.18)	−0.0263(t−1) (−2.28)*	1.0306 (13.20)**	0.9948	0.9884	0.0340	850.6508	2.3468

Note: **Significant at the 1% level, *significant at the 5% level.
The independent variables in Equations 3 and 6 have one year of time lag.

60

Table 8. Stock Price and Real Income Regression Results in Log
(Quarterly Data, 1962 II-1976 IV)

	Intercept	lnGNP/P	ln(i+ΔP/P)	$\ln S_{t-1}$	R	$\bar{R}^2$	S.E.	F	D.W.
ln S (1)	2.6685	0.9144 (5.62)**	−0.1638 (−2.11)*		0.6760	0.4376	0.1231	23.5631	0.3585
(2)	0.3825	0.3104 (2.81)**	−0.1388 (−3.08)**	0.8112 (10.56)**	0.9059	0.8109	0.0714	83.9037	1.7454
(3)	0.5266	0.2662(t−1) (2.06)*	−0.1031(t−1) (−2.03)*	0.7881 (9.76)**	0.8965	0.7931	0.0747	75.0926	1.6455

	Intercept	ln S	ln(i+ΔP/P)	$\ln(GNP/P)_{t-1}$	R	$\bar{R}^2$	S.E.	F	D.W.
ln GNP/P (4)	−0.0079	0.3943 (5.62)**	0.3081 (9.24)**		0.8763	0.7596	0.0808	92.6434	0.3526
(5)	−0.1371	0.0419 (3.20)**	−0.0219 (−2.55)**	0.9988 (47.90)**	0.9973	0.9943	0.0125	3355.8735	2.2136
(6)	−0.1361	0.0415(t−1) (3.11)**	−0.0235(t−1) (−2.80)**	1.0004 (46.79)**	0.9973	0.9944	0.0123	3432.0230	2.4293

Note: **Significant at the 1% level, *significant at the 5% level.
The indepenent variables in Equations 3 and 6 have one quarter of time lag.

61

Appendix Note

The derivation of the security market line may be briefly explained: Given two variables X and Y, where Y is the dependent variable and X is the independent variable, the regression equation is given by:

$$Y = a + b\ X + e$$

where

$$b = \frac{\Sigma(X - \overline{X})\ (Y - \overline{Y})}{\Sigma(X - \overline{X})^2} = \frac{Cov(X,\ Y)}{V(X)} \qquad \text{(a)}$$

or

$$b = \frac{\Delta Y}{\Delta X} \qquad \text{(b)}$$

Now in order to determine the relationship between the expected return on security i and the market return, assume that the security i's return depends upon the market return R_m:

$$E(R_i) = F_1(R_m,\ e_1) \qquad \text{(c)}$$

where e_1 = the error term. Applying formula (a), we obtain the regression equation:

$$E(R_i) = R_F + \frac{Cov(R_i, R_m)}{V(R_m)}\ R_m = R_F + \beta_i\ R_m \qquad \text{(d)}$$

Similarly, for security j,

$$E(R_j) = R_F + \frac{Cov(R_j, R_m)}{V(R_m)}\ R_m = R_F + \beta_j\ R_m \qquad \text{(e)}$$

The regression lines thus obtained are called the β characteristic lines, and are depicted in panel (a) of Figure 1.

The β-coeffident is regarded as a measure of the systematic, non-diversifiable risk. It defines the relationship between a firm's stock return and the market return. The stock return of a firm which has a larger value of β will rise more rapidly than the stock return of another firm which has a lower β value in prosperity, and the stock return of a firm which has a higher β value will fall more rapidly than another firm which has a lower β value in depression years. As long

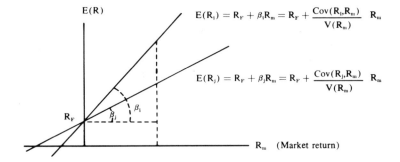

(a) Characteristic Line (β Coefficient for Each Security)

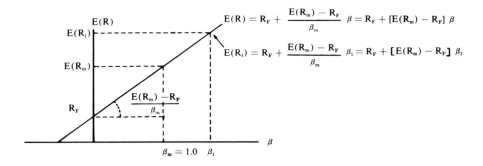

(b) Security Market Line

Figure 1   Derivation of the Security Market Line

as every firm's stock return is related to the market return positively or negatively, the variation of the stock return which is related to the market return cannot be eliminated by purchasing stocks of different firms.

In addition to the systematic, non-diversifiable risk, there is the variation of the stock return which is caused by factors which are unique to a particular firm such as efficient or inefficient management, strikes, inventions, discoveries, a sudden change of consumer taste, advertisement policies, and the like. Such a variation in the stock return of a particular firm is regarded as a non-systematic, diversifiable risk because an investor could minimize his total investment risk by purchasing stocks of many different firms.

Let $R_i = R_F + \beta R_m + e$ where e = the error term

The variance of the equation is,

$$V(R_i) = V(R_F + \beta R_m + e) = \beta^2 V(R_m) + V(e) + 2\beta Cov(R_m, e)$$
$$= \beta^2 V(R_m) + V(e)$$

where $V(R_F) = 0$, since R_F is a constant. Also $Cov(R_m, e) = 0$. Since the variance of the market return $V(R_m)$ is a constant over a given period, β^2 or β is taken as a measure of the systematic risk and $V(e)$ is regarded as a measure of the unsystematic or diversifiable risk.

Since the security return and the market return determine the β value, if we know the β value and the market return, we can also predict the security return. So assume that the security return depends upon the β value:

$$E(R) = F_2(\beta, e_2) \tag{f}$$

Applying formula (b), we obtain regression equation (g), which is also depicted in panel (b) of Figure 1. Note that $\beta_m = 1.0$ since when the market return is regressed on the market return itself, the slope should be equal to one:

$$E(R) = R_F + \frac{E(R_m) - R_F}{\beta_m} \beta$$

$$= R_F + [E(R_m) - R_F] \beta \tag{g}$$

Equation (g) is the so-called security market line. To predict a particular security return, we substitute the β value of the security to obtain the expected return for that security. For security i,

$$E(R_i) = R_F + [E(R_m) - R_F] \beta_i \tag{h}$$

In Equation (h), the average return of all securities may be used for $E(R_m)$, and the Treasury bill rate may be used for R_F.

In contrast to the security market line, the capital market line is defined in the space of the expected return and the standard deviation of the security return.

$$E(R) = R_F + b\,\sigma(R) = R_F + \frac{E(R_p) - R_F}{\sigma(R_p)}\,\sigma(R) \qquad (i)$$

where

$E(R_p) =$ return on the portfolio.
$\sigma(R_p) =$ standard deviation of the portfolio return

In Figure 2, R_FAB line is the capital market line which is tangent at point A with the efficient frontier EF which does not contain any riskless asset. Thus the capital market line is the new efficient frontier which consists of both riskless and risky assets.

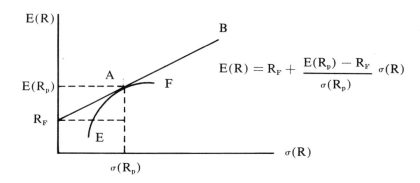

$$E(R) = R_F + \frac{E(R_p) - R_F}{\sigma(R_p)}\,\sigma(R)$$

Figure 2   Capital Market Line

REFERENCES

Auerbach, R.D., "Money and Stock Prices," *Monthly Review*, Federal Reserve Bank of Kansas City, Sept./Oct. 1976, pp. 3-11.

Cooper, R.V.L., "Efficient Capital Markets and the Quantity Theory of Money," *Journal of Finance*, Sept./Oct., 1975, pp. 18-26.

Fama, E., "Efficient Capital Markets: A Review of Theory and Empirical Work," *Journal of Finance, Papers and Proceedings*, May, 1970, pp. 383-417.

Hamburger, M.J., and L.A. Kochin, "Money Stock and Stock Prices: The Channels of Influence," *Journal of Finance*, May 1972, pp. 231-249.

Homa, K.E., and D.M. Jaffee, "The Supply of Money and Common Stock Prices," *Journal of Finance*, Dec., 1971, pp. 1056-66.

Keran, M.W., "Expectations, Money, and the Stock Market," *Review*, Federal Reserve Bank of St. Louis, Jan., 1971, pp. 16-31.

LeRoy, S.F., "Explaining Stock Prices," *Monthly Review*, Federal Reserve Bank of Kansas City, March 1972, pp. 10-19.

Lintner, J., "Inflation and Common Stock Prices in Cyclical Context," *NBER Annual Report*, 1973.

Miller, M.H., "Discussion," *Journal of Finance, Papers and Proceedings*, May, 1972, pp. 294-298.

Nelson, C.R., "Inflation and Rates of Return on Common Stocks," *Journal of Finance*, May 1976, pp. 471-483.

Palmer, M., "Money Supply, Portfolio Adjustments and Stock Prices," *Financial Analysts Journal*, July/August 1970, pp. 19-22.

Pesando, J.E., "The Supply of Money and Common Stock Prices: Further Observations on the Econometric Evidence," *Journal of Finance*, June 1974, pp. 909-921.

Reilly, F.K., G.L. Johnson, and R.E. Smith, "Inflation, Inflation Hedges, and Common Stocks," *Financial Analysts Journal*, Jan./Feb. 1970, pp. 104-11.

Reilly, F.K. et al., "Individual Common Stocks as Inflation Hedges," *Journal of Financial and Quantitative Analysis*, June 1971, pp. 1015-1024.

Reilly, F.K., and J.E. Lewis, "Monetary Variables and Stock Prices," Working Paper, No. 38, University of Kansas, Lawrence, March 1971.

Rozeff, M.S., "Money and Stock Prices: Market Efficiency and the Lag Effect of Monetary Policy," *Journal of Financial Economics*, Dec. 1974, pp. 245-302.

Rozeff, M.S., "The Money Supply and the Stock Market," *Financial Analysts Journal*, Sept./Oct. 1975, pp. 18-26.

Sprinkel, B.W., *Money and Stock Prices*, 1964.

Sprinkel, B.W., *Money and Markets: A Monetarits View*, 1971.

Chapter 3

The Rate of Interest and Inflation: An International Comparison

I. Introduction
II. The Hypotheses
III. The Statistical Results
IV. Conclusions

I. Introduction

A statistical survey shows that there is a large variation in the rate of interest among countries. As average of 1963-66, it ranges from the highest rate of 19.18% in South Korea to the lowest rate of 2.25% in Portugal (Table 5).[1] Also, the survey shows that low income countries on the average have a higher rate of interest than high income countries. The average rate of interest for the 23 low income countries with per capita GNP less than 900 U.S. dollars[2] was 6.99%, while the average rate

---

*Reprinted from *Economia Internazionale*, Aug./Nov. 1973, pp. 603-622.

*The author is indebted to William P. Snavely and Jerral C. Raymond for very useful comments.

[1]To mitigate cyclical factors, an average rate of interest is calculated for the period 1963-65, based mainly on discount rates of central banks. See Table 5 for the basic data.

[2]GNP was calculated as an average for 1963-65 for most countries by Lotz and Morss (1967).

of interest for the 15 high income countries with per capita
GNP more than 900 U.S. dollars was 4.93% (Table 1).

A question is, what factors are responsible for the differences in the rate of interest among countries? Many empirical
studies of demand for money functions have been made pre-
viously by other writers for the U.S. data and for a number of
countries by time series and cross-section analyses. This study
explicitly aims to explain the variations in the rate of interest
among countries by cross-section analysis.[3]

II. Hypotheses

To establish the hypotheses to explain the variations in the
rate of interest among countries, it may be useful to start with
a brief review of relevent theories of the determination of the
rate of interest within a given economy. According to the
Keynesian theory of liquidity preference, the equilibrium rate of
interest is determined by the demand for and the supply of
money. The demand for money (M) is a function of the rate of
interest (i) and the level of money income (Y).[4]

$$M = F(Y, i) \qquad\qquad (1)$$

where

$$\partial M/\partial Y > 0, \quad \partial M/\partial i < 0$$

---

[3]In Adekunle's paper (1968), the dependent variable is the money-income
ratio (M/Y), while in our study, the dependent variable is the rate of interest.
An extensive study of interest rate functions is found in Gibson and Kaufman
(1967, 1968) for the U.S. data. See references.

[4]When there exists the money illusion, the real demand for money should
be a function of the level of real income and the rate of interest.

And the supply of money (M^S) is given as an exogenous variable:

$$M^S = \overline{M} \qquad (2)$$

At equilibrium, the supply of and the demand for money should be equal:

$$\overline{M} = F(Y,\ i) \qquad (3)$$

Equation (3) states that the rate of interest is determined by the supply of money and the level of money income.[5]

According to the modern quantity theory of money, the money-income ratio is a function of the market rate of interest (i), the expected rate of change in prices ($\Delta P^*/P$), the ratio of income from non-human wealth to income from human wealth (w), and real income (Q).[6]

$$\frac{M}{Y} = G(i,\ \Delta P^*/P,\ w,\ Q,\ e) \qquad (4)$$

If the market rate of interest is assumed to be the only significant variable, Equation (4) can be rewritten as:

---

[5]If we assume a Cobb-Douglas type of demand for money function, in equilibrium

$$M = A Y^{\alpha} i^{-\beta} = \overline{M}$$

In logarithms,

$$\ln \overline{M} = \ln A + \alpha \ln Y - \beta \ln i$$

$$\ln i = (1/\beta)\ln A + (\alpha/\beta)\ln Y - (1/\beta)\ln \overline{M}$$

[6]In Friedman's equation, the rate of interest is divided into three types: interest rate on bonds, interest rate on equities, and the general interest rate, i.e., a weighted average rate of the above two interest rates plus the rates applicable to human wealth and to physical goods (Friedman, 1956).

$$\frac{M}{Y}=H(i) \tag{5}$$

where

$$\frac{d(M/Y)}{di} < 0$$

In Equation (5), the dependent variable is the money-income ratio and the independent variable is the rate of interest. However, reversing the direction of causation, we may assume that the money-income ratio determines the rate of interest (Latane, 1954, 1960).

$$i=J\left(\frac{M}{Y}\right) \tag{6}$$

where

$$\frac{di}{d(M/Y)} < 0$$

Equation (6) states that the rate of interest is a function of the money-income ratio.[7]

Rewriting Equation (5) in a linear relationship,

$$\frac{M}{Y}=a-bi \tag{7}$$

$$i = \frac{a}{b} - \frac{1}{b}\frac{M}{Y} \tag{8}$$

---

[7]The money-income ratio is the reciprocal of the income velocity of money. It may be called the average propensity to hold money. The marginal propensity to hold money can be defined as $\partial M/\partial Y$.

And taking the reciprocal of the rate of interest, a non-linear interest rate equation can be written as,

$$\frac{1}{i} = c + g\frac{M}{Y} \qquad (9)$$

If the current rate of interest rises, the speculative demand for money decreases to minimize the interest foregone and to maximize the capital gain in the future (See Keynes, 1936; Tobin, 1958). What will happen if the expected rate of increase in the prices of goods and services rises? People should be less willing to make loans or to purchase bonds, if the rate of interest does not rise, since by the time the loans are repaid or the bonds are redeemed the value of money will have decreased by the amount of a realized rate of inflation. As an alternative way of minimizing the loss of the value of money, people will wish to convert their money asset to other assets whose values are expected to rise, to remain constant, or to decrease less rapidly than the value of money. For these two reasons, both the speculative demand and the transactions demand for money will increase when the expected rate of change in prices rises.[8] Thus Equation (5) can be rewritten as,

---

[8]Thus when the expected rate of increase in prices rises, the demand curve for money will shift upward instead of downward; and the rate of interest will rise. However, if the expected rate of increase in the price of bonds rises, the demand curve for money will shift downward.

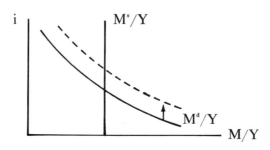

$$\frac{M}{Y} = J\left(i, \frac{\Delta P^*}{P}\right) \qquad (10)$$

where

$$\frac{\partial(M/Y)}{\partial i} < 0, \quad \frac{\partial(M/Y)}{\partial(\Delta P^*/P)} > 0$$

Assuming a linear relationship, the money-income ratio or the average propensity to hold money can be rewritten as,

$$\frac{M}{Y} = a - bi + c\,\frac{\Delta P^*}{P} \qquad (11)$$

Equation (11) states that people wish to hold less money relative to income if the rate of interest rises, and as the expected rate of inflation falls. Taking the rate of interest as a dependent variable, the interest rate equation becomes,

$$i = \frac{a}{b} - \frac{1}{b}\frac{M}{Y} + \frac{c}{b}\frac{\Delta P^*}{P} \qquad (12)$$

Equation (12) states that as people hold more money relative to their income, the rate of interest falls, and as the expected rate of inflation rises, the rate of interest also rises.

To test the above hypothesis, a difficulty arises as to the measurement of the expected rate of change in prices. As a simple but not too ingenious assumption, we shall assume that the expected rate of change in prices is a function of the actual rate of change in prices.[9] Assuming a linear relationship, we can write,

---

[9]The expected rate of change in prices may be calculated as a weighted average of the past rates of change in prices as was calculated by Phillip Cagan in his hyperinflation study (1956). His formula for the expected rate of change in prices is

$$\frac{\Delta \; P^*}{P}=e\;\frac{\Delta \; P}{P} \tag{13}$$

where 'e' may be called the elasticity of price expectation.[10] Substituting Equation (13) in Equation (12), we have the fundamental interest rate function which we wish to test in this paper:

$$i= \alpha - \beta \frac{M}{Y} + \gamma \frac{\Delta P}{P} \tag{14}$$

$$E_t=(1-e^{-\beta}) \sum_{i=0}^{T} C_{t-i}e^{-\beta i}$$

where E_t=the expected rate of change in prices at time t. C_t the actual rate of change in prices at time t. β=the coefficient of expectation. Applying the formula, and letting $\beta=0.4$, I have calculated the expected rate of change in prices for the South Korean economy during the 1945-60 high inflation period. The relationship between the expected rate of change in prices and the actual rate of change in prices was given by

$$\Delta P^*/P=6.5073+0.4786 \; \Delta P/P$$
$$(0.0528)^{**}$$
$$R=0.7884 \quad R^2=0.6216 \quad S.E.=7.2908 \quad D.W.=0.8180$$

For the calculation, quarterly data were used. Mimeographed paper, <The high inflation and the supply of money in South Korea, 1945-60>, 1963. In this study, instead of calculating the weighted average rate of change in prices, we have used the simple average rate of change in prices during 1963-66.

[10]The elasticity of price expectation may be divided into two types:

$$E_1= \frac{\Delta P_{t+1} / P_t}{\Delta P_t / P_{t-1}} \qquad E_2= \frac{\Delta P^*_t / P_{t-1}}{\Delta P_t / P_{t-1}} = \frac{\Delta P^*_t}{\Delta P_t}$$

Note that <e> in Equation (13) is equal to the elasticity of price expectation in the sense of the second formula, E_2.
If the expected rate of change in prices is equal to the realized rate of change in prices, then $e=E_2=1$. During the <normal> period of the economy, the elasticity may be close to 1. If $e>1$, it implies that the expected rate of change in prices was greater than the realized rate of change in prices.

where

$$a/b = \alpha, \quad 1/b = \beta, \quad \text{and} \quad (c/b)e = \gamma$$

Equation (14) states the hypothesis that the rate of interest depends upon the money-income ratio or the average propensity to hold money and the actual rate of change in prices.[11] Taking the reciprocal of the rate of interest to formulate a non-linear relationship, Equation (14) may be rewritten as,

$$\frac{1}{i} = \alpha' + \beta' \frac{M}{Y} - \gamma' \frac{\Delta P}{P} \qquad (15)$$

Finally, for the purpose of statistical test, in the above model, we assume that the demand for money is equal to the supply of money at equilibrium and the latter is assumed to be an exogenous variable given by the monetary authority.[12]

---

[11]Time lags may be introduced in Equation (14). Gibson and Kaufman (1967) calculated the following function:

$$i_t = f(M, Y, \Delta P / P_{t-n}) \qquad n = 0 \sim 8$$

in logarithms and with U.S. monthly and quarterly data for the period of 1952-66. Meiselman suggests:

$$i_t = f(M_{t-j}, Y_{t-k}, \Delta P^* / P_{t-n})$$

where the expected rate of change in prices is to be calculated by the method of distributed lags.

[12]It is recognized that the supply of money is a function of the rate of interest in a simultaneous model. For extensive analyses of the supply of money, see Teigen (1964, 1965) and Brunner (1962).

If the above hypothesis expressed in Equations (14) or (15) is applied to the international data, we expect that a country tends to have a higher rate of interest if the country has a higher money-income ratio and/or a higher rate of inflation. The main objective of our simple model is to test the statistical significance of the rate of inflation in explaining variations in the rate of interest among countries. However, if the objective were to increase the multiple correlation coefficient, in addition to these two variables, the following factors may be included as the independent variables: political stability, industrial composition, the balance of payment situation, responsiveness of foreign capital to domestic rate of interest, government deficit spending, government debt outstanding, other financial intermediaries (Gurley and Shaw, 1956), the rate of return on capital, the rate of unemployment, the capital-labor ratio, the openness of the economy, the degrees of monetization and commercialization of the economy, the development of banking and other financial institutions and markets, etc.[13]

III. The Statistical Results

First, we may discuss the source and the reliability of the statistical data (see Table 5). The rate of change in prices was calculated from the data given in IMF, *International Financial Statistics*, Oct. 1968. To represent the dependent variable, viz., the rate of interest, the market rate of interest may be more desirable. However, since it was not available for many countries, we have chosen the discount rate of a central bank to

---

[13]Economic policies for internal and external stability will also affect the rate of interest. Mundell (1962).

represent the rate of interest. Since the discount rate is a policy variable, we may expect that it would be affected little by market forces, or may be affected with a time lag. However, by taking the average of the discount rates for the three years, we may reasonably assume that a high discount rate reflects a high market rate of interest. As to the rate of change in prices, we face the question of whether we should use the wholesale price index or the consumer price index. Since more countries provided the consumer price index, we have chosen it. It may be assumed, however, that in the long run the consumer price index and the wholesale price index move together although there may be a time lag in the short run. The money-income ratio was obtained by dividing the supply of money by GNP in current prices.[14] To mitigate the short run bias, the rate of interest, the rate of change in prices and the money-income ratio were averaged for the period 1963-66, instead of taking a particular year.

With the above data, the ordinary least squares method of regression was used to estimate the parameters of Equations (8), (9), (14) and (15). The results are summarized in Tables 1, 2, 3, and 4, and the relevant equations are listed below.

(A) The following two equations were obtained for the 38 countries as a whole. Both the money-income ratio and the rate of change in prices are significant at the 1% level, but the non-linear interest rate equation shows a higher R^2. All the signs of

---

[14]The supply of money=currency+demand deposits. Also, most countries provided the supply of money in this definition. The supply of money in broader definitions may be tested when more data are available. As will be seen later, for the U.S. data, the supply of money including the time deposits was also tested.

the partial regression coefficients are consistent with the hypotheses. (Table 1, Equation IV; Table 2, Equation IV. The standard errors of the regression coefficients are shown in the parentheses.)

$$i = 8.0651 - 0.1275 \frac{M}{Y} + 0.1205 \frac{\Delta P}{P} \qquad R^2 = 0.392 \quad (1)$$
$$(0.9853)** \quad (0.0389)** \quad (0.0394)**$$

$$\frac{1}{i} = 12.2727 + 0.3950 \frac{M}{Y} - 0.2227 \frac{\Delta P}{P} \qquad R^2 = 0.570 \quad (2)$$
$$(1.7555)** \quad (0.0694)** \quad (0.0701)**$$

(B) For the 23 low income countries with per capita GNP below 900 U.S. dollars, the money-income ratio and the rate of change in prices are significant at the 5% level and the 1% level respectively. Further we note that the non-linear interest rate equation has a higher multiple R^2, although they are both significant at the 1% level. (Table 1, Equation V; Table 2, Equation V).

$$i = 8.7551 - 0.12175 \frac{M}{Y} + 0.1205 \frac{\Delta P}{P} \qquad R^2 = 0.389 \quad (3)$$
$$(1.3621)* \quad (0.0580)* \quad (0.0501)*$$

$$\frac{1}{i} = 10.7767 + 0.4660 \frac{M}{Y} - 0.2188 \frac{\Delta P}{P} \qquad R^2 = 0.688 \quad (4)$$
$$(1.9189)** \quad (0.0817)** \quad (0.0706)**$$

(C) When the data are fitted to the 15 high income countries, none of the two independent variables is significant at the 5% level for both linear and non-linear interest rate equations. The multiple correlation coefficients are also lower than those for the 23 low income countries. (Table 1, Equation VI; Table 2, Equation VI).

$$i = 4.4349 - 0.0310 \frac{M}{Y} + 0.3193 \frac{\Delta P}{P} \qquad\qquad R^2 = 0.327 \quad (5)$$

$$(1.4346)^{**} \ (0.0351) \quad (0.2139)$$

$$\frac{1}{i} = 23.2019 + 0.1229 \frac{M}{Y} - 1.2196 \frac{\Delta P}{P} \qquad\qquad R^2 = 0.301 \quad (6)$$

$$(5.9670)^{**} \ (0.1458) \quad (0.8895)$$

(D) For the purpose of comparison, the same interest rate functions (8), (9), (14), and (15) were fitted to the U.S. data (Table 8) for the period of 1948-66. The results are summarized in Tables 6 and 7. For the results of Table 6, M_1 (currency + demand deposits) was used to calculate the money-income ratio. The money-income ratio is significant at the 1% level for both linear and non-linear equations, but the rate of change in prices is not significant at the 5% level for both equations. The multiple R^2 is 0.904 for the linear interest rate equation (Table 6, Equation II), and 0.924 for the non-linear interest rate equation (Table 6, Equation IV). They are significant at the 1% level, although the Durbin-Watson statistic indicates the existence of a serial correlation.

For the results of Table 7, M_2 (M_1 + time deposits) was used to calculate the money-income ratio. The result is similar to the case where M_1 is used. That is, the money-income ratio is significant at the 1% level, but the rate of change in prices is not significant at the 5% level for the linear and non-linear interest rate equations, and the multiple R^2 is decreased from 0.904 and 0.924 to 0.638 and 0.723 respectively. Also, the Durbin-Watson statistic suggests a serial correlation.

$$i = 7.4294 - 0.1179 \frac{M_1}{Y} + 0.0229 \frac{\Delta P}{P} \qquad\qquad R^2 = 0.904 \quad (7)$$

$$(0.3256)^{**} \ (0.0101)^{**} \quad (0.0279) \qquad\qquad D.W. = 0.813$$

$$\frac{1}{i} = -1.3620 + 0.9358 \frac{M_1}{Y} - 0.1731 \frac{\Delta P}{P} \qquad R^2 = 0.961 \quad (8)$$
$$(2.2585) \quad (0.0703)** \quad (0.1932) \qquad\qquad D.W. = 0.795$$

$$i = 10.1645 - 0.1376 \frac{M_2}{Y} + 0.0098 \frac{\Delta P}{P} \qquad R^2 = 0.638 \quad (9)$$
$$(1.3086)** \quad (0.0279)** \quad (0.0539) \qquad\qquad D.W. = 0.266$$

$$\frac{1}{i} = -26.1535 + 1.1581 \frac{M_2}{Y} - 0.0947 \frac{\Delta P}{P} \qquad R^2 = 0.723 \quad (10)$$
$$(8.9749)** \quad (0.1915)** \quad (0.3700) \qquad\qquad D.W. = 0.309$$

Note: For more recent U.S. time series data we have obtained the following results:

(1) 1946-76 Annual Data

$i = 8.9695 - 21.5419\ M_1/Y + 0.2050\ \Delta P/P \qquad \overline{R}^2 = 0.8468 \quad D.W. = 1.5768[a]$
$\qquad\quad (-12.70)** \qquad\quad (4.58)**$

$i = 16.5061 - 31.6092\ M_2/Y + 0.4008\ \Delta P/P \qquad \overline{R}^2 = 0.6732 \quad D.W. = 1.2711$
$\qquad\quad (-7.79)** \qquad\quad (5.40)**$

(2) 1962 II-1976 IV Quarterly Data

$i = 8.5722 - 21.0184\ M_1/Y + 1.0361\ \Delta P/P \qquad \overline{R}^2 = 0.5508 \quad D.W. = 0.6448$
$\qquad\quad (-12.70)** \qquad\quad (4.58)**$

$i = -17.6285 - 32.2138\ M_2/Y + 1.2904\ \Delta P/P \qquad \overline{R}^2 = 0.5329 \quad D.W. = 0.7630$
$\qquad\quad (-2.02)* \qquad\qquad (6.30)**$

where i=Three-month Treasury bill rate on new issues. $\Delta P/P$=The rate of inflation, the implicit GNP deflator. The numbers in parentheses are t-ratios. "a" indicates no serial correlation at the 5% level.

Table 1. Interest Rate Regression Equations (International Data) (1963-66 Average Data): i(%)

		Intercept	M/Y(%)	ΔP/P(%)	R	R²	d.f.	S.E.E.
(I)	i(%)	8.9969	-0.1323				36 (38 countries)	2.997
	S.E.R.	(1.0403)**	(0.0432)**					
	Ave. 6.18(%)		21.2974		0.479	0.229		
(II)	i(%)	9.6614	-0.1409				21 (23 low-income countries, below $900)	3.665
	S.E.R.	(1.4245)**	(0.0634)*					
	Ave. 6.99(%)		18.9478		0.437	0.191		
(III)	i(%)	6.1320	-0.0481				13 (15 high-income countries, above $900)	1.180
	S.E.R.	(0.9158)**	(0.0347)					
	Ave. 4.93(%)		24.9000		0.385	0.148		
(IV)	i(%)	8.0651	-0.1275	0.1205			35 (38 countries)	2.699
	S.E.R.	(0.9853)**	(0.0389)**	(0.0394)**				
	Ave. 6.18(%)		21.2974	6.8947	0.626	0.392		
(V)	i(%)	8.7451	-0.1454	0.1140			20 (23 low-income countries)	3.348
	S.E.R.	(1.3621)**	(0.0580)*	(0.0501)*				
	Ave. 6.99(%)		18.9478	8.7913	0.624	0.389		
(VI)	i(%)	4.4349	-0.0310	0.3193			12 (15 high-income countries)	1.128
	S.E.R.	(1.4346)**	(0.0351)	(0.2139)				
	Ave. 4.93(%)		24.9000	3.9867	0.572	0.327		

Note: See Table 5 for the basic data. **Significant at the 1% level. *Significant at the 5% level. d.f.: Degrees of freedom. Ave.: Average S.E.R.: Standard error of the regression coefficient. S.E.E.: Standard error of the estimate.

Estimating equations: (1) $i = \alpha - \beta M/Y$ (2) $i = \alpha - \beta M/Y + \gamma \Delta P/P$

Table 2. Interest Rate Regression Equations (International Data) (1963-66 Average Data): 1/i.

		Intercept	M/Y(%)	ΔP/P(%)	R	R²	d.f.	S.E.E.
(I)	1/i	10.5510	0.4038				36 (38 countries)	5.382
	S.E.R.	(1.8683)**	(0.0778)**					
	Ave.	19.15	21.2974		0.668	0.440		
(II)	1/i	9.0180	0.4573				21 (23 low income countries)	5.599
	S.E.R.	(2.1761)**	(0.0969)**					
	Ave.	17.68	18.9479		0.733	0.537		
(III)	1/i	16.7201	0.1879				13 (15 high income countries)	4.847
	S.E.R.	(3.7623)**	(0.1425)					
	Ave.	21.40	24.9000		0.431	0.186		
(IV)	1/i	12.2727	0.3950	−0.2227			35 (38 countries)	4.810
	S.E.R.	(1.7555)**	(0.0694)**	(0.0701)**				
	Ave.	19.15	21.2974	6.8947	0.755	0.570		
(V)	1/i	10.7767	0.4660	−0.2188			20 (23 low income countries)	4.716
	S.E.R.	(1.9189)**	(0.0817)**	(0.0706)**				
	Ave.	17.68	18.9478	8.7913	0.829	0.688		
(VI)	1/i	23.2019	0.1229	−1.2196			12 (15 high income countries)	4.691
	S.E.R.	(5.9670)**	(0.1458)	(0.8895)				
	Ave.	21.40	24.9000	3.9867	0.549	0.301		

Note: See footnote for Table 1.

Estimating equations: (1) $1/i = \alpha + \beta M/Y$ (2) $1/i = \alpha + \beta M/Y - \gamma \Delta P/P$

81

Table 3. Actual and Predicted Interest Rates (International Data):i(%)

Country	(1) Actual(%)	(2) Predicted(%)	Residual (1)-(2)
1. Australia	4.94	5.71	−0.77
2. Austria	4.50	5.77	−1.27
3. Belgium	4.75	3.72	1.03
4. Brazil	8.00	12.47	−4.47
5. Canada	4.56	6.10	−1.54
6. Ceylon	4.50	5.55	−1.05
7. Chile	15.00	10.69	4.31
8. China (Taiwan)	14.00	6.49	7.51
9. Columbia	8.00	7.73	0.27
10. Costa Rica	4.75	6.22	−1.47
11. Denmark	6.25	5.48	0.77
12. Ecuador	5.00	6.90	−1.90
13. El Salvador	6.00	6.44	−0.44
14. Finland	7.00	7.73	−0.73
15. France	3.75	3.44	0.31
16. Germany (West)	3.75	6.41	−2.66
17. Greece	5.50	6.11	−0.61
18. Iran	4.25	6.64	−2.39
19. Ireland	5.89	4.68	1.21
20. Israel	6.00	6.59	−0.59
21. Italy	3.50	3.52	−0.02
22. Jamaica	4.88	6.98	−2.10
23. Japan	5.84	4.53	1.30
24. Korea (South)	19.18	9.38	9.80
25. Mexico	4.50	6.84	−2.34
26. Netherlands	4.38	5.50	−1.12
27. New Zealand	7.00	5.68	1.31
28. Nicaragua	6.00	6.88	−0.88
29. Norway	3.50	5.85	−2.35
30. Peru	9.50	8.16	1.34
31. Philippines	5.69	7.06	−1.37
32. Portugal	2.25	0.41	1.84
33. South Africa	5.00	5.98	−0.98
34. Spain	4.60	4.60	−0.19
35. Thailand	5.00	6.11	−1.11
36. Turkey	7.50	7.27	0.23
37. United Kingdom	6.00	3.98	2.02
38. United States	4.13	5.07	−0.94

Note: See Table 1, Eq. IV: For the basic data. See Table 5: 1963-66 average data.

Estimating equation: $i = 8.0651 - 0.1275 M/Y + 0.1205 \Delta P/P$

$(0.9853)^{**} \ (0.0389)^{**} \quad (R=0.626 \quad R^2=0.392)$

Table 4. Actual and Predicted Interest Rates (International Data): 1/i.

Country	Actual 1/i	(1) (i)	(2) Predicted 1/i	Residual (1)-(2)
1. Australia	20.2	(4.94)	20.1	0.1
2. Austria	22.2	(4.50)	19.9	2.3
3. Belgium	21.1	(4.75)	26.3	−5.2
4. Brazil	12.5	(8.00)	8.4	4.1
5. Canada	21.9	(4.56)	18.8	3.1
6. Ceylon	22.2	(4.50)	20.2	2.0
7. Chile	6.7	(15.00)	9.0	−2.3
8. China (Taiwan)	7.1	(14.00)	17.3	−10.2
9. Columbia	12.5	(8.00)	15.4	−2.9
10. Costa Rica	21.1	(4.75)	18.1	3.0
11. Denmark	16.0	(6.25)	21.1	−5.1
12. Ecuador	20.0	(5.00)	16.5	3.5
13. El Salvador	16.7	(6.00)	17.3	−0.6
14. Finland	14.3	(7.00)	14.3	0.0
15. France	26.7	(3.75)	26.8	−0.1
16. Germany	26.7	(3.75)	17.9	8.8
17. Greece	18.2	(3.50)	18.8	−0.6
18. Iran	23.5	(4.25)	17.0	6.5
19. Ireland	17.0	(5.89)	23.5	−6.5
20. Israel	16.7	(6.00)	17.9	−1.2
21. Italy	28.6	(3.50)	27.0	1.6
22. Jamaica	20.5	(4.88)	16.0	4.5
23. Japan	17.1	(5.84)	24.0	−6.9
24. Korea (South)	5.2	(19.18)	10.9	−5.7
25. Mexico	22.2	(4.50)	16.5	5.7
26. Netherlands	22.8	(4.38)	21.0	1.8
27. New Zealand	14.3	(7.00)	20.1	−5.8
28. Nicaragua	16.7	(6.00)	16.5	0.2
29. Norway	28.6	(3.50)	19.8	8.8
30. Peru	10.5	(9.50)	13.8	−3.3
31. Philippines	17.6	(5.69)	16.3	1.3
32. Portugal	44.4	(2.25)	36.6	7.8
33. South Africa	20.0	(5.00)	19.2	0.8
34. Spain	21.7	(4.60)	23.8	−2.1
35. Thailand	20.0	(5.00)	18.7	1.3
36. Turkey	13.1	(7.50)	15.5	−2.2
37. United Kingdom	16.7	(6.00)	25.5	−8.8
38. United States	24.2	(4.13)	21.9	2.3

Note: See Table 2, Sq. IV: For the basic data. See Table 5: 1963-66 average data.

Estimating Equation: $1/i = 12.2727 + 0.3950\ M/Y - 0.2227\ \Delta P/P$

$(1.7555)^{**}\ \ (0.0694)^{**}\ \ \ \ \ (0.0702)^{**}$

$(R = 0.7555\ \ R^2 = 0.570)$

Table 5. International Basic Statistical Data
(1963-66 Average Data)

Country	i (%)	M/Y (%)	Per Capita GNP ($)	ΔP/P (%)	1/i
1. Australia	4.94 g	21.5	1913	3.2	20.2
2. Austria	4.50	21.3	1181	3.5	22.2
3. Belgium	4.75	38.0	1416	4.2	21.1
4. Brazil	8.00	27.0	194	65.1	12.5
5. Canada	4.56 b	17.9	2293	2.6	21.9
6. Ceylon	4.50 a	20.7	143	1.0	22.2
7. Chile	15.00	10.1	632	32.5	6.7
8. China (Taiwan)	14.00 c	13.0	196	0.7	7.1
9. Columbia	8.00 dc	15.6	316	13.7	12.5
10. Costa Rica	4.75 dc	15.4	399	1.0	21.1
11. Denmark	6.25	25.1	1897	5.1	16.0
12. Ecuador	5.00	13.1	206	4.2	20.0
13. El Salvador	6.00 dc	13.0	264	0.3	16.7
14. Finland	7.00	8.6	1431	6.3	14.3
15. France	3.75	37.8	1815	1.6	26.7
16. Germany (West)	3.75	16.0	1845	3.2	26.7
17. Greece	5.50	18.1	546	2.9	18.2
18. Iran	4.25	13.1	251	2.0	23.5
19. Ireland	5.89	31.1	825	4.8	17.0
20. Israel	6.00	18.1	1249	6.9	16.7
21. Italy	3.50	39.6	1032	4.2	28.6
22. Jamaica	4.88 b	10.7	479	2.3	20.5
23. Japan	5.84	32.8	720	5.4	17.1
24. Korea (South)	19.18	6.9	110	18.2	5.2
25. Mexico	4.50	12.6	397	3.2	22.2
26. Netherlands	4.38	25.2	1398	5.4	22.8
27. New Zealand	7.00	21.7	1853	3.2	14.3
28. Nicaragua	6.00	13.0	324	3.9	16.7
29. Norway	8.50	21.6	1709	4.5	28.6
30. Peru	9.50	10.8	317	12.2	10.5
31. Philippines	5.69	13.3	159	5.7	17.6
32. Portugal	2.25	63.7	344	3.9	44.4
33. South Africa	5.00	19.4	543	3.2	20.0
34. Spain	4.60	34.1	500	8.9	21.7
35. Thailand	5.00	17.5	199	2.3	20.0
36. Turkey	7.50	10.8	256	4.8	13.3
37. United Kingdom	6.00 b	35.7	1705	3.9	16.7
38. United States	4.13	25.4	3112	2.0	24.2

Source: (1) i, M/Y and ΔP/P were calculated from IMF, *International Financial Statistics*, Oct. 1968. Average for 1963-66. (2) Per capita GNP in U.S. $:, J.R. Lotz and E.R. Morss, "Measuring 'Tax Effort' in Developing Countries," *IMF Staff Papers*, Nov. 1967, pp. 478-497. Average for 1963-66. (3) i: discount rate, except the following: g: government bond yield; b: bank loan rate; c: call loan rate, dc: discount rate (commercial), a: advance rate...as listed in IMF, *International*. All the data are calculated as the average for 1963-66.

Table 6. Interest Rate Regression Equations (U.S.A., 1948-66): i(%)

	Intercept	M/Y(%)	ΔP/P(%)	R	R²	D.W.	d.f.	S.E.R.
(I) i(%)	7.42052	−0.11622		0.948**		0.693	17	0.265
S.E.R.	(0.3222)**	(0.0098)**			0.898			
Ave. 3.677(%)		(32.2053)						
(II) i(%)	7.4294	−0.1179	0.0229	0.951**		0.813	16	0.267
S.E.R.	(0.3256)**	(0.0101)**	(0.0279)		0.904			
Ave. 3.677(%)		(32.2053)	(2.0211)					
(III) 1/i	−1.2952	0.9229		0.964**		0.729	17	1.843
S.E.R.	(2.2441)	(0.0684)**			0.930			
Ave. 28.43		(32.2053)						
(IV) 1/i	−1.3620	0.9358	−0.1731	0.961**		0.795	16	1.853
S.E.R.	(2.2585)	(0.0703)**	(0.1932)		0.924			
Ave. 28.32		(32.2053)	(2.0211)					

Note: See footnote for Table 1. See Table 8 for the basic data.

$M_t/Y = (\text{currency} + \text{demand deposits})/Y$.

Estimating equations:

$i = \alpha - \beta M/Y$ $i = \alpha - \beta M_t/Y + \gamma P\Delta/P$

$1/i = \alpha + \beta M/Y$ $1/i = \alpha + \beta M_t/Y - \gamma \Delta P/P$

Table 7. Interest Rate Regression Equations (U.S.A., 1948-66): 1/i

	Intercept	M/Y(%)	ΔP/P(%)	R	R²	D.W.	d.f.	S.E.R.
(I) i(%)	10.1361	-0.1366				0.249	17	0.503
S.E.R.	(1.2617)**	(0.0266)**		0.796	0.634			
Ave. 3.677%		47.2947						
(II) i(%)	10.1645	-0.1376	0.0098			0.266	16	0.560
S.E.R.	(1.3086)**	(0.0279)**	(0.0539)	0.799	0.638			
Ave. 3.677(%)		47.2947	2.0211					
(III) 1/i	-25.8788	1.1482				0.288	17	3.453
S.E.R.	(8.6622)**	(0.1824)**		0.872	0.761			
Ave. 28.43		47.2947						
(IV) 1/i	-26.1535	1.1581	-0.0947			0.309	16	3.552
S.E.R.	(8.9749)**	(0.1915)**	(0.3700)	0.850	0.723			
Ave. 28.43		47.2947	2.0211					

Note: See Table 8 for the basic data.

Estimating equations:

$$i = \alpha - \beta M_2/Y \qquad\qquad i = \alpha - \beta M_2/Y + \gamma \Delta P/P$$

$$1/i = \alpha + \beta M_2/Y \qquad\qquad 1/i = \alpha + \beta M_2/Y - \gamma \Delta P/P$$

Table 8. U.S.A. Basic Statistical Data (1948-66)

Year	i(%)	M_1/Y(%)	M_2/Y(%)	$\Delta P/P$(%)	1/i
1948	2.82	43.3	57.3	7.7	35.5 (1/0.0282)
1949	2.66	43.7	57.5	−1.0	37.6
1950	2.62	40.8	53.7	1.0	38.2
1951	2.86	37.4	49.0	8.0	35.0
1952	2.96	36.9	48.8	2.2	33.8
1953	3.20	35.3	47.5	0.8	31.3
1954	2.90	36.3	49.5	0.4	34.5
1955	3.06	33.3	46.5	−0.3	32.7
1956	3.36	32.7	45.0	1.5	29.8
1957	3.89	30.8	43.8	3.5	25.7
1958	3.79	31.5	46.2	2.8	26.4
1959	4.38	29.3	43.3	0.8	22.8
1960	4.41	28.0	42.5	1.6	22.7
1961	4.35	28.0	43.9	1.1	23.0
1962	4.33	26.3	43.8	1.2	23.1
1963	4.26	25.9	44.9	1.2	23.5
1964	4.40	25.2	45.2	1.3	22.7
1965	4.49	24.3	45.9	1.7	22.3
1966	5.13	22.9	44.3	2.9	19.5

Note: i=The yield on corporate bonds (Aaa)=the rate of interest (%).

$\Delta P/P$=The rate of change in consumer prices (%).

M_1/Y=The supply of money (currency plus demand deposits) divided by GNP=the money-income ratio.

M_2/Y=The supply of money (M_1+time deposits)/GNP.

1/i=The reciprocal of the rate of interest.

$M_1/Y, M_2/Y, \Delta P/P$, i and 1/i are taken or calculated from U.S. Council of Economic Advisers, *Economic Report of the President*, 1968.

IV. Conclusions

From the above statistical results we may derive the following tentative conclusions:

(1) For the 38 countries as a whole, the statistical results support the two hypotheses: (a) a country tends to have a higher rate of interest if the money-income ratio is lower; and (b) a country tends to have a higher rate of interest if the rate of change in prices is higher. Also the two hypotheses are supported for the 23 low income countries.

(2) However, the second hypothesis that the rate of interest is an increasing function of the rate of change in prices is not supported for the 15 high income countries as a whole and for the U.S.[15] These two results may be said to be consistent. If the rate of change in prices increases, the market rate of interest must rise according to our hypothesis, but this hypothesis is not supported for the U.S. and the 15 high income countries. One possible reason may be that the rate of change in prices in high income countries was much lower and stable, and thus it was insignificant in influencing the rate of interest during the observation period. The average rate of change in prices was 8.79% in the 23 low income countries; 3.99% in the 15 high income countries during 1963-66, and 2.02% in the United States during 1948-68.[16]

(3) Since the hypothesis that a country with a low money-income ratio and/or a higher rate of change in prices tends to have a higher rate of interest is supported for the low income

---

[15]In Gibson and Kaufman's study (1967), the rate of change in prices was significant for the U.S. quarterly and monthly data for 1952-56.

[16]Alternatively, a strong institutional convention could make the rate of interest not sufficiently flexible in high income countries.

countries, it may be helpful to adopt a strong anti-inflationary policy in order to achieve a low rate of interest.

The significance of the correlation between the rate of inflation and the rate of interest might suggest an automatic adjustment cycle: inflation—a high interest rate—low investment ratio—low economic growth rate—high rate of unemployment—low rate of increase in money wage rate (the Phillips relation)—low rate of increase in prices. For the better half of the cycle, the low rate of inflation would lead to a lower rate of interest—high investment ratio—high economic growth rate—low rate of unemployment—high rate of increase in money wage rate—high rate of inflation...and the second round will start.

However, the above automatic adjustment cycle is not necessarily proved in many low income countries where a chronic high rate of inflation and a high rate of unemployment co-exist. In such countries, the solution for a high economic growth rate, a higher private investment ratio, a lower rate of interest, or a lower rate of inflation does not seem to lie in a higher rate of unemployment. Our study shows that the excessive rate of increase in the supply of money, particularly to finance certain unproductive government expenditures, is the major cause of inflation. If the major cause of inflation is the excessive rate of increase in the supply of money, and as long as there exist rigidities in price, wage, and interest rate, the above automatic adjustment cycle could not take place, unless the government takes discretionary fiscal and monetary policies for price stabilization.

(4) Finally, the above statistical results may be different (1) if more refined data become available for the market rate of interest and the expected rate of inflation; (2) if other additional variables are included in the interest rate equipment; (3) if the period of observation is different; (4) if the grouping of the high and low income countries is different; and (5) if the time lag is introduced. There is need for continued study in order to develop a fully satisfactory explanation of the variations in the rate of interest among countries as well as within country.

RIASSUNTO

Tasso di interesse e inflazione: un confronto internazionale

Lo studio si propone di individuare le variabili statisticamente significative dalle quali dipendono le variazioni del tasso di interesse nei vari paesi utilizzando un'analisi di regressione settoriale. Si suppone che il tasso di interesse sia funzione del rapporto moneta-reddito (propensione media al risparmio) e del presunto tasso di variazione dei prezzi. Dall'analisi si rileva che i 38 paesi a reddito alto e basso considerati come un complesso tendono ad avere un alto tasso di interesse, se il rapporto moneta-reddito è basso e l'effettivo tasso di inflazione è alto. Specie per i paesi sottosviluppati, l'analisi dimostra che la maggior causa di inflazione è data dal forte aumento dell'offerta di moneta per finanziare spese pubbliche improduttive.

REFERENCES

Adekunle, J.O., "The Demand for Money: Evidence from Developed and Less Developed Economics," *IMF Staff Papers*, July 1968, pp. 220-264

Bronfenbrener, M., and Mayer, T., "Liquidity Functions in the American Economy," *Econometrica*, Oct. 1960, pp. 810-834.

Brunner, K., "A Schema for the Supply Theory of Money," *International Economic Review*, Jan. 1962, pp. 79-109

Brunner, K., and Meltzer, A., "Some Further Investigations of Demand and Supply Functions of Money," *Journal of Finance*, Vol. 19, 1964, pp. 240-283.

Cagan, P., "he Monetary Dynamics of Hyperinflation," in M. Friedman, ed., *Studies in the Quantity Theory of Money*, 1956, pp. 25-117.

Chow, G.C., "On the Long-run and Short-run Demand for Money," *Journal of Political Economy*, Vol. 74, 1966, pp. 111-131: "Comment" and "Reply" by K. Brunner and A.H. Meltzer, *J.P.E.*, Dec. 1968, pp. 1234-1243.

Christ, C.F., "Interest Rates and Portfolio Selection among Liquid Assets in the U.S.," in Christ G.F. et al., *Measurement in Economics*, 1963, pp. 201-218.

Courchene, T., and Shapiro, H., "The Demand for Money: A Note from the Time Series," *Journal of Political Economy*, Vol. 72, 1964, pp. 498-508: "Reply" by A. Meltzer.

Friedman, M., "The Demand for Money: Some Theoretical and Empirical Results," *Journal of Political Economy*; Aug. 1959, pp. 327-351.

Friedman, M., "The Quantity Theory of Money: A Restatement," in M. Friedman, ed., *Studies in the Quantity Theory of Money*, 1956, pp. 3-21.

Gibson, W.E., *Effects of Money on Interest Rates*, Board of Governors, Federal Reserve System, *Staff Economic Studies*, No. 43, Jan. 1968.

Gibson, W.E., and Kaufman, G.G., *The Relative Impact of Money and Income on Interest Rates: An Empirical Investigation*, Federal Reserve System, Staff Economic Studies, No. 26, Feb. 1967: "Comments" by Hester, pp. 48-50 and D.I. Meiselman, pp. 51-55.

Gurley, J., and Shaw, E.S., "Financial Aspects of Economic Developments," *American Economic Review*, Sept. 1952, pp. 515-538.

Kane, E.J., *Economic Statistics and Econometrics*, 1968, pp. 336-348.

Keynes, J.M., *The General Theory of Employment, Interest, and Money*, 1936.

Latane, H.A., "Cash Balances and the Interest Rate: A Pragmatic Approach," *Review of Economics and Statistics*, Nov. 1954, pp. 456-460.

Latane, H.A., "Income Velocity and Interest Rates: A Pragmatic Approach," *Review of Economics and Statistics*, Nov. 1960, pp. 445-449.

Laidler, D., "The Rate of Interest and the Demand For Money: Some Empirical Evidence," *Journal of Political Economy*, Dec. 1966, pp. 543-555.

Lotz, J.R. and Morss, E.R., "Measuring 'Tax Effort' in Developing Countries," *IMF Staff Papers*, Nov. 1967, pp. 478-497.

Meltzer, A.H., "The Demand for Money: The Evidence from the Time Series," *Journal of Political Economy*, June 63, pp. 219-246.

Mundell, R.A., "The Appropriate Use of Monetary and Fiscal Policy for Internal and External Stability," *IMF Staff Papers*, March 1962, pp. 70-77.

Polak, J.J. and White, W.H., "The Effect of Income Expansion on the Quantity of Money," *IMF Staff Papers*, Aug. 1955, pp. 398-433.

Stedry, A.C., "A Note on Interest Rates and the Demand for Money," *Review of Economics and Statistics*, Aug. 1959, pp. 303-307.

Teigen, R.L., "Demand and Supply Functions for Money in the United States: Some Structural Estimates," *Econometrica*, Oct. 1964, pp. 476-509.

Teigen, R.L., "The demand for and Supply of Money," in W.L. Smith and R.L. Teigen, eds., *Readings in Money, National Income and Stabilization*, 1965, pp. 44-76.

Tobin, J., "Liquidity Preference as Behavior towards Risk," *Review of Economic Studies*, Feb. 1958, pp. 65-86.

Chapter 4

The Burden of Tax and Inflation: An International Comparison

I. Introduction
II. The Model
III. Statistical Results
IV. Conclusions

I. Introduction

Several studies have been made on differences in tax ratio (total tax revenue divided by GNP) among countries. Martin and Lewis[1] (1956) have found that there is a pattern in which countries with higher per capita GNP have higher shares of government expenditures and revenues. The same observation was made by Oshima (1957)[2], who held that the differences are generally caused

---

*Reprinted from "International Differences in Tax Ratio," *The Review of Economics and Statistics*, May 1969, pp. 213-220.

*I am indebted to Otto Eckstein of Harvard University for very helpful suggestions.

[1]Martin, A., and W.A. Lewis, "Patterns of Public Revenue and Expenditure," *The Manchester School of Economic and Social Studies* (Sept. 1956), pp. 203-244.

[2]Oshima, H.T., "Share of Government in Gross National Product for Various Countries," *American Economic Review* (June 1957), pp. 381-390. See also Wai, U.T., "Taxation Problems and Policies of Underdeveloped Countries," *IMF Staff Papers* (Nov. 1962), pp. 428-445.

by productivity differences. Williamson (1961)[3] has confirmed the statistical significance of the correlation by calculating regression equations. Subsequently, Lewis (1963),[4] Hinrichs (1966),[5] and Lotz and Morss (1967)[6] have added the foreign trade ratio as a measure of openness of a country to the per capita GNP in their regression equations. Lewis and Hinrichs found that the foreign trade ratio is statistically a more significant variable than the per capita GNP, while Lotz and Morss together have found that both per capita GNP and the foreign trade ratio are statistically significant for low but not high income cuntries. Why were the results so different? Possible causes may be one or a combination of the following: (1) different periods, (2) different countries, (3) different groupings of low and high income countries, (4) different independent variables.

The purpose of this study is to include some additional variables in the empirical tax ratio functions to see if the results are different from previous studies.

---

[3]Williamson, J.G., "Public Expenditure and Revenue: An International Comparison," *The Manchester School of Economic and Social Studies* (Jan. 1961), pp. 43-56.

[4]Lewis, S.R., Jr., "Government Revenue from Foreign Trade: An International Comprison," *The Manchester School of Economic and Social Studies* (Jan. 1963), pp. 39-45.

[5]Hinrichs, H.H., *A General Theory of Tax Structure Change during Economic Development*, 1966, chap. 2, pp. 7-31. See excellent bibliography. See also Hinrichs, H.H., and R. Bird, "Government Revenue Shares in Developed and Less Developed Countries," *Canadian Tax Journal* (Sept.-Oct. 1963), pp. 431-437.

[6]Lotz, J.R., and E.R. Morss, "Measuring 'Tax Effort' in Developing Countries," *IMF Staff Papers* (Nov. 1967), pp. 478-497.

II. The Model

Other than the per capita GNP and the foreign trade ratio, the following factors may be responsible for differences in tax ratio among countries: the size distribution of income, industrial composition, the composition of government expenditures, the degrees of industrialization and urbanization,[7] the rate of change in prices, the rate of growth in population, the development in money and banking system, the degree of monetization of the economy, political stability, foreign grant and loan, functional income distribution, development of commercial system, climatic and geographical conditions, educational level of taxpayers, occupational structure, wealth, the development of tax and general administration, the development of social security system,[8] and the political and military dependency on other powerful nations, etc.

Among these variables, we shall select the agricultural income ratio as a measure of industrialization, commercialization and urbanization; the rate of change in prices, and the rate of growth in population in addition to per capita GNP and the foreign trade ratio. Our tax ratio function to be fitted to the empirical data is:

$$\frac{T}{Y} = F(Y, \ \frac{F}{Y}, \ \frac{A}{Y}, \ \frac{\Delta P}{P}, \ \frac{\Delta N}{N}, \ \ e) \qquad (1)$$

where

T/Y = tax ratio to GNP

---

[7]Lotz and Morss, op. cit.

[8]Eckstein, O., "The Tax Structure and the Functioning of the American Economy," *National Tax Journal, Proceedings* (1962), pp. 236-249. Hinrichs, H., *A General Theory*, op. cit., pp. 19-22.

Y=per capita GNP

F/Y=the size of foreign trade [sum of export and import (absolute value)] divided by GNP; foreign trade ratio.

A/Y=agricultural income ratio (to GNP)

ΔP/P=the rate of change in the level of consumer prices

ΔN/N=the rate of growth in population

e=the error term

The expected partial regression coefficients are:

$$\frac{\partial(T/Y)}{\partial Y} \ , \ \frac{\partial(T/Y)}{\partial(F/Y)} \ , \ \frac{\partial(T/Y)}{\partial(\Delta P/P)} > 0$$

and

$$\frac{\partial(T/Y)}{\partial(A/Y)} \ , \ \frac{\partial(T/Y)}{\partial(\Delta N/N)} < 0$$

An explanation for the significance of the above factors is briefly attempted:

First, we may expect the tax ratio to be higher when the per capita GNP is higher. The underlying assumption is that the government can extract tax from the surplus of total income over physical subsistence. The higher the total income, the larger will be the relative share of the surplus and thus the potential tax ratio.[9] It is possible for a government to take away the portion of income of subsistence and return it to the tax-payers. In such a case, the tax ratio can be higher even if the per capita GNP is lower. However, this possibility does not

---

[9]See H. Oshima, op. cit.; Lotz and Morss, op. cit.

seem to be what most governments are doing. That is, the social security program is underdeveloped in low income countries, and major expenditures are on public goods and services such as general administration, national defense, police, education, highway construction, etc.

The inclusion of per capita GNP in the tax ratio function assumes an increasing marginal tax rate among countries, or a progressive tax system.[10] However, if the progressiveness is insignificant, the per capita GNP would be also insignificant. As a second factor, the size of foreign trade is expected to have a positive coefficient. Since in many underdeveloped countries a high portion of revenue is derived from custom duties.[11] we may expect that the higher the foreign trade ratio, the higher the tax ratio.

Third, the agricultural income ratio is expected to reflect the industrial composition or the degree of industrialization,

---

[10]A linear form of the "average tax ratio function" is:

$$\frac{T}{Y} = a+bY+c\ \frac{F}{Y}\ +d\ \frac{A}{Y}\ +e\ \frac{\Delta P}{P} + f\ \frac{\Delta N}{N}$$

The "tax function" is:

$$T = aY+bY^2+c\frac{F}{Y}Y+d\ \frac{A}{Y}\ Y +e\frac{\Delta P}{P}\ Y +f\ \frac{\Delta N}{N}\ Y$$

The "marginal tax rate" is:

$$\frac{\partial T}{\partial Y} = a+2bY+\ e\ \frac{\Delta P}{P}\ + f\ \frac{\Delta N}{N}$$

As income rises, the marginal tax rate rises.

[11]Meier, G.M., and R.E. Baldwin, *Economic Development* (1964), pp. 301-302; Crockett, J.P., "Tax Patterns in Latin America," *National Tax Journal* (March 1962), pp. 93-104; Hinrichs, H., op. cit., pp. 19-22.

urbanization and commercialization. When a country is dependent largely on the agricultural sector, we may expect that the private surplus which government can take away as tax, is small. In addition, with a lower degree of commercialization[12] the country will have lower sales taxation and income taxation. A low degree of urbanization will probably have the same disadvantage.

Fourth, as to the rate of change in prices, a country which has a higher rate of inflation may have a higher tax ratio, if the country has any degree of progressive tax system. However, if a country relies upon an indirect tax system or proportional personal and corporate income taxes, or if the progressiveness of personal and corporate income taxes is insignificant, the rate of inflation may be neutral.

Finally, the significance of the rate of increase in population may be briefly discussed. If the population of a country grows more rapidly it may be expected that the country may have a lower tax revenue even if all other conditions are the same, because the number for tax exemption increases. However, if the portion of income tax revenue is very small, a higher rate of population growth may increase the tax ratio because consumption expenditures and thus the payment of sales tax will increase.

III. Statistical Results

To test the above hypothesis, due to the limitation of the available statistical data, only 47 nations were selected. The

---

[12]Jacoby estimates that "less than 10 percent of the product of Laos is 'monetized' in the sense of being sold in markets for money." Jacoby, N.H., "Taxation in Laos: Policies for a New Country with an Underdeveloped Economy," *National Tax Journal* (June 1961), pp. 145-162, pp. 148-149.

statistical data for the tax ratio, per capita GNP and the foreign trade ratio were taken from the laborious calculations of Lotz and Morss. The agricultural income ratio and the rate of increase in population were taken from United Nations, *Statistical Yearbook*, 1966. The rate of change in consumer prices was calculated from International Monetary Fund, *International Financial Statistics*, February 1968. Variables are generally the average figures for the period of 1963-1965. (See Table 4.)

With the method of the ordinary least squares regression, first, three empirical international tax ratio functions were calculated, as shown in Table 1. Equation (1) is for the 47 nations. Equation (2) is for 16 nations with income equal to or greater than $800. (Average per capita GNP was $777.) Equation (3) is for 31 nations with per capita GNP less than $800. Lotz and Morss selected $800 as a rough criterion which divides high and low income countries; these may roughly correspond to developed and underdeveloped countries.

Table 1 shows the following:

1) For the 47 countries, the five independent variables, namely, per capita GNP, the foreign trade ratio, the agricultural income ratio, the rate of change in prices, and the rate of increase in population, explained 73 per cent of the total variation in the tax ratio. However, only the per capita GNP and the rate of increase in population were significant at the 5 per cent level. All the coefficients, however, showed the expected signs.

2) For the 16 high income countries, the 5 independent variables explained only 18.9 per cent of the total variation in the tax ratio, and none of the independent variables was significant at the 5 per cent level.

3) For the 31 low income countries, the 5 independent variables explained only 47.4 per cent of the total variation in the tax ratio. Significant variables were the rate of increase in the

level of prices and the rate of increase in population. All the
coefficients had expected signs.

4) For all the three regression equations, the foreign trade
ratio was not significant at the 5 per cent level and had the
smallest t-ratios among the independent variables. To see the
effect of excluding the foreign trade ratio from the regression
equation, the following equation was fitted to the same empirical
data:

$$\frac{T}{Y} = F(Y, \ \frac{A}{Y}, \ \frac{\Delta P}{P}, \ \frac{\Delta N}{N}, \ e) \qquad\qquad (2)$$

The results are shown in Table 2, and can be summarized as
follows:

1) For the 47 countries, the significant variables were per
capita GNP, the agricultural income ratio, and the rate of increase in population. That is, the agricultural income ratio has
now become a significant variable. R^2 decreased from 0.736 to
0.722. The signs of all the coefficients were consistent with the
expectation.

2) For the 16 high income countries, again none of the independent variables was significant. All the coefficients had
negative signs as in Table 1. R^2 decreased from 0.189 to 0.082.

3) For the 31 low income countries, significant variables
were the agricultural income ratio, and the rate of change in
prices. That is, the rate of increase in population lost the significance and the agricultural income ratio became significant. The
rate of increase in population was significant at the 10 prcent
level. R^2 decreased from 0.474 to 0.449.

Table 1. Statistical Results (Equation 1)

	Intercept	Y(U.S.$)	F/Y(%)	A/Y(%)	$\Delta P/P$(%)	$\Delta N/N$(%)	$\bar{R}$	$\bar{R}^2$	S	d.f.
(1)[a]										
T/Y per cent	18.5598	0.0060	0.0695	−0.1013	0.0977	−1.9941				
S.E.	(3.1357)	(0.0011)	(0.0387)	(0.0538)	(0.0521)	(0.6587)				
T.R.	(5.9189)[e]	(5.9189)[e]	(1.7976)[f]	(−1.8851)[f]	(1.8731)[f]	(−2.9520)[e]	0.858	0.736	4.0	41
(19.75) M.V.		(777.38)	(34.82)	(23.34)	(6.87)	(2.17)				
(2)[b]										
T/Y per cent	39.1990	−0.0018	−0.0105	−0.2256	−0.6124	−1.0181				
S.E.	(12.2328)	(0.0040)	(0.0818)	(0.1671)	(1.3003)	(1.6401)				
T.R.	(3.2044)[e]	(−0.4520)	(−0.1289)	(−1.3505)	(−0.4709)	(−0.6208)	0.435	0.189	5.17	10
(29.04) M.V.		(1667.13)	(40.97)	(12.50)	(4.06)	(1.38)				
(3)[c]										
T/Y per cent	18.7159	0.0006	0.0652	−0.0866	0.1096	−1.7162				
S.E.	(3.1342)	(0.0037)	(0.0435)	(0.0476)	(0.0373)	(0.6783)				
T.R.	(5.9714)[e]	(0.1612)	(1.4967)	(−1.8201)[f]	(2.9420)[e]	(−2.5303)[d]	0.689	0.474	2.71	25
(14.95) M.V.		(318.16)	(31.65)	(28.94)	(8.32)	(2.58)				

[a]For 47 countries. [b]For 16 countries with per capita GNP equal to or greater than $800. [c]For 31 countries with per capita GNP less than $800. [d]Significant at the 5 per cent level. [e]Significant at the 1 per cent level. [f]Significant at the 10 per cent level. S.E.: standard error of the regression coefficient; T.R.: T-ratio; M.V.: mean value; S: standard error of the estimate.

Table 2. Statistical Results (Equation 2)

	Intercept	Y(U.S.$)	A/Y(%)	ΔP/P(%)	ΔN/N(%)	R̄	R̄²	S	d.f.
(1)									
T/Y per cent	21.9902	0.00582	−0.1246	0.0707	−1.9992				
S.E.	(2.5534)	(0.0011)	(0.0535)	(0.0512)	(0.6751)				
T.R.	(8.6122)[e]	(5.1432)[e]	(−2.3264)[d]	(1.3798)	(−2.9613)[e]				
(19.75) M.V.		(777.38)	(23.34)	(6.87)	(2.17)	0.850	0.722	4.16	42
(2)									
T/Y per cent	38.3769	−0.0015	−0.2257	−6.6079	−0.9700				
S.E.	(9.9605)	(0.00356)	(0.1594)	(1.2404)	(1.5240)				
T.R.	(3.8529)[e]	(−0.4555)	(−1.4160)	(−0.4901)	(−0.6365)				
(29.04) M.V.		(1667.13)	(12.50)	(4.06)	(1.38)	0.287	0.083	4.94	11
(3)									
T/Y per cent	19.9756	0.00163	−0.10267	0.0856	−1.2738				
S.E.	(3.0903)	(0.00379)	(0.0474)	(0.0344)	(0.6249)				
T.R.	(6.464)[e]	(0.4311)	(−2.1645)[d]	(2.4868)[d]	(−2.0386)[d]				
(14.95)		(318.16)	(28.94)	(8.32)	(2.58)	0.670	0.449	2.777	26

Note: See Table 1.

Table 3. A Comparison of Statistical Results for Low Income Countries

Regression Equations

Williamson

$$T/Y = 0.0378\,Y^{0.298}$$
$$(0.048)^a$$

R=0.73; N=33; Y<\$1908

(period: 1951-1957)

Lewis

$$\log Y = 1.76 + 0.096 \log F/Y - 0.730 \log Y$$
$$(1.10)\quad(0.640)\qquad\qquad(0.334)$$

R=0.78; N=41; Y<\$2577

$$\log Y = 0.945 - 0.575 \log F/Y - 0.097 \log Y$$
$$(0.396)\quad(0.181)^a\qquad\quad(0.162)$$

R=0.63; N=18; Y<\$275

$$\log Y = 0.707 + 1.13 \log F/Y - 0.497 \log Y$$
$$(0.870)\quad(0.290)^a\qquad\quad(0.243)^c$$

R=0.72; N=23; Y>\$275

(period: 1957)

Hinrichs

$$T/Y = 4.202 + 0.480Y + 0.011\,F/Y$$
$$(\quad)\qquad(\quad)^b$$

$\overline{R^2}=0.415$; N=30; Y<\$300

$$T/Y = 0.299 + 0.237\,Y + 0.0114\,F/Y$$
$$(2.236)\quad(0.089)\qquad(0.006)^b$$

$\overline{R^2}=0.216$; N=30; Y<\$500

(period: 1957-1960)

Lotz & Morss

$$T/Y = 10.21 + 0.0085Y + 0.0712\,F/Y$$
$$((2.963))^a\qquad((2.573))^b$$

$\overline{R^2}=0.197$; N=52; Y<\$800

$$T/Y = 11.04 + 0.000013\,Y^2 + 0.0733\,F/Y$$
$$((2.998))^b\qquad\qquad((2.650))^b$$

$\overline{R^2}=0.200$; N=52; Y<\$800

(period: 1963-1965)

Table 3. A Comparison of Statistical Results for Low Income Countries—Continued

Shin

$$T/Y = 18.7159 + 0.0006Y + 0.0652 \, F/Y - 0.0866 \, A/Y + 0.1096 \, \Delta P/P - 1.7162 \, \Delta N/N$$

$$\quad (3.1342) \quad (0.0037) \quad (0.0435) \quad (0.0476)^c \quad (0.0373)^b \quad (0.6783)^b$$

$$\bar{R}^2 = 0.474; \ N = 31; \ Y < \$800$$

$$T/Y = 19.90756 + 0.00163 \, Y - 0.10267 \, A/Y + 0.0856 \, \Delta P/P - 1.2738 \, \Delta N/N$$

$$\quad (3.0903)^b \quad (0.00379) \quad (0.0474)^b \quad (0.0344)^b \quad (0.6249)^b$$

$$\bar{R}^2 = 0.449; \ N = 31; \ Y < \$800$$

$$(\text{period: } 1963\text{-}1965)$$

[a]Significant at the 1 per cent level, [b]Significant at the 5 per cent level, [c]Significant at the 10 per cent level.
The numbers in parentheses are the standard errors of the regression coefficients.
The numbers in double parentheses are the t-ratios, i.e., the regression coefficients divided by the standard errors.
N: the number of countries observed. Y: per capita GNP in United States dollars.

Table 4. The Basic Data

(1)	(2) Countries	(3) Period for T/Y	(4) T/Y (%)	(5) Per Capita GNP ($)	(6) Year for A/Y	(7) A/Y (%)	(8) ΔP/P (%)	(9) ΔN/N (%)	(10) F/Y (%)
1.	Australia	1964-66	23.6	1913	1965	14	2.9	2.1	28.4
2.	Austria	1963-65	34.5	1181	1965	10	4.0	0.5	39.3
3.	Belgium	1963-65	28.7	1416	1965	6	3.4	0.6	84.0
4.	Brazil	1963-65	21.4	194	1964	29	74.2	3.0	16.5
5.	Canada	1963-65	27.8	2293	1965	6	2.2	2.0	32.8
6.	Ceylon	1963-65	18.6	143	1964	7	2.0	2.6	47.4
7.	Chile	1963-65	20.9	632	1965	10	39.4	2.3	22.5
8.	China (Taiwan)	1963-65	15.0	196	1965	26	0.5	3.4	32.4
9.	Colombia	1962-64	10.9	316	1965	32	17.2	3.2	19.2
10.	Costa Rica	1963-65	13.8	399	1964	31	2.1	4.2	45.9
11.	Denmark	1963-65	28.7	1897	1965	22	5.5	0.8	51.8
12.	Ecuador	1963-65	16.7	206	1965	34	4.1	3.2	27.9
13.	El Salvador	1963-65	10.9	264	1964	32	1.0	3.4	48.0
14.	Finland	1962-64	20.9	1431	1965	18	6.5	0.8	38.2
15.	France	1963-65	37.7	1815	1965	8	3.5	1.3	21.5
16.	Germany (West)	1963-65	34.8	1845	1965	13	3.0	1.3	30.3
17.	Greece	1962-64	20.4	546	1965	25	1.2	0.6	23.3
18.	Honduras	1963-65	9.9	211	1965	44	3.8	3.3	44.6
19.	India	1963	12.5	81	1964	51	8.5	2.3	10.9
20.	Iran	1964-66	16.3	251	1965	30	1.6	2.5	33.4
21.	Ireland	1962-64	23.4	825	1964	22	4.4	0.1	60.5
22.	Israel	1963-65	26.4	1249	1965	9	6.5	3.6	37.7
23.	Italy	1963-65	29.6	1032	1965	13	5.8	0.7	25.6
24.	Jamaica	1964-66	15.6	479	1963	13	2.2	1.9	58.4
25.	Japan	1963-65	19.4	720	1965	12	6.4	1.0	18.7
26.	Korea (South)	1962-64	9.0	110	1965	41	18.8	2.8	16.6
27.	Mexico	1962-64	9.9	397	1965	17	1.5	3.4	14.4

Table 4. The Basic Data—Continued

(1)	(2) Countries	(3) Period for T/Y	(4) T/Y (%)	(5) Per Capita GNP ($)	(6) Year for A/Y	(7) A/Y (%)	(8) ΔP/P (%)	(9) ΔN/N (%)	(10) F/Y (%)
28.	Netherlands	1963-65	32.9	1398	1968	8	5.3	1.4	74.3
29.	New Zealand	1964-66	26.0	1953	1965	35	3.2	2.1	41.7
30.	Nicaragua	1963-65	13.5	324	1965	35	2.4	3.2	49.4
31.	Nigeria	1963-65	11.3	60	1962	65	2.2	2.0	22.4
32.	Norway	1963-65	34.6	1709	1965	9	4.0	0.8	51.8
33.	Panama	1963-65	15.1	484	1964	48	1.0	3.2	41.6
34.	Paraguay	1963-65	10.2	202	1965	36	2.5	2.7	21.3
35.	Peru	1963-65	16.0	317	1964	20	11.3	3.0	34.7
36.	Philippines	1964-65	10.8	159	1965	34	5.7	3.3	31.3
37.	Portugal	1962-64	17.9	344	1965	21	2.8	0.8	35.4
38.	South Africa	1963-65	17.2	543	1965	10	2.5	2.4	34.6
39.	Spain	1962-65	12.2	500	1964	21	7.3	0.8	17.6
40.	Sudan	1963-65	13.3	101	1964	54	2.1	2.8	36.1
41.	Thailand	1963-65	12.6	119	1965	33	1.3	3.0	33.6
42.	Trinidad & Tobago	1964-66	16.7	645	1962	10	2.3	3.1	70.3
43.	Turkey	1963-65	15.1	256	1065	36	4.3	2.6	13.2
44.	United Arab Republic	1962-64	18.5	139	1961	25	0.7	2.6	31.7
45.	United Kingdom	1963-65	28.9	1705	1965	3	3.5	2.5	30.5
46.	United States	1963-65	26.2	3112	1965	4	1.3	1.5	7.1
47.	Uruguay	1962-64	21.8	525	1963	15	24.9	1.4	27.7

Source: T/Y: Tax ratio (to GNP)(%). Lotz, J.R., and Morss, E.R., "Measuring 'Tax Effort' in Developing Countries," IMF Staff Papers, Nov. 1967, pp. 479-497. Y: Per capita GNP (Lotz and Morss, op cit.) in U.S. dollars, A/Y: Agricultural income ratio to GNP (the ratio of income originated from agricultural industries as classified in U.N., Statistical Yearbook, 1966)(%). ΔP/P: Rate of increase in consumer prices (calculated from IMF, International Financial Statistics, Feb. 1968 (%). ΔN/N: Rate of growth in population, 1950-1965 (U.N., Statistical Yearbook, 1966)(%). F/Y: The foreign trade ratio (openness) (the ratio of the sum of export and import (absolute value) to GNP) (Lotz and Morss, op. cit.).

Table 5. Actual Tax Ratio and Predicted Tax Ratio (Equation 2)

(1) Rank[a]	(2) Country	(3) T^A/Y	(4) T^P/Y	(5) Deviation	(6) Deviation %	(7) Tax Effort ranking Shin	(8) Tax Effort ranking Lots and Morss
1.	France	37.7	29.20	8.50	22.54	2	4
2.	Germany (West)	34.8	28.72	6.08	17.47	8	7
3.	Norway	34.6	29.49	5.11	14.76	10	9
4.	Austria	34.5	26.90	7.60	22.02	3	2
5.	Netherlands	32.9	26.70	6.20	18.84	7	12
6.	Italy	29.6	25.38	4.22	14.25	11	3
7.	United Kingdom	28.9	26.78	3.96	7.33	18	18
8.	Belgium	28.7	28.52	0.18	0.62	22	24
9.	Denmark	28.7	29.07	-0.37	-1.28	25	26
10.	Canada	27.8	30.74	-2.94	-10.57	32	30
11.	Israel	26.4	21.40	5.00	18.93	6	14
12.	United States	26.2	36.69	-10.49	-40.03	44	43
13.	New Zealand	26.0	24.44	-1.56	-6.00	29	28
14.	Australia	23.6	27.38	-3.78	-16.01	37	33
15.	Ireland	23.4	24.16	-0.76	-3.24	28	20
16.	Uruguay	21.8	22.14	-0.34	-1.55	26	6
17.	Brazil	21.4	18.75	2.65	12.38	13	1
18.	Chile	20.9	22.61	-1.71	-8.18	30	11
19.	Finland	20.9	26.93	-6.03	-28.85	41	34
20.	Greece	20.4	20.94	-0.54	-2.64	27	8
21.	Japan	19.4	23.14	-3.74	-10.22	39	17
22.	Ceylon	18.6	16.89	1.71	9.19	15	10
23.	United Arab Republic	18.5	14.54	3.96	21.40	5	5
24.	Portugal	17.9	19.97	-2.07	-11.56	33	16
25.	S. Africa	17.2	19.28	-2.08	-12.09	34	25
26.	Ecuador	16.7	12.85	3.85	23.05	1	13
27.	Trinidad	16.7	18.46	-1.76	-10.53	31	38

Table 5. Actual Tax Ratio and Predicted Tax Ratio (Equation 2)—Continued

(1) Rank[a]	(2) Country	(3) TA/Y	(4) TP/Y	(5) Deviation	(6) Deviation %	(7) Tax Effort ranking Shin	(8) Tax Effort ranking Lots and Morss
28.	Iran	16.3	14.83	1.47	9.01	16	19
29.	Peru	16.0	16.14	-0.14	-0.87	24	23
30.	Jamaica	15.6	19.51	-3.91	-25.06	40	35
31.	Panama	15.1	12.50	2.60	17.21	9	32
32.	Turkey	15.1	14.10	1.00	6.55	19	15
33.	China (Taiwan)	15.0	13.13	1.87	12.46	12	22
34.	Costa Rica	13.8	12.20	1.60	11.59	14	36
35.	Nicaragua	13.5	13.29	0.21	1.55	21	37
36.	Sudan	13.3	10.40	2.90	21.80	4	27
37.	Thailand	12.6	12.67	-0.07	-0.55	23	29
38.	India	12.5	12.11	0.39	3.12	20	21
39.	Spain	12.2	21.20	-9.00	-73.68	47	39
40.	Nigeria	11.3	10.40	0.90	7.76	17	31
41.	Colombia	10.9	14.66	-3.76	-34.49	43	40
42.	El Salvador	10.9	12.81	-1.91	-17.52	38	46
43.	Philippines	10.8	12.49	-1.69	-15.64	36	41
44.	Paraguay	10.2	13.46	-3.26	-31.86	42	42
45.	Mexico	9.9	15.49	-5.59	-56.46	46	45
46.	Honduras	9.9	11.41	-1.51	-15.25	35	47
47.	Korea (South)	9.0	13.25	-4.25	-47.22	45	44

[a]Ranked in the order of the actual tax ratio.
TA/Y: Actual tax ratio. TP/Y: Predicted tax ratio, Equation (2) is used. Deviation:=TA/Y − TP/Y. Percentage deviation: (Deviation ÷ TA/Y × 100. Tax effort rank. Column (7): If the positive percentage deviation is the largest, Rank 1 is assigned. Tax effort rank. Column (8): Rank numbers assigned by Lotz and Morss with their Equation (2). Since the number of countries is larger in their observation, the rank number was rearranged.

108

Table 6. Ranking by Percentage Deviation of Tax Ratio (Equation 2)

Countries[a]	Rank	T^A/Y	T^P/Y	% Deviation
Equador	1	16.7	12.85	23.05
France	2	37.7	29.20	22.54
Austria	3	34.5	26.90	22.02
Sudan	4	13.3	10.40	21.80
United Arab Rep.	5	18.5	14.54	21.40
Israel	6	26.4	21.40	18.93
Netherlands	7	3.9	26.70	18.84
Germany (West)	8	34.8	28.72	17.47
Panama	9	15.1	12.50	17.21
Norway	10	34.6	29.49	14.76
Italy	11	29.6	25.38	14.25
China (Taiwan)	12	15.0	13.13	12.46
Brazil	13	21.4	18.75	12.38
Costa Rica	14	13.8	12.20	11.59
Ceylon	15	18.6	16.89	9.19
Iran	16	16.3	14.83	9.01
Nigeria	17	11.3	10.40	17.96
United Kingdom	18	28.9	26.78	7.33
Turkey	19	15.1	14.10	6.55
India	20	12.5	12.11	3.12
Nicaragua	21	13.5	13.29	1.55
Belgium	22	28.7	28.52	0.62
Thailand	23	12.6	12.67	−0.55
Peru	24	16.0	16.14	−0.87
Denmark	25	28.7	29.07	−1.28
Uruguay	26	21.8	22.14	−1.55
Greece	27	20.4	20.94	−2.64
Ireland	28	23.4	24.16	−3.24
New Zealand	29	26.0	24.44	−6.00
Chile	30	20.9	22.61	−8.18
Trinidad	31	16.7	18.46	−10.57
Canada	32	27.8	30.74	−10.57
Portugal	33	17.9	19.97	−11.56
S. Africa	34	17.2	19.28	−12.09
Honduras	35	9.9	11.41	−15.25
Philippines	36	10.8	12.49	−15.64
Australia	37	23.6	27.38	−16.01
El Salvador	38	10.9	12.81	−17.52
Japan	39	18.4	23.14	−19.22
Jamaica	40	15.6	19.51	−25.06
Finland	41	20.9	26.93	−28.85
Paraguay	42	10.2	13.46	−31.86
Colombia	43	10.9	14.66	−34.49
United States	44	26.2	36.69	−40.03
Korea (South)	45	9.0	13.25	−47.22
Mexico	46	9.9	15.49	−56.46
Spain	47	12.2	21.20	−173.68

[a]Ranked in the order of the percentage deviation from the actual tax ratio.

IV. Conclusions

From the statistical results of Tables 1 and 2, we may derive the following conclusions:

1) When countries are divided into two groups, we confirm that a high income country tends to have a higher tax ratio than a lower income country. The difference in the tax ratios between the two groups may be caused not only by differences in per capita GNP and openness, but also by differences in the degree of industrialization, the rate of change in prices and the rate of growth in population.

2) Our results suggest that variations in the tax ratio among low income countries may be caused by differences in the rate of change in prices, the rate of growth in population, and the degree of industrialization. Neither the per capita GNP nor openness was found to be a significant factor. This result does not support the results of the former studies that openness is a significant factor (see Table 3). This difference may be accounted for by the four reasons which were mentioned in the introduction.

3) Our results do not reject the conclusion of Lotz and Morss that "...the tax ratio of high income countries is more an index of political preference for the appropriate size of the government's role than the index of taxable capacity."[13]

4) Finally, as a policy implication, we reach a rather pessimistic conclusion in raising the burden of tax or the tax ratio in low income countries at least in the short run. First, in order to increase the tax ratio, we may have to increase, as a method, per capita GNP. But how can we increase per capita GNP?

---

[13]Lotz and Morss, op. cit., pp. 487-488.

Certainly this goal cannot be achieved in the short run. Secondly, if the agricultural income ratio measures the industrial composition or the degree of commercialization or industrialization, it may be also impossible to change it in the short run.[14]

We may not suggest a higher rate of increase in prices although it is positively correlated with the tax ratio. Not the rate of change in prices, but the higher tax ratio may be the cause of the higher rate of change in prices.[15]

As to the rate of growth in population, how can we decrease the population growth rate? It is doubtful if the people in underdeveloped countries are increasing the number of babies rapidly to avoid taxes.[16] Then any fiscal measures to curb the birth rate may not be as powerful as one may argue. However, any measures to decrease the overpopulation in underdeveloped countries may be of benefit in the long run not only for taxation but also for solving many economic problems caused by overpopulation.

It has been often suggested in economics of development that a government can increase the tax ratio and then the government investment ratio. Our empirical result is pessimistic to this idea. What the government can do to increase the investment ratio and GNP is to increase the portion of government

---

[14]The possibility of increasing tax revenue from higher taxes on rent in countries which rely more on agricultural sector may be difficult without changing political structure, because landlords exercise powerful influence on government policy in many underdeveloped countries.

[15]Clark, C., "Public Finance and Changes in the Value of Money," *Economic Journal* (Dec. 1945), pp. 371-389.

[16]Taylor, M.C., "Income Taxation in the Federation of Malaya," *National Tax Journal* (June 1961), pp. 198-204. An exemption is allowed for one wife. Exemptions for children follow declining amounts: For the first child, $750, $500 for the second and third, $300 for the fourth and fifth, and no allowance for over five, p. 199.

investment in the given total government revenue. In other words, the government will have to shift from consumption to investment,[17] if it wishes to increase the investment ratio.

---

[17]For instance, South Korea, which has a low tax ratio, spent about 35 percent of the "general government" expenditures on national defense during 1963-65. The Bank of Korea, *Economic Statistics Yearbook*, 1966, p. 23.

REFERENCES

Clark, C., "Public Finance and Changes in the Value of Money," *Economic Journal*, Dec. 1945, pp. 371-389.

Crockett, J.P., "Tax Patterns in Latin America," *National Tax Journal*, March 1962, pp. 93-104.

Eckstein, O., "The Tax Structure and the Functioning of the American Economy," *National Tax Journal Proceedings*, 1962, pp. 236-249.

Hinrichs, H.H., *A General Theory of Tax Structure Change during Economic Development*, 1966.

Hinrichs, H.H., and Bird, R., "Government Revenue Shares in Developed and Less Developed Countries," *Canadian Tax Journal*, Sept.-Oct., 1963, pp. 431-437.

Jacoby, N.H., "Taxation in Laos: Policies for a New Country with an Underdeveloped Economy," *National Tax Journal*, June 1961, pp. 145-162.

Lewis, S.R., Jr. "Government Revenue from Foreign Trade: An International Comparison," *The Manchester School of Economics and Social Studies*, Jan. 1963, pp. 39-45.

Lotz, J.R., and Morss, E.R., "Measuring 'Tax Effort' in Developing Countries," *IMF Staff Papers*, Nov. 1967, pp. 478-497.

Martin, A., and Lewis, W.A., "Patterns of Public Revenue and Expenditures," *The Manchester School of Economics and Social Studies*, Sept. 1956, pp. 203-244.

Meier, G.M., and Baldwin, R.E., *Economic Development*, 1965.

Oshima, H.T., "Share of Government in Gross National Product for Various Countries," *American Economic Review*, June 1957, pp. 381-390.

Taylor, M.C., "Income Taxation in the Federation of Malaya," *National Tax Journal*, June 1961, pp. 198-204.

Wai, U.T., "Taxation Problems and Policies of Underdeveloped Countries," *IMF Staff Papers*, Nov. 1962, pp. 428-445.

Williamson, J.G., "Public Expenditure and Revenue: An International Comparison," *The Manchester School of economics and Social Studies*, Jan. 1961, pp. 43-56.

Chapter 5

The Investment Ratio and Inflation: An International Comparison

I. The Problem
II. The Model
III. The Statistical Results
IV. Conclusions

I. The Problem

If the major determinant of the economic growth rate is the investment ratio,[1] then the question is what factors determine

---

*The writer is indebted to Morris Singer for very useful comments on the earlier draft of the manuscript.

[1]Harrod, R.F., *Towards a Dynamic Economics*, 1947: Domar, E.D., "Expansion and Employment," *American Economic Review*, March, 1947, pp. 34-35; "Capital Expansion, Rate of Growth, and Employment," *Econometrica*, April 1946, pp. 137-147. Given the growth rate equation $\Delta Y/Y = (\Delta Y/\Delta K)I/Y$, the growth rate will be determined by the marginal output-capital ratio and the investment ratio. Cheng (1974) obtained the following results for seven industrialized countries with the annual data:

$$\Delta Y/Y = -6.42 + 0.53 \ I/Y \qquad R^2 = 0.90$$
$$(3.87) \quad (7.20) \qquad S.E. = 0.81$$

The numbers in the parentheses are t-ratios. The seven countries are Canada, France, Germany (West), Italy, Japan, U.K., and U.S.A. (Cheng, H.S., In-the investment ratio. This problem is important not only for underdeveloped countries where rapid economic growth is urgent but also for developed countries where stabilization as well as economic growth is one of the major goals of economic policy.

For the domestic investment function, numerous empirical studies have been published. However, the international investment function has not been studied. The purpose of this paper is to test the statistical significance of some empirical factors which may be responsible for differences in the international investment ratio. Some conceivable factors include: per capita GNP or aggregate GNP, the rate of economic growth, the rate of interest, the rate of change in prices, the degree of industrialization, the size of foreign trade, tax systems, the development of monetary and banking systems, the rate of increase in population, political and social stability, wealth, foreign aid, personal and functional income distributions, geographical and climatic conditions, etc.

If we include government investment expenditures in the investment ratio, then the size of the tax ratio, and the composition of government expenditures may be also important variables.

II. The Model

If the statistical data are available, one may attempt to include all of the above variables into the empirical investment ratio function. However, due to the limitation of the data, we select only five factors: namely, the per capita GNP, the agricultural income ratio, the rate of change in prices, the rate of change in

---

vestment Ratios and Economic Growth Rates," *Review*, Federal Reserve Bank of San Francisco, Spring 1974, pp. 9-19.

population, and the foreign trade ratio. The international investment ratio function to be fitted to the empirical data is:[2]

$$\frac{I}{Y} = F(Y, \frac{A}{Y}, \frac{\Delta P}{P}, \frac{\Delta N}{N}, \frac{F}{Y}, e)$$

where

I/Y = gross private and government domestic investment ratio to GNP

Y = per capita GNP in U.S. dollars

A/Y = agricultural income ratio to GNP (Income originated from the agricultural sector)

ΔP/P = the rate of change in the level of consumer prices

ΔN/N = the rate of growth in population

F/Y = the foreign trade ratio: the ratio of the sum of export and import (absolute value) to GNP

e = the error term.

This hypothesis may be explained a little more in detail for each of the above factors: First, if a country has a high per capita GNP, we may expect that the investment ratio would be higher. Since investment can take place only after at least a subsistence level of consumption is subtracted out of a given GNP, the higher the per capita GNP is, the larger will be the surplus, and the investment ratio. However, a simple correlation between the investment ratio and the per capita GNP for 39 countries for 1965 shows that only 23% of the total variation in the investment ratio is associated with the per capita GNP. This suggests that the per capita GNP alone is not a strong explanatory factor for variations in the investment ratio among nations.

---

[2]The rate of interest is not included in the model due to unavailability of the statistical data for many countries.

$$I/Y = 17.3807 + 0.00393GNP \qquad R^2 \quad = 0.233$$
$$(1.2425) \quad (0.00110)** \qquad SE \quad = 5.088$$

As a second factor, we include the agricultural income ratio.[3] It is expected to measure the degrees of industrialization, urbanization[4] and commercialization. In other words, as an economy becomes more industrialized, the incentive for investment may increase. If a country is less industrialized, without much foreign trade, it may be said that the country is still closer to the stage of subsistence level of living without sufficient funds to invest.

As a third factor, the effects of inflation on investment and economic growth have been controversial. As an advantage, inflation may increase profit more rapidly than cost and thus investment.[5] Also when the government spends printed money on investment, both forced saving and investment may rise. However, as a disadvantage, inflation may cause unstable expectation over future profits and may decrease investment. A high rate of inflation will push up the rate of interest, and investment may be discouraged. Also it may decrease the real value of savings, and thus personal saving may be discouraged.[6] As a result, investment fund and investment may decrease. Especially, in many underdeveloped countries, if the government spends printed money on consumption rather than on in-

---

[3]The degree of industrialization may be measured by the percentage of the labor force employed in manufacturing industry. (Bain, J.S., *International Differences in Industrial Structure*, 1966, pp. 13 ff.

[4]Bain, op cit., p. 18.

[5]Ruggles, R., "Summary of the Conference on Inflation and Economic Growth in Latin America," *Inflation and Growth in Latin America*, 1964, pp. 29 ff.

[6]Higgins, B., *Economic Development*, 1959, pp. 463 ff, pp. 455.

vestment, inflation and a low investment ratio will co-exist.

The fourth factor is the rate of growth in population. It may increase the investment activities due to increases in demand. But it may discourage capital-using investments.

Lastly, the effect of the foreign trade ratio on the investment ratio is uncertain. The foreign trade ratio is often used as an index of "openness" of a country. When a country is "open", it may be subject to both consumption and investment emulation effects. Depending upon the nature of imports and exports, domestic investment activities will be different. Thus we may have to wait for the empirical results on its net effect on the investment ratio.

III. The Statistical Results

Due to the limitation of the available statistical data, we have selected 39 countries. The per capita GNP and the foreign trade ratio were taken from Lotz and Morss.[7] The investment ratio, the rate of growth in population, the agricultural income ratio, and the index of consumer prices were obtained from U.N., *Statistical Yearbook*, 1966. For some countries, the consumer price index was obtained from IMF, *Financial Statistics*, Feb. 1968. (For detailed notes, see Table A-3.)

By the ordinary least squares method of regression, three regression equations were calculated for (1) 39 countries as a whole, (2) 15 high income countries and (3) 24 low income countries. The results are shown in Table 1 and can be summarized as follows:

---

[7]Lotz, J.R. and Morss, E.R., "Measuring 'Tax Effort' in Developing Countries," *IMF Staff Papers*, Nov. 1967, pp. 478-497.

Table 1. Statistical Results: The International Investment Ratio

	Intercept	Y(U.S.$)	A/Y(%)	ΔP/P(%)	ΔN/N(%)	F/Y(%)	R̄	R̄²	S	d.f.
I/Y (1)	24.4865	0.00159	−0.1280	−0.0637	−1.0504	0.0026	0.508	0.258	5.00	33
(%) S.E.	(4.4250)	(0.0016)	(0.1020)	(0.0656)	(0.8688)	(0.0524)				
T.R.	(5.5337)**	(1.0114)	(−1.2549)	(−0.9717)	(−1.2091)	(0.0492)				
(20.72)M.V.		(845.44)	(19.82)	(7.70)	(2.08)	(34.88)				
I/Y (2)	15.7149	0.00023	0.1281	0.9820	1.9892	0.0123	0.399	0.159	5.08	9
(%) S.E.	(12.1210)	(0.0039)	(0.3133)	(1.4556)	(1.9570)	(0.0821)				
T.R.	(1.2965)	(0.0579)	(0.4088)	(0.6746)	(1.0165)	(0.1494)				
(24.70)M.V.		(1654.73)	(11.00)	(4.12)	(1.33)	(40.92)				
I/Y (3)	19.7411	0.0112	−0.0362	−0.0794	−0.9242	−0.0412	0.464	0.215	4.46	18
(%) S.E.	(7.0076)	(0.0080)	(0.1210)	(0.0627)	(1.2438)	(0.0854)				
T.R.	(2.8171)	(1.4117)	(−0.2988)	(−1.2658)	(−0.7430)	(−0.4818)				
(18.21)M.V.		(339.63)	(25.33)	(9.94)	(2.55)	(31.11)				

Note: I/Y = Gross private and government domestic investment ratio (to GNP) (%).

Y = Per capita GNP in U.S. dollars (Lotz and Morss, op. cit.).

A/Y = Agricultural income ratio to GNP (%). (The ratio of income originated from agricultural industries as classified in U.N., *Statistical Yearbook*, 1966.)

ΔP/P = The rate of increase in consumer prices (Calculated from IMF, *International Financial Statistics*, Feb. 1968) (%).

ΔN/N = The rate of growth in population, the average of 1950-65 (U.N., *Statistical Yearbook*, 1966).

F/Y = Foreign trade ratio (%). (The ratio of the sum of export and absolute value of import to GNP (Lotz and Morss, op. cit.)

(1) The statistical results support the hypothesis that high income countries tend to have a higher investment ratio since the surplus income that can be saved and invested above the subsistence level is larger.[8] But the per capita GNP explains only 23% of the total international variation in the investment ratio. When all the five independent variables, namely, per capita GNP (Y), the agricultural income ratio (A/Y), the rate of inflation (ΔP/P), the rate of increase in population (ΔN/N), and the foreign trade ratio (F/Y) are put together into the multiple regression equation, the coefficient of determination R^2 increases negligibly to 0.258 from 0.233 for the 39 countries as a whole (Equation 1, Table 1).

(2) When the 39 countries are divided into high and low income countries, the coefficient of determination R^2 becomes much smaller, i.e., 0.159 for the 15 high income countries and 0.215 for the low income countries (Equations 2 and 3 in Table 1). Further we note that the per capita GNP loses the statistical significance in all the three multiple regression equations, perhaps partly due to multicollinearity.

(3) As to the signs of the partial regression coefficients, though none of them is significant at the 5% level, we note that the regression signs for the 15 high income cuntries are contrary to the signs of the regression equations for the 39 countries as a whole and for the 24 low income countries. If the signs of the coefficients were significant, the statistical results would support the following propositions for the 39 countries as a whole: (a) A higher per capita income country can afford a higher percentage of GNP for investment. (b) A more indus-

---

[8]The gross private and government domestic investment ratio was 20.71% for the 39 countries as a whole, 24.71% for the 15 high income countries, and 18.21% for the 24 low income countries in 1965. See Table 1.

Table 2. International Basic Data

(1) Rank	(2) Countries	(3) I/Y	(4) Per capita GNP (U.S.$)	(5) Year for A/Y	(6) A/Y (%)	(7) ΔP/P (%)	(8) ΔN/N (%)	(9) F/Y (%)
1	Australia	29.5	1913	1965	14	2.9	2.1	28.4
2	Austria	28.0	1181	1965	10	4.0	0.5	39.3
3	Belgium	20.0	1416	1965	6	3.4	0.6	84.0
4	Brazil	17.0	194	1964	29	74.2	3.0	16.5
5	Canada	25.5	2293	1965	6	2.2	2.0	32.8
6	Ceylon	14.0	143	1964	7	2.0	2.6	47.4
7	Chile	12.0	632	1965	10	39.4	2.3	22.5
8	China (Taiwan)	21.5	196	1965	26	0.5	3.4	32.4
9	Colombia	19.0	316	1965	32	17.2	3.2	19.2
10	Costa Rica	16.5	399	1964	31	2.1	4.2	45.9
11	Denmark	23.0	1897	1965	22	5.5	0.8	51.8
12	Ecuador	15.0	206	1965	34	4.1	3.2	27.9
13	El Salvador	14.5	264	1964	32	1.0	3.4	48.0
14	Finland	29.5	1431	1965	18	6.5	0.8	38.2
15	France	21.5	1815	1965	8	3.5	1.3	21.5
16	Germany (West)	27.0	1845	1965	13	3.0	1.3	30.3
17	Greece	26.0	546	1965	25	1.2	0.6	23.3
18	Honduras	13.5	211	1965	44	3.8	3.3	44.6
19	India	18.0	81	1964	51	8.5	2.3	10.9
20	Iran	19.0	251	1965	30	1.6	2.5	33.4
21	Israel	32.0	1249	1965	9	6.5	3.6	37.7

Table 2. International Basic Data—Continued

(1) Rank	(2) Countries	(3) I/Y	(4) Per capita GNP (U.S.$)	(5) Year for A/Y	(6) A/Y (%)	(7) ΔP/P (%)	(8) ΔN/N (%)	(9) F/Y (%)
22	Italy	22.0	1032	1965	13	5.8	0.7	25.6
23	Jamaica	21.0	479	1963	13	2.2	1.9	58.4
24	Japan	34.0	720	1965	12	6.4	1.0	18.7
25	Korea (South)	11.5	110	1965	41	18.8	2.8	16.6
26	Mexico	15.5	397	1965	17	1.5	3.4	14.4
27	Netherlands	26.5	1398	1968	8	5.3	1.4	74.3
28	Nicaragua	16.0	324	1965	35	2.4	3.2	41.7
29	Norway	30.5	1709	1965	9	4.0	0.8	49.4
30	Peru	21.5	317	1964	20	11.3	3.0	51.8
31	Philippines	17.5	159	1965	34	5.7	3.3	34.7
32	Portugal	17.5	344	1965	21	2.8	0.8	31.3
33	South Africa	25.5	543	1965	10	2.5	2.4	35.4
34	Spain	20.0	500	1964	21	7.3	0.8	34.6
35	Thailand	19.5	119	1965	33	1.3	3.0	17.6
36	Turkey	14.5	256	1965	36	4.3	2.6	33.6
37	United Kingdom	18.5	1705	1965	3	3.5	2.5	13.2
38	United States	18.0	3112	1965	4	1.3	1.5	30.5
39	Uruguay	16.0	525	1963	15	24.9	1.4	7.1

Note: For sources, see Table 1.

123

trialized country will have a higher investment ratio. (c) Inflation tends to decrease the investment ratio. (d) A high rate of population growth tends to decrease the investment ratio. (e) A country with a higher percentage of foreign trade tends to have a high investment ratio. However, we note that contrary propositions should be true for the 15 high income countries excepting proposition (a). The propositions would be true for the 24 low income countries excepting proposition (e), that is, a low income country with a high percentage of foreign trade tends to have a low investment ratio.

IV. Conclusions

The above overall statistical results suggest that some institutional variables or some policy variables may be more significant factors in determining the investment ratio of an economy. Such institutional or policy variables may include political stability, the lack of profitable investment opportunities, the lack of entrepreneurship, the underdevelopment of banking and financial systems, a high rate of interest, a large share of military and other government consumption expenditures, a low productivity of labor, and foreign economic domination, etc.[9]

---

[9]For investment and development strategies, see, for example, Nurkse, R., *Problems of Capital Formation in Underdeveloped Countries*, 1953; Hirshman, A.O., *The Strategies of Economic Development*, 1958; Nelson, R.R., "A Theory of Low-Equilibrium Trap," *American Economic Review*, Dec. 1956, pp. 894-908.

REFERENCES

Bain, J.S., *International Differences in Industrial Structure*, 1964

Domar, E.D., "Expansion and Employment," *American Economic Review*, March 1947, pp. 34-35.

Harrod, R.F., *Towards a Dynamic Economics*, 1948.

Harrod, R.F., "An Essay in Dynamic Theory," *Economic Journal*, March 1939, pp. 14-33.

Higgins, B., *Economic Development*, 1959, 2nd ed., 1958.

Hirschman, A.O., *The Strategy of Economic Development*, 1958.

Lotz, J.R., and Morss, E.R., "Measuring 'Tax Effort' in Developing Countries," *IMF Staff Papers*, Nov. 1967, pp. 478-497.

Nelson, R.R., "A Theory of the Low-Level Equilibrium Trap," *American Economic Review*, Dec. 1956, pp. 894-908.

Nurkse, R., *Problems of Capital Formation in Underdeveloped Countries*, 1953.

Ruggles, R., "Summary of the Conference on Inflation and Economic Growth in Latin America," *Inflation and Growth in Latin America*, 1964.

Chapter 6

The Causes of High Inflation
in South Korea, 1945-60

I. Introduction
II. The Quantity Theory Hypothesis
III. Determinants of the Demand for Money
IV. Determinants of the Supply of Money
V. Summary and Conclusions

I. Introduction

The end of World War II in 1945 brought the liberation to the people of Korea from 36 years of Japanese military occupation. But the country was immediately occupied by the U.S. army in the south of the 38th parallel line, and by the Soviet army in the North. In 1948 the South established the ''Republic of Korea'' headed by Syngman Rhee and backed by the United States, and the North established the ''Democratic People's Republic of Korea'' headed by II Sung Kim and backed by the Soviet Union.

On June 25, 1950, the two Koreas were thrown into the Korean War, destroying lives and production facilities, and bringing the United States and the People's Republic of China into the battlefield. The ceasefire agreement was signed on July 27, 1953 after three years of destruction of people and land.

---

*The author is indebted to Phillip Cagan for very useful suggestions and comments on an earlier draft. The author is responsible for subjective political views, if any.

The recovery of the South Korean economy was slow. Unemployment continued to grow; the balance of trade and the government budget continued to show deficits which were largely financed by foreign aid, the remainder being financed by printing paper money. On April 26, 1960, President Syngman Rhee was forced to resign by the national movement spearheaded by college students. After the fall of the Rhee government, an interim goverment was established, and after a congressional amendment, on July 29, 1960, Myung Chang was elected as premier. However, in less than a year on May 16, 1961, the Chang government was overthrown by a military coup d'etat led by Chung Hee Park.[1]

The period 1945-60 was indeed years of mixed emotional experiences for the people of Korea: the joy for their liberation from the 36 years of Japanese military occupation, frustration at the separation from family due to a sudden blockade which divided the country into two parts, shock at the assassinations of many political figures, lamentation over the loss of lives in the American air raids during the war and by the South Korean army's executions of the persons who joined the North Korean cause during the North Korean occupation of the Southern part of the country, and more social unrest due to the political dictatorship and the long-lasting economic stagnation.

During the period 1945-60, the Seoul wholesale price index increased from 17 to 25,547 or 1,502 times, the annual average rate of increase in prices being 55%. On the other hand, the supply of

---

[1]For the political setting and general economic development in South Korea during the period 1945-50, see excellent articles by A.I. Bloomfield, and J.P. Jensen, in *Banking Reform in South Korea*, 1951, pp. 9-41.

money increased from 114 million "whan"[2] to 219,077 million whan or 1,921 times, the annual average rate of increase in the supply of money being 48%. Comparing the 55% annual rate of increase in the level of prices and the 48% annual rate of increase in the supply of money, it may be said that prices and the supply of money increased almost together.

The apparent close relationship between the level of prices and the supply of money provides a good testing ground for a few economic hypotheses.[3] According to the modern quantity theory of money, inflation is caused by the discrepancies between the supply of and the demand for money. In the following section II we will test the classical quantity theory of money. In section III we will discuss the modern quantity theory by testing the demand function for real money balances. In section III we will examine the factors responsible for the rapid increases in the supply of money. In the final section IV a summary and conclusions are derived.

---

[2]Korean monetary unit during the period. The foreign exchange rate was 0.5 whan to the U.S. dollar in 1945, 650 whan in 1960, and 1,300 whan in Feb. 1961. The monetary unit was "won" up to 1953, when it was changed to "whan" by denomination of 100 won=1 whan. In 1961, again, 100 whan was denominated to 1 won.

[3]Inflation may be divided into: creeping inflation (1—3% price rise per year), trotting inflation (4—6%), cantering inflation (7—9%), galloping inflation (10, 20, 50, 70%, P.A. Samuelson), and Hyperinflation. Phillip Cagan defines hyperinflation as price rises about 50% per month. In the Korean case, the 55% annual average rate of inflation during the priod 1945-60 belongs to the category of galloping inflation. But the inflations during the immediate aftermath of World War II, and during the earlier months of the Korean War period fall into the category of hyperinflation. See P.A. Samuelson, *Economics*, 9th ed., 1973, p. 827, footnote. P. Cagan, "The Monetary

II. The Quantity Theory Hypothesis

The quantity theory of money is divided into the classical quantity theory and the modern quantity theory.

According to the classical rigid quantity theory of money, the level of prices should rise in proportion to the increase in the supply of money, or the rate of change in prices should be equal to the rate of change in the supply of money, since the velocity of money and the real output are held constant in the classical world of the quantity theory. No reliable GNP data are available for the earlier years of the period 1945-60, and for the Korean War years. However, the political and economic situations such as the division of the country, the war, and the social unrest suggest that real GNP remained almost stable during the period. Thus assuming the real GNP growth rate almost equal to zero, the variations in the level of prices, or the rate

---

Dynamics of Hyperinflation," in M. Friedman, ed., *Studies in the Quantity Theory of Money*, p. 25.

We have chosen the period 1945-60 as a political and historical period in which the Korean people have experienced rapid political, social and emotional changes, and in which the statistical data and economic institutions are incomplete. For example, only after 1953, reliable GNP data are available, and the social order seems to have started to be restored.

The galloping inflation in South Korea did not come to an end after the Park government started to rule the country by military coup d'etat in 1961. The supply of money increased from 24,509 million won in 1960 to 41,161 million won in 1972, the average annual rate of increase in the supply of money being 29.46%. The level of wholesale prices increased from 31.0 (1970=100) to 123.8 during the same period, the average annual rate of increase in prices being 29.46%. In terms of the elasticity of price with respect to the money supply, it was about 1.14 during the period 1945-60, and it was about 0.84 during the period 1961-72. The elasticity of price with respect to money supply is defined as:

$$\frac{\Delta P}{P} \bigg/ \frac{\Delta M}{M} = \frac{dP}{dM} \cdot \frac{M}{P} = E_{PM}$$

of change in prices, should be largely explained by the rate of change in the supply of money, if the velocity of money stayed almost stable, and the classical quantity theory should be found to be valid during such a period. Thus, according to the quantity theory, the supply of money or its rate of change should be a major determinant of the level of prices or the rate of change in prices. These hypotheses are expressed in Equations 1 and 2:[4]

$$P = F_1(M_{t-i}, e_1) \qquad\qquad (1)$$

$$\Delta P/P = F_2(\Delta M/M_{t-i}, e_2) \qquad\qquad (2)$$

where

P = the level of prices, the Seoul wholesale price index (1947 = 100)

M = the supply of money, currency + demand deposits in million whan

$\Delta P/P$ = the rate of change in prices (%)

$\Delta M/M$ = the rate of change in the supply of money (%)

e = the error term

i = time lag, 0, 1, 2,...

The annual and the quarterly data are shown in Tables 8 and 9. The basic annual data for the period 1945-60 are taken from the Bank of Korea, *Economic Statistics Yearbook*, 1961; and the basic quarterly data for the period September 1945-December 1949 are taken from A.I. Bloomfield and J.P. Jensen *Banking Reform in South Korea*, 1951, and the basic data for the period March 1950 to December 1960 are taken from the Bank of Korea, *Annual Economic Review*, 1955-59 editions and

---

[4]Given the quantity equation of money $MV = PQ$, $P = MV/Q$ and $P = F_1$ (M, e_1). Total differentiation of the quantity equation gives $\Delta P/P = \Delta M/M + \Delta V/V - \Delta Q/Q$ and $\Delta P/P = F_2$ $(\Delta M/M, e_2)$.

Table 1. The Level of Prices, The Rate of Change in Prices, and the Supply of Money: The Regression Results

A. Annual Data (1945–60)

(1) $P = 1171.67 + 0.1144\,M$
$(17.00)^{**}$

$R = 0.9766 \quad R^2 = 0.9538 \quad F = 288.98 \quad SE = 2158.69 \quad DW = 1.0517$

(2) $\Delta P/P = -419.1430 + 7.8882\,\Delta M/M$
$(5.38)^{**}$

$R = 0.8211 \quad R^2 = 0.6742 \quad F = 28.97 \quad SE = 30.8248 \quad DW = 1.0219$

B. Annual Data (1946–60)

(3) $P = 1307.48 + 0.5627\,M$
$(16.13)^{**}$

$R = 0.9759 \quad R^2 = 0.9524 \quad F = 260.12 \quad SE = 2203.07 \quad DW = 2.3568[a]$

(4) $\Delta P/P = -45.4246 + 1.8460\,\Delta M/M$
$(3.12)^{**}$

$R = 0.6549 \quad R^2 = 0.4289 \quad F = 9.76 \quad SE = 105.888 \quad DW = 2.3568[a]$

C. Quarterly Data (1948 I–1960 IV)

(5) $P = 2441.68 + 0.1132\,M$
$(17.53)^{**}$

$R = 0.9274 \quad R^2 = 0.8601 \quad F = 307.30 \quad SE = 3579.50 \quad DW = 1.4592$

(6) $\Delta P/P = 9.2100 + 0.2057\,\Delta M/M$
(1.22)

$R = 0.1697 \quad R^2 = 0.0288 \quad F = 1.48 \quad SE = 19.2402 \quad DW = 1.6949[a]$

(7) $\Delta P/P = 6.1387 + 0.3653\Delta M/M_{t-2}$
(2.81)**

R=0.3696 R²=0.1366 F=7.91 SE=18.1408

(8) $\Delta P/P = 1.9507 + 0.3228\Delta M/M_{t-2} + 0.3351\Delta M/M_{t-3}$
(2.55)* (2.21)*

R=0.4636 R²=0.2149 F=6.71 SE=17.47

(9) $\Delta P/P = -0.5531 + 0.2356\Delta M/M_{t-2} + 0.3425\Delta M/M_{t-3}$ $0.2621\Delta M/M_{t-1}$
(1.76) (2.30)* (1.73)

R=0.5109 R²=0.2610 F=5.65 SE=17.1297

(10) $\Delta P/P = 0.2494 + 0.3046\Delta M/M_{t-2} + 0.3046\Delta M/M_{t-3} + 0.2430\Delta M/M_{t-1} + 0.1273\Delta M/M_{t-4}$
(1.84) (1.95) (1.58) (0.81)

R=0.5208 R²=0.2712 F=4.37 SE=4.37

(11) $\Delta P/P = -1.4293 + 0.2648\Delta M/M_{t-2} + 0.2927\Delta M/M_{t-3} + 0.3610\Delta M/M_{t-1} + 0.1653\Delta M/M_{t-4}$
(1.94) (1.87) (1.84) (1.02)
$- 0.2050\Delta M/M_t$
(0.97)

R=0.5347 R²=0.2855 F=3.68 SE=17.2012 DW=1.8334[a]

Note: **Significant at the 1% level. *Significant at the 5% level. [a]The serial correlation is not significant at the 5% level. The numbers in the parentheses are t-ratios.

Economic Statistics Yearbook, 1961.[5] As the index of price level, we have chosen the Seoul wholesale price index because the consumer price index is not available for the earlier years of the period. However, for the period 1951-53 the Pusan retail price index is used because the Seoul wholesale price index is not available due to the fact that Seoul was a battleground and the capital was moved to Pusan during that period. As the supply of money we have used the ordinary definition of the supply of money, i.e., currency plus demand deposits, and these data are the only available data for the supply of money.

The regression results are summarized in Table 1 and below:

Annual data (1945-60):

$$P = 1171.67 + 0.1144M \qquad\qquad R^2 = 0.9538 \qquad (3)$$
$$(7.00)** \qquad\qquad\qquad DW = 1.0517$$

$$\Delta P/P = -419.1430 + 7.8882 \Delta M/M \qquad R^2 = 0.6742 \qquad (4)$$
$$(5.38)** \qquad\qquad\qquad DW = 1.0219$$

where the numbers in parentheses are the t-ratios. **Significant at the 1% level, *significant at the 5% level.

For the level of prices, Equation 3 shows that the supply of money explains 95% of the total variation in the level of prices, Equation 4 shows that the rate of change in the supply of money explains about 67% of the total variation in the rate of change in prices. The regression coefficient has a positive sign as expected, and is significant at the 1% level. Almost the same results are obtained for the period 1946-60.

---

[5]We note that the supply of money decreased from 1,276 million whan to 1,193 million whan during the period December 1949 and March 1950. This decrease may be due to the discrepancy in the two series and it may not be a real decrease in the supply of money. However, we left the two series intact without an attempt to reconcile them.

The regression results for the quarterly data are not as good as for the annual data. For the level of prices, $\Delta R^2 = 0.861$, but for the rate of change in prices, $\Delta R^2 = 0.029$. For possible existence of time lags, four lagged variables of the rate of change in the supply of money are introduced. In Table 1, Equations 7 to 11 are stepwise regression results with 5 rates of change in the supply of money. Equations 2 and 8 show that $\Delta M/M_{t-2}$ and $\Delta M/M_{t-3}$ are significant in explaining the variations in the rate of change in prices. However, R^2 is only 0.2149 in Equation 8. Though the regression results for the quarterly data do not yield high coefficients of determination, the regression results of the annual data support the hypothesis that the supply of money is a major determinant of the level of prices, and the rate of change in the supply of money is a major determinant of the rate of inflation.

However, we note that the price elasticity of money supply $(\Delta P/P)/(\Delta M/M)$ is 7.89 which is far greater than one. This result does not support the classical rigid quantity theory which expects the price elasticity of money supply to be about one.

As a variation of the quantity theory of money, we wish to test the expectation hypothesis: the actual rate of change in prices depends upon the expected rate of change in prices and the expected rate of change in prices is determined by the rate of change in the supply of money:

$$\Delta P/P = F_3(\Delta P^*/P, \ e_3) \qquad\qquad (5)$$

$$\Delta P^*/P = F_4(\Delta M/M_{t-i}, \ e_4) \qquad\qquad (6)$$

where

$\Delta P/P$ = the actual rate of change in prices
$\Delta P^*/P$ = the expected rate of change in prices
   i = time lag, 0, 1, 2,...

Equations 5 and 6 are based on the following assumptions: If people expect that prices will rise in the future, they will wish to spend more now before the level of prices does increase. This will increase spending, the aggregate demand for goods and services, and thus the level of prices. But what will determine the expected rate of change in prices? Some factors which may influence the expected rate of change in prices include: predictions of a bad harvest, war anticipation, population increase anticipated, and the rate of increase in the supply of money.

Nevertheless, the expected rate of change in prices is widely calculated as a weighted average of the past rates of change in prices. A pioneering formula for the expected rate of change in prices is given by Phillip Cagan.[6]

$$\Delta P^*/P = (1 - e^{-\beta}) \sum_{i=0}^{T} C_{t-i} \, e^{-\beta i} \qquad (7)$$

where

$\Delta P^*/P$ = the expected rate of change in prices
C_t = actual rate of change in prices at time t
e = the base of natural logarithm

---

[6]Equation (7) is derived by Cagan (1956, p. 39) from the following assumption:

$$\left(\frac{dE}{dt} \right)_t = \beta(C_t - E_t)$$

and the solution of the differential equation is:

$$E_t = H e^{-\beta t} + e^{-\beta t} \int_{-T}^{t} C_x \, e^{\beta x} \, dx$$

where β is a coefficient of expectation, H is the constant of integration and T is an arbitrary lower limit of the time lag. $E = \Delta P^*/P$.

β=a constant, the coefficient of expectation. Its
time lag determines the rapidity with which the
expected rate of change in prices adjusts, to actual
rate of change in prices. The smaller β, the
slower is the adjustment.

i=time lag from 0 to T

T=an arbritrary lower limit of the time lag

Equation 7 states that the expected rate of change in prices is a
weighted average of past rates of change in prices with weights
given by the exponential function, $e^{-\beta i}$.

For the β value, we have used 0.4 per quarter as being a reasonable estimate of the true value, based on other empirical studies,
rather than estimating it from our data. The calculated weight values
are shown in the following table:

Weight Values

$e^{-\beta}$	$(i-e^{-\beta})$	$e^{-\beta i}$	$(1-e^{-\beta})e^{-\beta i}$
$e^{-0.4}=0.67032$	0.32968	$e^{-0.4(0)}=1.00000$	0.330
		$e^{-0.4(1)}=0.67032$	0.221
		$e^{-0.4(2)}=0.449329$	0.148
		$e^{-0.4(3)}=0.301194$	0.099
		$e^{-0.4(4)}=0.210897$	0.067
		$e^{-0.4(5)}=0.135335$	0.045
		$e^{-0.4(6)}=0.090718$	0.030
		$e^{-0.4(7)}=0.60810$	0.020

Note: The expected rate of change in prices is defined as:

$$\Delta P^*/P=(1-e^{-\beta}) \sum_{i=0}^{T} C_{t-i} e^{-\beta i}$$

The calculated expected rate of change in prices, calculated with Equation (7), and the above weight values are shown in Table 9. Since the number of observations is small for the annual data, the expected rate of change in prices is calculated only for the quarterly data. The regression results are summarized in Table 2 and below:

Quarterly data (1948 I—1960 IV):

$$\Delta P/P = -3.9321 + 1.2988 \Delta P^*/P \tag{8}$$
$$(9.06)^{**} \quad R^2 = 0.6216 \quad DW = 2.0421$$

$$\Delta P^*/P = -0.1790 + 0.2199 \Delta M/M_{t-2} + 0.1955 \Delta M/M_{t-4}$$
$$(3.47)^{**} \qquad\qquad (2.67)^{**}$$
$$+ 0.2081 \Delta M/M_{t-1} + 0.2108 \Delta M/M_{t-3}$$
$$(2.89)^{**} \qquad\qquad (2.88)^{**} \tag{9}$$
$$R^2 = 0.5673$$

The Regression Equation 8 shows that the sign of the regression coefficient of the expected rate of change in prices is positive as expected and significant at the 1% level. The expected rate of change in prices explains about 62% of the total variation in the actual rate of change in prices. Equation 9 is calculated by taking the expected rate of change in prices as a dependent variable.

In Table 2, Regression Equations 2 to 7 are the stepwise regression results with the five rates of change in the supply of money. The stepwise regression includes first the variable with the largest simple correlation coefficient and then other variables are included in the order of significance in increasing R^2. We note that all the regression coefficients of the rates of

---

$$= (1 - e^{-0.4}) \sum_{i=0}^{T=7} C_{t-i} e^{-0.4i} \tag{7}'$$

where $C = \Delta P/P$, the actual rate of change in prices.

Table 2. The Rate of Change in Prices, the Expected Rate of Change in Prices, and the Rate of Change in the Supply of Money: The Regression Results (Quarterly Data, 1948 I—1960 IV)

(1) $\Delta P/P = -3.9321 + \underset{(9.06)^{**}}{1.2988\Delta P^*/P}$

    R=0.7884 R²=0.6216 F=82.12 SE=12.01 DW=2.0421[a]

(2) $\Delta P^*/P = 6.5073 + \underset{(3.18)^{**}}{0.4786\Delta P/P}$

    R=0.7884 R²=0.6216 F=82.12 SE=7.29 DW=0.8780

(3) $\Delta P^*/P = 7.2870 + \underset{(4.29)^{**}}{0.3111\Delta M/M_{t-2}}$

    R=0.5186 R²=0.2690 F=18.40 SE=10.1331

(4) $\Delta P^*/P = 3.0391 + \underset{(4.87)^{**}}{0.3169\Delta M/M_{t-2}} + \underset{(3.64)^{**}}{0.2846\Delta M/M_{t-4}}$

    R=0.6514 R²=0.4243 F=18.06 SE=9.0837

(5) $\Delta P^*/P = 1.6523 + \underset{(3.78)^{**}}{0.2529\Delta M/M_{t-2}} + \underset{(3.44)^{**}}{0.2586\Delta M/M_{t-4}} + \underset{(2.50)^{*}}{0.1929\Delta M/M_{t-1}}$

    R=0.7006 R²=0.4908 F=15.42 SE=8.6316

(6) $\Delta P^*/P = -0.1790 + \underset{(3.47)^{**}}{0.2199\Delta M/M_{t-2}} + \underset{(2.67)^{**}}{0.1955\Delta M/M_{t-4}} + \underset{(2.89)^{**}}{0.2081\Delta M/M_{t-1}} + \underset{(2.88)^{*}}{0.2108\Delta M/M_{t-3}}$

    R=0.7532 R²=0.5673 F=15.40 SE=8.0413

(7) $\Delta P^*/P = -0.2124 + \underset{(3.39)^{**}}{0.2185\Delta M/M_{t-2}} + \underset{(2.52)^{*}}{0.1921\Delta M/M_{t-4}} + \underset{(2.13)^{*}}{0.1975\Delta M/M_{t-1}} + \underset{(2.86)^{**}}{0.2118\Delta M/M_{t-3}} + \underset{(0.18)}{0.0183\Delta M/M_{t}}$

    R=0.7534 R²=0.5676 F=12.08 SE=8.1252 DW=0.7261

Note: See footnote of Table 1.

change in the supply of money are positive and significant either at the 1% or the 5% level, except the current rate of increase in the supply of money in Equation 7. The above regression results support the hypotheses that the rates of change in the supply of money influence the expected rate of change in prices, which in turn, affects the actual rate of change in prices.

III. The Determinants of the Demand for Money

According to the modern quantity theory of money, inflation takes place when the supply of money is greater than the demand for money. In terms of the real money balance, when the supply of real money balances exceeds the demand for real money balances, i.e., $\overline{M}/P > M/P$, people spend more to reduce the excess supply of money. As spending increases, the aggregate demand for goods and services increases, and the level of prices rises. As the price level rises, the real money balance $\overline{M}/P$ decreases to the desired equilibrium level of real money balances, $\overline{M}/P = M/P$. According to this real money balance theory, the Korean inflation may be explained in terms of the slow rates of increase in the demand for real money balances, and the rapid rates of increase in the supply of real money balances.

In this section, we will discuss the reasons for the slow rates of increase in the demand for real money balances by testing the demand function for real money balances, and in the next section, we will discuss the reasons for the rapid rates of increase in the supply of money.

According to the Classical rigid quantity theory of money, the real money balance (M/P) should be a constant when the real output and the velocity of money are held constant:[7]

---

[7]Given $MV = PQ$, $M/P = Q/V = k$.

$$M/P = k \qquad\qquad (7)$$

However, according to the Cambridge cash balance theory, real money balance theory, or a more general theory of demand for money, the demand for real money balances is expressed as a function of several independent variables:[8]

$$M/P = F_5(Q, W, r, \Delta P^*/P, \ldots e_5) \qquad\qquad (8)$$

where

M/P = the demand for real money balances, the stock of money divided by the level of prices

Q = real output

W = real wealth

r = the rate of interest

$\Delta P^*/P$ = the expected rate of change in prices

e_5 = the error term or other factors which are influenced by institutional systems, social and individual customs, habits, political and social conditions, develop-

---

[8]In the classical rigid quantity theory of money, given the quantity equation, $MV = PQ$, $M/P = Q/V$. When Q and V are held constant, M/P must be a constant. In the Cambridge cash balance theory, the demand for money is, $M/P = kQ$ or $M/P = k(W, r, \Delta P^*/P, \ldots)Q$. This may be rewritten as $M/P = F_5 (Q, W, r, \Delta P^*/P, \ldots)$.

The expected regression signs are:

$$\frac{\partial M/P}{\partial Q} > 0, \quad \frac{\partial M/P}{\partial W} > 0, \quad \frac{\partial M/P}{\partial r} < 0, \quad \frac{\partial M/P}{\partial \Delta P^*/P} < 0$$

For the cash balance theory see Pigou (1951), Cagan (1958), Tobin (1952). For the classical quantity theory of money, see Fisher (1911), and for the modern quantity theory see Friedman (1956). For a review see Humphrey (1974).

ment of monetary and financial organizations and
credit systems, and the like.

Equation 8 states the hypothesis that the demand for real money balances is a function of real income, real wealth, the rate of interest, the expected rate of change in prices, and other factors. To be more specific, first, how will an increase in real income affect the demand for real money balances? According to the Keynesian theory, as real income rises, the transactions and precautionary demands for money also increase. The modern quantity theory accepts the Keynesian theory.

However, according to the classical rigid quantity theory of money, an increase in real income does not imply an increase in money income when the supply of money and the velocity of money are held constant: $\overline{M}\,\overline{V}=PQ$. A real income increase means an increase in real output. As long as the supply of money and the velocity of money are held constant, money income is constant. Since money income or the aggregate demand is held constant while the real output is increased, the level of prices must decrease. This implies an increase in the purchasing power of money.

That is, a real income increase is equivalent to an increase in the purchasing power of money. As the level of prices decreases in proportion to an increase in real output, the real money balance also increases in proportion to the increase in real output according to the classical rigid quantity theory of money. However, the classical quantity theory does not recognize the existence of idle money balances. As the purchasing

---

The Keynesian demand for money function is given by:

$$M=F(\,Y,\,i\,)\quad\text{or}\quad M/P=F(\,Q,\,i)$$

in which the expected rate cf change in prices is absent.

power of money increases, people can and will have more both real output and idle money balances as a liquid asset, since the precautionary and speculative demand for money will increase as income rises. As the demand for idle money balances changes, the aggregate demand will also change. If the aggregate demand changes the level of prices will also change. For these reasons, the level of prices will not fall in proportion to the increase in real output when there exists a demand for idle money balances. Thus the real money balance will not necessarily increase in the same proportion to the increase in real income.[9]

As a second determinant of the demand for real money balances, an increase in real wealth will also increase the demand for real money balances.

As a third determinant, if the rate of interest falls, the opportunity cost of holding money decreases. If the utility gain from the low interest to be received per dollar falls below the utility gain from holding the convenient liquid money asset per dollar, an individual will prefer holding money. Keynes' explanation is that when the rate of interest is low the price of bonds is so high that an individual expects the price of bonds

---

[9]Given the classical rigid quantity equation, $MV=PQ$, $M/P=Q/V$. Holding the velocity of money (V) constant, total differentiation gives $d(M/P)=dQ/V$. Dividing by $M/P=Q/V$, we obtain $d(M/P)/(M/P)=dQ/Q$. Under the Cambridge cash balance equation, where the velocity of money is a variable, total differentiation of $M/P=Q/V$ gives:

$$d(M/P) = \frac{VdQ+QdV}{V^2}$$

Dividing by $M/P=Q/V$, we obtain

$$\frac{d(M/P)}{M/P} = \frac{dQ}{Q} - \frac{dV}{V}$$

to fall in the near future. To avoid a capital loss, he will rather hold idle money balances instead of buying bonds until the price of bonds falls. Tobin's explanation is that when the rate of interest is low it is not worthy to risk to purchase bonds whose future prices are uncertain. So, as the rate of interest falls, he wishes to convert securities and assets of higher degrees of risk and less liquidity into less risky and more liquid assets and money. On the other hand, if the rate of interest rises, the portfolios of the wealth holders move toward more risky and less liquid assets.[10] For these reasons, when the rate of interest falls, the demand for idle money balances increases. When the idle money balance increases, the aggregate demand for goods and services decreases and the level of price decreases. Through these processes, the real money balance (M/P) increases to a desired level.

As to the fourth factor, what will happen with the demand for real money balances if the level of prices is expected to rise rapidly in the near future? A person who had planned to purchase goods and services in the future period will want to purchase them if he can afford, during the current period before the purchasing power of money further decreases. Some people or firms will wish to purchase goods and services even by borrowing the necessary amount of money if the extra cost of borrowing now is less than the expected increase in the level of prices. Instead of holding idle money balances, people will want to purchase inflation-hedging assets such as gold, land, and buildings.[11] As a result the aggregate demand will increase and the

---

[10]J.M. Keynes, *The General Theory of Employment, Interest, and Money*, 1936, chs. 13 and 15. J. Tobin, "Liquidity Preference as Behavior towards Risk," *Review of Economic Studies*, Feb. 1958, pp. 65-86.

[11]If the expected rate of change in prices rises, the demand for bonds will decrease since the face value of bonds is fixed, and thus bond is not a hedge against a rapid inflation. Unless the bond price is extremely low,

level of prices will rise more rapidly than before the expectation of inflation took place, and the real money balance will decrease.

However, an opposite result is theoretically possible. If an individual has a fixed income or if an individual expects that his money income will not increase as much as the level of prices in the future period, and if his income is not sufficient to purchase gold or real estate, he will have to reduce current spending to finance the expected high cost of living in the future period. Due to reductions in the aggregate spending by these persons, the level of prices will fall, if other conditions are the same, and the real money balance will increase.

To test the hypothesis expressed in Equation 8, we need the statistical data for real income, real wealth, the rate of interest and the expected rate of change in prices as the major determinants. However, no quarterly data are available except for the expected rate of change in prices. So, we will test the following simplified real money balance function:[12]

$$M/P = F_6(\Delta P^*/P, \quad e_6) \tag{9}$$

---

therefore, people will want to convert bonds to stocks and real estate whose prices do not have ceilings. This will cause the price of bonds to fall and the rate of interest to rise. However, there is a question whether or not stocks are infla-hedging assets. Another explanation of the same phenomenon is that people will demand a high rate of interest if the rate of change in prices is expected to rise to cover the loss of the value of money due to the realized inflation. See S.F. LeRoy, "Interest Rates and the Inflation Premium," Federal Reserve Bank of Kansas City, *Monthly Review*, May 1973, pp. 11-18.

[12]Phillip Cagan tests the following semi log function:

$$\ln M/P = -aE - b$$

or

$$M/P = e^{-aE - b}$$

where E is the expected rate of change in prices, a and b are parameters to estimate. P. Cagan, op. cit., p. 35.

The results of linear regression are summarized in Table 3 and below:

Annual data (1946—60)

$$M/P = 104.0090 - 0.1365\Delta P/P \qquad\qquad R^2 = 0.3575 \qquad (10)$$
$$(-2.69)** \qquad\qquad DW = 1.1021$$

Quarterly data (1948 I—1960 IV)

$$M/P = 6.9226 - 0.1418\Delta P^*/P \qquad\qquad R^2 = 0.5674 \qquad (11)$$
$$(-8.10)** \qquad\qquad DW = 0.2313$$

For the annual data we have used the actual rate of change in prices instead of calculating the expected rate of change in prices since the number of observations is too small to calculate the expected rate of change in prices. Equation 10 is for the period 1945-60. We note that the actual rate of change in prices has a negative sign. The sign is significant at the 1% level for the period 1946-60.

For the quarterly data, the expected rates of change in prices were calculated for the period 1948 I—1960 IV by the method which was explained in Section II, and are shown in Table 9. That is, the expected rate of change in prices is assumed to be a weighted average of past rates of change in prices, weighted according to an exponential function. The regression Equation 11 shows that the expected rate of change in prices is negative and significant at the 1% level, supporting the real money balance hypothesis that if the expected rate of change in prices rises, the demand for real money balances decreases. We note that Equation 11 explains about 57% of the total variation in the real money balance. To see if the coefficient of determination can be increased, we have added five rates of change in the supply of money. The stepwise regression equations 3 to 8 in Table 3 show that only the expected rate of change in prices is significant and none of the money supply variables is significant at the 5% level.

Table 3. The Real Money Balance and the Expected Rate of Change in Prices: The Regression Results

A. Annual Data (1945—60)

(1) $M/P = 93.1543 - 0.0026 \Delta P/P$
$\quad(-0.22)$

$R = 0.0584 \quad R^2 = 0.0034 \quad F = 0.05 \quad SE = 30.8284 \quad DW = 0.9586$

B. Annual Data (1946—60)

(2) $M/P = 104.0090 - 0.1365 \Delta P/P$
$\quad(-2.69)^{**}$

$R = 0.5979 \quad R^2 = 0.3575 \quad F = 7.23 \quad SE = 25.6422 \quad DW = 1.1012$

C. Quarterly Data (1948 I—1960 IV)

(3) $M/P = 6.9226 - 0.1418 \Delta P^*/P$
$\quad(-8.10)^{**}$

$R = 0.7533 \quad R^2 = 0.5675 \quad F = 65.50 \quad SE = 1.4675 \quad DW = 0.2313$

(4) $M/P = 7.0056 - 0.1348 \Delta P^*/P - 0.0117 \Delta M/M_{t-3}$
$\quad(-6.91)^{**} \quad (-0.83)$

$R = 0.7573 \quad R^2 = 0.5735 \quad F = 32.95 \quad SE = 1.4720$

(5) $M/P = 7.0755 - 0.1304 \Delta P^*/P - 0.0102 \Delta M/M_{t-3} - 0.0098 M/M_{t-4}$
$\quad(-6.35)^{**} \quad (-0.72) \quad (-0.71)$

$R = 0.7602 \quad R^2 = 0.5779 \quad F = 21.90 \quad SE = 1.4796$

(6) $M/P = 7.0335 - 0.1359 \Delta P^*/P - 0.0099 \Delta M/M_{t-3} - 0.0083 \Delta M/M_{t-4} + 0.0051 \Delta M/M_{t-2}$
$\quad(-5.45)^{**} \quad (-0.69) \quad (-0.57) \quad (0.39)$

$R = 0.7611 \quad R^2 = 0.5793 \quad F = 16.18 \quad SE = 1.4928$

(7) $M/P = 7.0494 - 0.1346 \Delta P^*/P - 0.0104 \Delta M/M_{t-3} - 0.0078 \Delta M/M_{t-4} + 0.0055 \Delta M/M_{t-2}$
$\quad(-5.15)^{**} \quad (-0.70) \quad (-0.52) \quad (0.41)$
$\quad - 0.0028 \Delta M/M_t$
$\quad (-0.19)$

$R = 0.7613 \quad R^2 = 0.5796 \quad F = 12.68 \quad SE = 1.5084$

(8) $M/P = 7.0441 - 0.1353 \Delta P^*/P - 0.0103 \Delta M/M_{t-3} - 0.0076 \Delta M/M_{t-4} + 0.0054 \Delta M/M_{t-2}$
$\quad(-4.89)^{**} \quad (-0.68) \quad (-0.50) \quad (0.40)$
$\quad - 0.0038 \Delta M/M_t + 0.0010 \Delta M/M_{t-1}$
$\quad (-0.20) \quad (\ )$

$R = 0.7613 \quad R^2 = 0.5797 \quad F = 10.34 \quad SE = 1.5240 \quad DW = 0.2524$

Note: See footnote of Table 1.

147

Table 4. Simple Correlation Coefficients (1945-60, Annual Data)

	(1) M (in Million whan)	(2) M (1947=100)	(3) ΔM/M	(4) P (1947=100)	(5) M/P (1955=100)	(6) ΔP/P (%)
(1) M	1.000	1.000	−0.689	0.977	0.747	−0.299
(2) M(1947=100)		1.000	−0.689	0.977	0.747	−0.299
(3) ΔM/M(%)			1.000	−0.704	−0.336	0.821
(4) P				1.000	0.658	−0.323
(5) M/P					1.000	−0.323
(6) ΔP/P(%)						1.000

Note: If $r>0.6055$, it is significant at the 1% level, and if $r>0.4821$, it is significant at the 5% level. $n=15$. For the basic statistical data see Table 8.

148

Table 5. Simple Correlation Coefficients (Quarterly Data, 1948 I–1960 IV)

	(1) M	(2) P	(3) M/P	(4) $\Delta P/P$	(5) M/P	(6) $\Delta P^*/P$	(7) $\Delta M/M_t$	(8) $\Delta M/M_{t-4}$	(9) $\Delta M/M_{t-1}$	(10) $\Delta M/M_{t-2}$	(11) $\Delta M/M_{t-3}$
1. M	1.000	0.927	0.909	-0.402	0.895	-0.632	-0.405	-0.345	-0.446	-0.421	-0.389
2. P		1.000	0.784	-0.371	0.763	-0.570	-0.391	-0.276	-0.482	-0.416	-0.349
3. M/P			1.000	-0.492	0.975	-0.753	-0.311	-0.358	-0.344	-0.339	-0.398
4. $\Delta P/P$				1.000	-0.374	0.788	0.170	0.200	0.331	0.370	0.333
5. M/P (Index)					1.000	-0.701	-0.298	-0.329	-0.336	-0.362	-0.399
6. $\Delta P^*/P$						1.000	0.405	0.381	0.482	0.519	0.435
7. $\Delta M/M_t$							1.000	0.243	0.673	0.311	0.028
8. $\Delta M/M_{t-4}$								1.000	0.119	-0.025	0.285
9. $\Delta M/M_{t-1}$									1.000	0.377	0.031
10. $\Delta M/M_{t-2}$										1.000	0.152
11. $\Delta M/M_{t-3}$											1.000

Note: The critical value of r is 0.35 for the 1% level of significance, and 0.27 for the 5% level of significance. n=52.

149

Table 6. Means and Standard Deviations
(1948-60, Annual Data)

Variables	Means	Standard deviation
1. The supply of money (in million 'whan') (M)	68,548.9	82,847.2
2. The supply of money (1947 = 100) (m)	13,836.9	16,716.2
3. The rate of change in the supply of money $(\Delta M/M, \%)$	85.2	70.2
4. The Seoul wholesale price index (1947 = 100) (P)	9,011.4	9,701.8
5. The real money balance (M/P, 1955 = 100)	92.5	29.8
6. The rate of change in prices ($\Delta P/P$) (%)	252.8	674.1

Table 7. Means and Standard Deviations
(Quarterly Data, 1948 I–1960 IV)

Variables	Means	Standard deviation
1. The supply of money in million whan (M)	74,897.8	77,628.1
2. The price level, Seoul wholesale price (P, 1947 = 100)	10,919.2	9,474.4
3. The real money balance (M/P, in million whan)	5.2	2.2
4. The rate of change in prices ($\Delta P/P$, %)	11.9	19.3
5. The real money balance (M/P, 1947 = 100)	150.3	62.2
6. The expected rate of change in prices ($\Delta P^*/P$, %)	12.2	11.7
7. The rate of change in the supply of money $(\Delta M/M, \%)$	13.2	16.0
8. $\Delta M/M_{t-4}$	13.2	15.9
9. $\Delta M/M_{t-1}$	14.6	16.3
10. $\Delta M/M_{t-2}$	15.8	19.6
11. $\Delta M/M_{t-3}$	14.5	16.3

150

Table 8. The Supply of Money and the Level of Prices in South Korea, 1945-60

	(1) M (million whan)[1]	(2) M (1947=100)	(3) ΔM/M (%)	(4) P (1947=100)[4]	(5) M/P (1955=100)	(6) ΔP/P (%)
(1944)	(32)	(6)		(0.6)	(730)	
1945	114	23	(293)[3]	17[5]	99	(2733)[3]
1946	249	50	117	55	66	223.5
1947	495	100	100	100	73	81.8
1948	696	141	41	163	63	63.0
1949	1,211	245	74	223	90	36.8
1950	2,831[2]	572	133	348	120	56.1
1951	7,304[2]	1,476	158	2,194[6]	49	530.5
1952	14,325	2,894	96	4,751[7]	45	116.5
1953	30,316	6,124	112	5,951[7]	75	25.3
1954	58,079	11,733	92	7,629	112	28.2
1955	93,523	18,894	61	13,816	100	81.1
1956	120,925	24,429	29	18,623	96	34.8
1957	145,184	29,330	20	22,070	97	18.5
1958	192,553	38,900	33	20,619	138	-6.6
1959	209,900	42,222	9	22,077	140	7.1
1960	219,077	44,258	5	25,547	127	15.7

Note: [1]at the end of the year. [2]estimated by the Bank of Korea. [3]estimated by the author. [4]average of the year. [5]estimated by the Bank of Korea. [6]average of April-December data. Pusan retail price index. [7]Pusan retail price index. The data in parentheses are incomplete.

M=the supply of money in million whan. ΔM/M=the rate of increase in the supply of money (%). P=the Seoul wholesale price index (1947=100). M/P=the real money balance (1955=100). ΔP/P=the rate of change in prices (%).

Source: Calculated from the Bank of Korea, *Economic Statistics Yearbook*, 1961 ed., pp. 28-29.

Table 9. The Real Money Balance and the Expected Rate of Change in prices, Quarterly Data, 1948 I—1960 IV

	(1) M (mill. whan)	(2) P (1947=100)	(3) M/P	(4) ΔP/P (%)	(5) M/P (1947=100)	(6) ΔP*/P (%)	(7) ΔM/M (%)
(1944.12)	(32)	(0.6)	(53.3)	(11.1)	(1523)		
1945.9	105	11	9.5	(1933.3)	271		228.1
12	118	12	9.8	9.1	280		12.4
46.3	128	49	2.6	308.3	74		8.5
6	147	52	2.8	6.1	80		14.8
9	188	90	2.1	73.1	60		27.9
12	272	74	3.7	−7.8	106		44.7
47.3	288	90	3.2	21.6	91		5.9
6	313	90	3.5	0	100		8.7
9	362	102	3.5	13.3	100		15.7
12	536	142	3.8	39.2	109		48.1
48.3	540	149	3.6	4.9	103	15.7	0.7
6	573	162	3.5	8.7	100	13.3	6.1
9	633	180	3.5	11.1	100	11.6	10.5
12	737	185	4.0	2.8	114	8.8	16.4
49.3	778	178	4.4	−3.8	126	6.9	5.6
6	818	202	4.0	13.5	114	7.4	5.1
9	1,087	255	4.3	26.2	123	13.4	32.9
12	1,276	290	4.4	13.7	126	13.0	17.4
50.3	1,193	332	3.6	13.8	103	13.2	6.5
6	(1,248)[e]	348	3.6	4.8	103	10.3	4.6
9	(1,524)	(659)[n]	2.3	89.4	166	36.3	22.1

12	(2,905)	831	3.5	26.1	100	32.9	90.6
51.3	(4,116)	(1,034)[n]	4.0	24.4	114	30.1	41.7
6	(5,125)	1,670	3.1	61.5	89	40.3	24.5
9	(5,966)	2,550	2.3	52.7	66	44.1	16.4
12	(7,304)	2,599	2.8	1.9	80	30.0	22.4
52.3	8,224	3,677	2.2	41.5	63	33.7	12.6
6	9,378	5,137	1.8	39.7	51	35.6	14.0
9	10,822	6,198	1.8	20.7	51	29.5	15.4
12	14,325	5,257	2.7	-15.2	77	14.3	32.4
1953.3	13,770	5,974	2.3	13.6	66	13.8	32.4
6	18,224	6,147	3.0	2.9	86	9.4	-3.9
9	25,409	5,870	4.3	-4.5	123	4.1	32.3
12	30,316	6,635	4.6	13.0	131	7.0	39.4
54.3	36,296	6,135	5.9	-7.5	169	1.7	19.3
6	45,783	6,730	6.8	9.7	194	3.8	19.7
9	50,238	9.108	5.5	35.3	157	13.9	26.1
12	58,079	10,037	5.8	10.2	166	12.9	9.7
55.3	58,142	11,508	5.1	14.7	146	13.3	15.6
6	65,062	14,012	4.6	21.8	131	16.1	0.1
9	75,586	17,729	4.3	26.5	123	19.3	11.9
12	93,523	14,330	6.5	-19.2	186	6.4	16.2
56.3	90,144	15,471	5.8	8.0	166	7.0	23.7
6	99,011	20,013	5.0	29.4	143	14.3	3.6
9	103,971	21,524	4.8	7.6	137	11.6	9.8
12	120,925	20,950	5.8	-2.7	166	6.7	16.3

Table 9. The Real Money Balance and the Expected Rate of Change in prices, Quarterly Data, 1948I–1960 IV—Continued

	(1) M (mill. whan)	(2) P (1947=100)	(3) M/P	(4) ΔP/P (%)	(5) M/P (1947=100)	(6) ΔP*/P (%)	(7) ΔM/M (%)
57.3	120,239	22,500	5.3	7.4	151	6.8	-0.6
6	119,288	23,427	5.1	4.1	146	5.6	-0.8
9	125,049	22,554	5.5	-3.7	157	2.2	4.8
12	145,184	19,503	7.4	-13.5	211	-2.7	17.0
58.3	147,056	19,873	7.4	1.9	211	1.2	1.3
6	149,141	20,707	7.2	4.2	206	0.1	1.4
9	165,781	21,268	7.8	2.7	223	1.0	10.7
12	192,553	21,142	9.1	-0.6	260	0.4	16.1
59.3	210,710	20,423	10.3	-3.7	294	-1.0	9.4
6	206,703	21,950	9.4	7.5	269	1.7	-2.9
9	203,714	23,617	8.6	7.6	246	3.7	-1.4
12	209,900	23,605	8.9	-0.1	254	2.6	3.0
60.3	211,072	24,727	8.5	4.8	243	3.3	0.6
6	206,892	25,804	8.0	4.4	229	3.6	-2.0
9	199,278	26,941	7.4	4.4	211	3.8	-3.8
12	219,077	25,689	8.5	-4.6	248	1.1	9.9

Note: e) estimate. n) Pusan retail price index. ΔP*/P = the expected rate of change in prices. See footnote of Table 8.

Source: Calculated from the Bank of Korea, *Annual Economic Review*, 1955-59 editions; *Economic Statistics Yearbook*, 1960-62 editions. For 1945-49, the data are from A.I. Bloomfield and J.P. Jensen, *Banking Reform in South Korea*, 1951, Table 2, p. 29. Figures are rounded.

The above statistical results, that the expected rate of change in prices is negatively correlated with the real money balance, are consistent with the Cagan's findings for Austria (Jan. 21– Aug. 1922), Germany (Sept. 1920–July 1923), Greece (Jan. 1943– Aug. 1944), Hungary (July 1922–Feb. 1924. July 1945–Feb. 1946), Poland (Apr. 1922–Nov. 1923), and Russia (Dec. 1921– Jan. 1924),[13] though Cagan uses the monthly data, while the Korean data are quarterly, and Cagan fits semilogarithmic function, while the Korean equation is a linear function.

IV. The Determinants of the Supply of Money

In the previous section, we have tested a demand function for real money balances. Now we turn to the reasons for the rapid increases in the supply of money in South Korea during 1945-60.

We have seen that the supply of money increased from 114 million whan to 219,077 million whan or 1,921 times during the 15 years from 1945 to 1960, the annual average rate being 48%. Meanwhile, the level of prices increased from 17 to 25,547 or 1,502 times during the period, the average annual rate being 55%. In section II we have seen that the rapid rate of increase in the supply of money was the major cause of the rapid inflation during that period in South Korea. Then the question is, what caused the supply of money to increase so rapidly? This section deals with the factors which caused the rapid and continuous increases in the supply of money. For this purpose we have to postulate the determinants of the supply of money.

---

[13]P. Cagan, op. cit. p. 43.

[14]For instance, see P. Cagan, *Determinants and Effects of Changes in the U.S. Money Stock, 1875-1955*, 1962.

The supply equation of money is derived from the definitions of the monetary base and the supply of money:[14]

$$M = C + D \qquad (12)$$

where

M = the supply of money

C = currency and coin held by the public (individuals and non-bank corporations), excluding the banks and the central government

D = demand deposits held by the public

Equation 12 states that the supply of money is defined as the sum of currency and demand deposits held by the public. On the other hand, the monetary base or the so-called high powered money is defined by:

$$B = C + R \qquad (13)$$

where

B = the monetary base or the high powered money, or tangible money which is defined as the sum of C and R.

R = currency and coins held by the commercial banks as reserves, and the reserves of banks with the central bank.

From Equations 12 and 13 we can derive the supply equation of money expressed by Equation 14:[15]

---

[15]Dividing Equation 12 by Equation 13:

$$\frac{B}{M} = \frac{C+R}{C+D} = \frac{\dfrac{C}{D} + \dfrac{R}{D}}{\dfrac{D}{D} + 1} \qquad \text{So, } M = B \; \frac{\dfrac{C}{D} + 1}{\dfrac{C}{D} + \dfrac{R}{D}}$$

$$M = B \frac{\dfrac{C}{D} + 1}{\dfrac{C}{D} + \dfrac{R}{D}} \qquad (14)$$

where

C/D=the currency-deposit ratio, or simply currency ratio
R/D=the actual reserve-deposit ratio, or simply actual
    reserve ratio

Equation 14 suggests that the supply of money will increase (1) if the currency-deposit ratio decreases, (2) if the actual reserve ratio decreases, and (3) if the monetary base increases.[16] From Equations 12 and 13 we can also derive Equation 15:[17]

---

[16]Letting C/D=c, R/D=r, where 1>r>0, c>0, differentiating Equation 14, $M = B(c + 1) / (c + r)$:

$$\frac{\partial M}{\partial B} = \frac{c+1}{c+r} > 0, \quad \frac{\partial M}{\partial c} = \frac{B(r-1)}{(c+r)^2} < 0, \quad \frac{\partial M}{\partial r} = \frac{-B(c+1)}{(c+r)^2} < 0$$

[17]Dividing Equation 13 by M,

$$\frac{B}{M} = \frac{R}{M} + \frac{C}{M} \qquad \frac{B}{M} = \frac{R}{D}\frac{D}{M} + \frac{C}{M} \qquad (a)$$

Dividing Equation 12 by M:

$$\frac{M}{M} = \frac{C}{M} + \frac{D}{M} \qquad \frac{D}{M} = 1 - \frac{C}{M} \qquad (b)$$

Substituting (b) in (a), we get:

$$\frac{B}{M} = \frac{R}{D}\left(1 - \frac{C}{M}\right) + \frac{C}{M} = \frac{R}{D} + \frac{C}{M} - \frac{R}{D}\frac{C}{M} \qquad (c)$$

From (c) we obtain Equation 15.

$$M = \frac{B}{\dfrac{R}{D} + \dfrac{C}{M} - \dfrac{R}{D}\dfrac{C}{M}} \qquad (15)$$

where C/M=the currency-money ratio.

Equation 15 suggests that the supply of money will increase (1) if the actual reserve ratio decreases, (2) if the currency-money ratio decreases, and (3) if the monetary base increases.[18]

The monetary base is issued largely in two forms by the central bank: (1) the loans to the government sector and (2) the loans to the private sector, or largely to the commercial banking institutions. Thus, the monetary base may be rewritten as:

$$B = B^g + B^p + e \qquad (16)$$

where

B^g=monetary loans to the government sector by the central bank[19]

B^p=loans to the private sector

e=omissions and errors

---

[18]In Equation 15, letting $R/D=r$, $C/M=m$, where $1>r>0$, $1>m>0$, $r+m-rm>0$, differentiating $M=B(r+m-rm)$,

$$\frac{\partial M}{\partial r} = \frac{-B(1-m)}{(r+m-rm)^2} < 0, \frac{\partial M}{\partial m} = \frac{-B(1-r)}{(r+m-rm)^2} < 0, \frac{\partial M}{\partial B} = \frac{1}{r+m-rm} > 0$$

[19]The Bank of Korea is the central bank of South Korea. It was established in 1901, and has branches in major cities of the country. Only the central bank can issue currency. It also underwrites the government bonds, makes loans to the commercial banks as well as to the government agencies. The central bank also keeps reserves of the commercial banks. Since the

The monetary loans to the government sector is further divided into: (1) the net government overdraft, (2) the loans to the government agencies, (3) and the government bonds undertaken and owned by the central bank:

$$B^g = G^1 + G^2 + G^3 \tag{17}$$

Substituting Equations 16 and 17 into Equation 15, and omitting the term of omissions and errors, we obtain Equation (18):

$$M \cong \frac{B^g + B^p}{\dfrac{R}{D} + \dfrac{C}{M} - \dfrac{R}{D}\dfrac{C}{M}} = \frac{G^1 + G^2 + G^3 + B^p}{\dfrac{R}{D} + \dfrac{C}{M} - \dfrac{R}{D}\dfrac{C}{M}} = \frac{B}{A} = B \; \cdot \text{(mbm)} \tag{18}$$

Equation 18 shows that the supply of money is determined by the loans to the government sector, the loans to the private sector, the actual reserve ratio, and the currency-money ratio. Or, we may simply say that the supply of money is determined by the monetary base (the numerator) and the monetary base multiplier.[20]

---

central bank is virtually controlled by the central government, the central government can increase the supply of currency through the forms of borrowing, overdraft, and national bonds. Besides this central bank, there were National Agricultural Cooperative Federation, and member cooperatives, the Medium Industrial Bank, and several large commercial banks which have branches throughout the country. "All Banking Institutions" refer to the above institutions, including the Bank of Korea, as used in publications of the Bank of Korea, and "Banking Institutions" refer to the above institutions excluding the Bank of Korea. There was the "Korean Reconstruction Bank" which is excluded from both of the definitions since the Reconstruction Bank was engaged exclusively in long-term lending activities with funds financed by the government, and was regarded rather as a government agency. See the Bank of Korea, *Economic Statistics Yearbook*, 1962 ed., p. 1.

[20]Letting $R/D + C/M - R/D \cdot C/M = A$, the monetary base multiplier (mbm) is: $mbm = 1/A$.

Table 10. The Actual Reserve Ratio, the Currency-Money Ratio and the Monetary Base Multiplier (1945-60)

	(1) R/D(%)	(2) C/M(%)	(3) $\frac{R}{D} + \frac{C}{M} - \frac{R}{D} \cdot \frac{C}{M}$ (%)	(4) 1/(3) (monetary base multiplier)
1945	24	73.8	80.1	1.25
1946	24	66.6	74.6	1.34
1947	21	63.0	70.8	1.41
1948	15	58.3	64.4	1.55
1949	14	58.4	64.2	1.56
1950	(10)	78.7	80.8	1.24
1951	11.5	73.8	76.8	1.30
1952	16.0	68.0	73.1	1.37
1953	19.4	73.7	78.8	1.27
1954	23.6	68.8	76.2	1.31
1955	23.2	62.8	71.4	1.40
1956	26.6	60.6	71.1	1.41
1957	21.7	59.3	68.5	1.46
1958	19.6	57.7	66.0	1.52
1959	19.5	58.9	66.9	1.49
1960	17.8	63.6	70.1	1.43

Source: The currency-money ratios are calculated from the Bank of Korea, *Economic Statistics Yearbook*, 1961 edition. The actual reserve ratios for 1945-49 are from A.I. Bloomfield and J.P. Jensen, *Banking Reform in South Korea*, 1951, p. 38. Figures are rounded. For 1950-60, the data are from the Bank of Korea, *Annual Economic Review*, 1955-59 editions, and *Economic Statistics Yearbook*, 1959-61 editions.

Table 11. The Supply of Money, the Monetary Base and the Loans to the Government Sector (1945-60)

	(1) M (bill. whan)	(2) B	(3) B^g	(4) B^p	(5) B^g/M(%)	(6) $\Delta B/B$(%)	(7) B^g/B(%)
1945	0.114	(0.012)	(0.003)	(0.009)	10.5		21.0
1946	0.249	(0.113)	(0.101)	(0.012)	45.4	841.7	89.4
1947	0.495	(0.257)	(0.244)	(0.013)	51.9	127.4	94.9
1948	0.696	(0.328)	(0.310)	(0.018)	47.1	27.6	94.5
1949	1.2	(0.7)	(0.6)	(0.030)	55.7	105.8	85.7
1950	2.8	2.6	2.2	0.4	94.3	288.2	84.6
1951	7.3	5.7	4.9	0.8	77.8	115.2	86.0
1952	14.3	11.1	7.3	3.8	77.6	95.4	65.8
1953	30.3	25.0	13.5	11.5	82.4	125.4	54.0
1954	58.1	48.9	38.9	10.2	84.1	95.7	79.6
1955	93.5	89.3	73.1	16.2	95.5	82.7	81.9
1956	120.9	102.0	67.0	35.0	84.4	14.2	65.7
1957	145.2	114.2	64.8	49.4	78.6	11.9	56.7
1958	192.6	128.0	96.9	31.1	66.4	12.1	75.7
1959	209.9	146.9	124.9	22.0	70.0	14.8	85.0
1960	219.1	152.3	93.5	58.8	69.5	3.7	61.4

Note: B = total monetary base. B^g = monetary base loaned to the government sector

B^p = monetary base loaned to the private sector, or the commercial banks.

B/M = the monetary base-money rate(%). $\Delta B/B$ = the rate of change in the monetary base.

B^g/B = the percent of the monetary base loaned to the government sector in the total monetary base(%).

Source: See footnote of Table 9.

Table 12. Government Expenditures, Tax Revenue, Defense Expenditures and Deficit Spending (1945—60) (in billion whan)

	(1) Gov't. exp.	(2) Defense exp.	(3) Tax revenue	(4) Gov't. deficit spending	(5) Defense expenditure ratio (2)/(4) (%)	(6) Deficit spending ratio (4)/(1) (%)
1945	0.019	(0.002)	0.004	0.010	(11)	53
46	0.134	(0.010)	0.012	0.079	(8)	59
47	0.192	(0.40)	0.030	0.162	(21)	84
48	0.152	(0.033)	0.028	0.124	(22)	82
49	0.911	0.24	0.144	0.542	(26)	60
50	2.4	1.3	0.434	1.5	55	63
51	(6.1)	(3.5)	(4.0)	(0.4)	(56)	(7)
52	(21.5)	(9.8)	(9.8)	(1.2)	(46)	(6)
53	52.7	3.8	21.0	22.2	73	42
54a)	108.7	73.0	52.0	26.5	67	24
55b)	243.1	112.5	117.4	54.1	46	22
57b)	223.6	106.4	110.5	33.1	48	15
58	278.0	127.3	146.6	40.3	46	15
59	309.4	139.2	220.9	13.5	45	4
60	351.6	147.1	249.7	20.0	42	5

Note: a) September 1955-December 1956. b) Since 1957, the fiscal year is equal to the calendar year, January-December. The data in the parentheses are incomplete.

Source: Calculated from the Bank of Korea, *Annual Economic Review*, 1949 edition, pp. 132-133, 1956 edition, pp. 99, 132; *Economic Statistics Yearbook*, 1961 edition, pp. 120-121, 1962 edition, pp. 124-125.

Figure 1   The Actual Reserve Ratio, the Currency-Money Ratio, the Base-Money Ratio and the Monetary Base Multiplier (1945–1960)

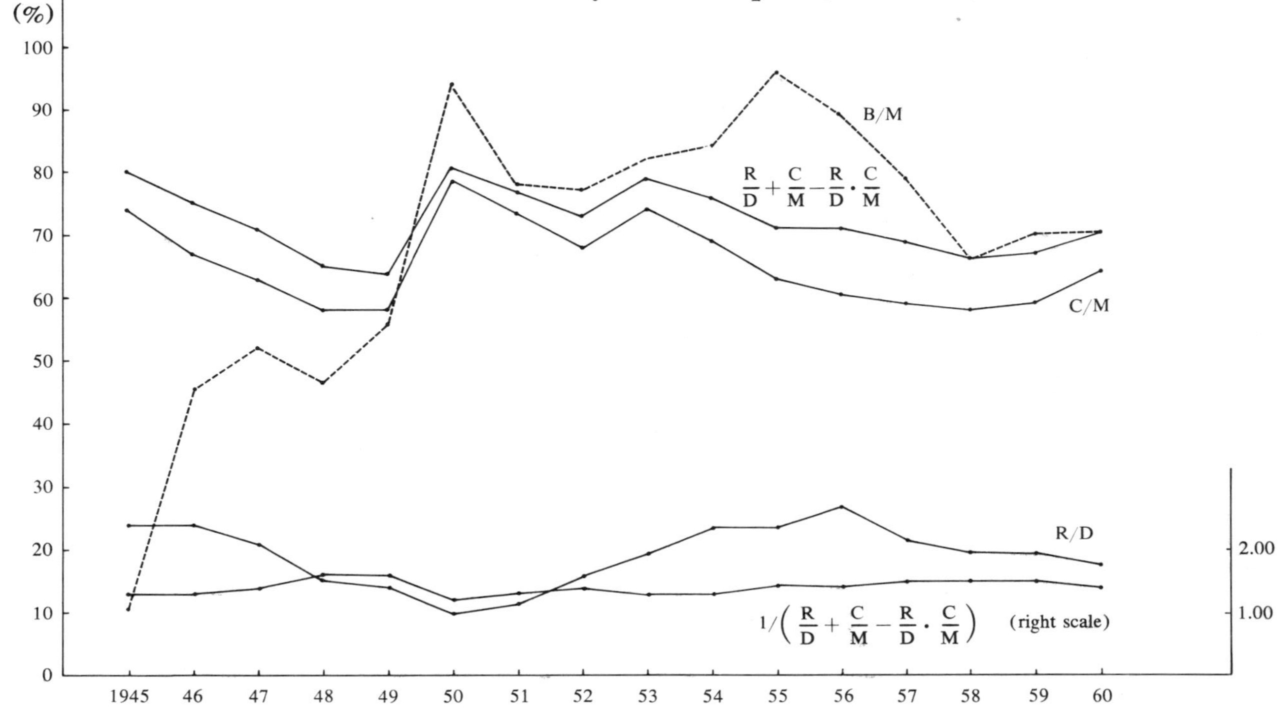

163

In order to see which of these determinants is largely responsible for the rapid increases in the supply of money, we have calculated the actual reserve ratio, the denominator, the monetary base multiplier, and the loans to the government sector, and the loans to the private sector. The results are shown in Tables 10 and 11, and some of these series are plotted in Figure 1. We note that the actual reserve ratio and ·the currency-money ratio show fluctuations reflecting the credit conditions during the period. The high actual reserve ratio during the post World War II period reflects a tightening credit situation, and the decreasing actual reserve ratio up to 1950 reflects an expanding credit situation. The actual reserve ratio started to rise at the outbreak of the Korean War, and reached a peak in 1956, and showed a downward trend thereafter. The currency-money ratio showed a falling tendency up to 1949. But at the outbreak of the Korean War, the currency-money ratio jumped up to 78.8%, and after the ceasefire in 1953, it showed a decreasing tendency up to 1958, and then it showed mild increases in 1959 and 1960. The denominator as a whole showed almost the same pattern as the currency-money ratio.

We note that though the actual reserve ratio and the currency-money ratio showed some fluctuations, the monetary base multiplier was very stable during the entire period, 1945-60, the average being 1.39.[21] This leads to the conclusion that the major factor responsible for the rapid increases in the supply of money during the period was the monetary base. Indeed we note in Table 10 that the supply of money increased from 0.249 billion whan in 1946 to 219.1 billion whan in 1960, and

---

[21]The monetary base multiplier was about 2.6 in the U.S. for the period August-October, 1973. Federal Reserve Bank of St. Louis, *U.S. Financial Data*, Oct. 12, 1973.

the monetary base increased from 0.113 billion whan to 152.3 billion whan during the period.

When the monetary base is divided into two categories, i.e., the government sector and the private sector, we note that the percentage of loans to the government sector ranges from 61.4% to 94.9% during 1946-60, excluding the year 1945 in which the ratio is low 21.0%, the average ratio being 77.4%. In other words, it may be concluded that rapid increases in the loans to the government sector by the central bank was the major cause of the increases in the monetary base, and thus it was the major cause of the rapid increases in the supply of money. In Table 11, we note that the deficit spending of the central government increased from 0.010 billion whan to 20 billion whan during 1945-60. The deficit ratio, or the ratio of the deficit spending in the total central government expenditures ranged from 8% in 1947 to 73% in 1953. This suggests that the deficit spending was the major cause of the rapid increases in the loans to the central government by the central bank. Then the question is, why did the government increase deficit spending so much? Why couldn't it finance its expenditures by increasing the tax revenue?

The following reasons may be given for the rapid increases in the deficit spending of the central government:

(1) First, to finance the war the Japanese government in Korea was increasing the volume of currency at an extremely high rate, and as World War II approached the end, the supply of currencies was accelerating. Thus with the end of the war, the country was flooded with the paper currencies which were piled up during the war. For example, the supply of currencies increased to 1,467 million "won" in 1943 and to 3,136 million "won" in 1944. And it increased to 4,800 million "won" by August 14, 1945, just a day before the day of liberation of Korea. However, this was just the beginning of the story. The

issue of money was increased to 8,500 million "won" on September 8, 1945, by the surrendering Japanese government in Korea, when the United States military force landed. This was an increase of 3,700 million "won" or 77% increase in 2 weeks.[22] This example shows how rapidly the issue of money was increasing in the aftermath of the war. During such a period, taxation was, of course, impossible.

Even during the period the U.S. military government was ruling the country until a new Korean government was established in 1948, the issue of money was increasing rapidly. The issue of money increased from 8,797 million "won" at the end of October 1945 to 30,480 million won at the end of July 1948. On August 15, 1948, the Rhee government was established to rule the following 12 years until it was overthrown in April 1960 by the "Student Revolution." We note that during the last two years of the U.S. military government in 1947 and 1948, about 95% of the total monetary base was the loans to the central government, as shown in Table 11.

(2) The second reason for the rapid increases in the deficit spending of the central government was the Korean War. Table 11 shows that the percentage of the loans to the government sector in the total monetary base was 85.7%, 84.6%, 86.0%, 65.8%, and 54.0% during the 5-year period 1949-53. However, in Table 12, we note that the ratio of deficit spending in the total central government expenditures is only 7% in 1951, and 6% in 1952, compared with 63% in 1951, and 42% in 1953. The low percentages of the deficit ratio during 1951-52 are probably due to incomplete data, i.e., due to the fact that most cities and villages were occupied by the North Korean forces

---

[22]C. Sung, *Hanguk Kyungje Ron* (Studies on the Korean Economy), 1957, p. 99.

during the period. The supply of money increased from 121,100 million "won" in 1949 to 1,432,500 million "won" in 1952. These tremendous increases in the supply of money required the monetary reform of February 14, 1953, and the 100 "won" was denominated to 1 "whan." In spite of the monetary reform, the increasing tendency in the supply of money did not cease because of the continuing government deficit spending. The supply of money increased to 30,136 million whan (3,031,600 million won) by the end of 1953. A large portion of the supply of money took the form of the loans to the United Nations forces during the war period. In 1953, the supply of money increased to about 30 times of the 1949 level.

(3) The end of the Korean War did not stop the government deficit spending. In 1953 the percentage of defense expenditures in the total central government expenditures reached the peak level of 73%. It was decreasing thereafter, but in 1960 it still remained at 42% of the total central government expenditures. During the pre-Korean War period, we note that the percentage of the defense expenditures ranged between 8% and 26%, which is extraordinarily high for a low income country. The defense expenditure ratio was on the average more than 40% of the total central government expenditures during 1949-60, and more than 50% during 1950-60.

We have seen that the major cause of the rapid increases in the supply of money was the continuing government deficit spending to finance the military expenditures throughout the period. Then the following questions arise: (1) Why was the government deficit spending largely financed by the Bank of Korea and not by the sale of government bonds and bills to the private sector? (2) Why didn't the government increase the tax rate to eliminate the government deficit spending?

As for the first question, people did not wish to purchase the government bonds for two major reasons. One, because of the rapid inflation; the other, because the people did not have any confidence in the government. As for the second question, the statistical data are not complete for the pre-Korean War period to measure the burden of tax. During the post Korean War priod, however, the burden of tax, measured by the ratio of tax revenue to GNP, increased from 6.7% in 1953 to 14.5% in 1960.[23] This is more than a two-fold increase in the burden of tax in only 7 years, though GNP increased only 37% during the priod.[24] More rapid increases in taxation must have faced difficulties because of the low per capita income, i.e., the small margin between income and the minimum subsistence level of consumption, and because of the political instability. So the government adopted an easier method of "taxation," i.e., printing the paper money!

V. Summary and Conclusions

Inflation, or the rapid and continuous rises in the level of prices, whether it be cost push inflation, demand pull inflation or demand shift inflation, is caused by discrepancies between the rate of increase in the aggregate demand and the rate of increase in the aggregate supply. According to the classical rigid quantity theory it is the change in the supply of money that causes the gap. The supply of money determines the aggregate demand together with the constant velocity of money. The velocity is fixed because it is determined by institutional customs and habits. Institutional customs and habits do not change suddenly simply because the supply of money changes. Thus the

---

[23]The Bank of Korea, *Monthly Economic Review*, Dec. 1972, p. 12.

[24]GNP in 1955 prices increased from 868.5 billion whan in 1953 to 1,189 billion whan in 1960. The average annual economic growth rate was 4.7% during the period.

velocity of money is held constant. In the classical world, there are no idle money balances held. The money received will be spent away or will be saved. The saving will soon finance an equal amount of investment. Thus the amount of money received will soon finance the same amount of spending. Thus the aggregate demand increases in proportion to an increase in the supply of money.

If the supply of money increases, will the real output increase? In the classical world of quantity theory, the answer is no, because real output can be increased only if capital stock, human labor, technology, or other real factors of production are increased or improved. The money itself is not a factor of production. If the aggregate demand increases, the firms may wish to produce more. But as aggregate demand rises, the price level and the money wage rate rise in the same proportion. So the real wage rate does not change, nor the demand for labor which is a function of real wage rate. So the real output does not increase.[25] Also the velocity of money remains constant. Then as the supply of money increases, the aggregate demand increases in proportion to the increase in the supply of money, and the level of prices also rises in proportion to the increase in the supply of money. This implies a constant real money balance, M/P.

However, the modern real money balance theory assumes neither full employment nor a constant velocity of money. It assumes, however, that people wish to hold a certain desired level of real money balances which is determined by real income, real wealth, the rate of interest, and the expected rate of change in prices among other factors. Thus if the supply of money and the real money balance increase beyond a certain desired level, people wish to convert the excess real money balance into other types of assets such as consumer goods, bonds, equities, or real estates. This attempt increases the aggregate

---

[25]See Chapter 1 for the quantity theory and its criticism.

demand and the level of prices on the one hand, and real output on the other. Since the level of prices will not increase proportionally under these circumstances, the real money balance, M/P, would not remain constant. However, when the supply of real money balances increases more rapidly than the demand for real money balances, inflation takes place.

In this paper, we have examined the supply of money and the level of prices in South Korea during the period 1945-60. The supply of money increased at an average annual rate of 48% during the period of social unrest and political instability, largely to finance the government deficit spending which was necessary to sustain a large percentage of defense expenditures. The rapid increases in the supply of money were indeed accompanied by a 55% average annual rate of increase in prices, as the quantity theory of money would expect. The regression results of the annual data show that 67.4% of the total variation in the rate of change in prices is explained by the rate of change in the supply of money.

As to the demand for real money balances, the empirical data indicate that the real money balance fluctuated with a wide range of variations. Since the quarterly data were not available for real income, real wealth, and the rate of interest among other factors, we have included only the expected rate of change in prices in the regression function of the demand for real money balances. The empirical results support the hypothesis that the real money balance is a function of the expected rate of change in prices. This result is consistent with other empirical analyses of real money balances and the expected rate of change in prices.

In short, according to the modern quantity theory or the real money balance hypothesis, inflation takes place when the supply of money increases more rapidly than the demand for money. Table 8 indicates that the demand for real money balances was decreasing with some fluctuations until the Korean war was over.

It shows some increases only after the war ended. The reasons for the decreasing demand for real money balances may include the stagnant real income, political instability and the expected high rate of inflation. On the other hand, the supply of money increased rapidly to finance the government military and other consumption expenditures since a higher taxation was impossible during such a period of political instability.

REFERENCES

Cagan, P., "The Monetary Dynamics of Hyperinflation," in Friedman, M., ed., *Studies in the Quantity Theory of Money*, 1956, pp. 25-117.

Cagan, P., *Determinants and Effects of Changes in the U.S. Money Stock, 1875-1955*, 1962.

Fisher, I., *The Purchasing Power of Money*, 1911, Ch. 5, rev. ed., 1913.

Humphrey, T.M., "The Quantity Theory of Money: Its Historical Evolution and Role in Policy Debates," *Economic Review*, Federal Reserve Bank of Richmond, May, June, 1974, pp. 2-19.

Keynes, J.M., *The General Theory of Employment, Interest, and Money*, 1936, Ch. 21.

Pigou, A.C., "The Value of Money," *Quarterly Journal of Economics*, Nov. 1917, pp. 38-65, rep. in AEA, ed., *Readings in Monetary Theory*, 1951, pp. 162-183.

Tobin, J., "Asset Holdings and Spending Decisions," *American Economic Review, Papers and Proceedings*, May 1952, pp. 109-123.

Tobin, J., "Liquidity Preference as Behavior towards Risk," *Review of Economic Studies*, Feb. 1958, pp. 65-86.

On the Korean Economy and the Statistical Data

Bank of Korea, *Annual Economic Review*, 1948-49 editions, 1955-59 editions.

_____, *Economic Statistics Yearbook*, 1960-62 editions.

_____, *Monthly Statistics Review*, 1946-62.

Bloomfield, A.I., *Report on Monetary Policy and Banking in Korea*, 1956.

Bloomfield, A.I., and J.P. Jensen, *Banking Reform in South Korea*, 1951.

Campbell, C.D., and Tullock, G., "Some Little-Understood Aspects of Korea's Monetary and Fiscal Policy," *American economic Review*, 1957, pp. 337-349; "Comments" and "Reply" by L.D. Allesi, R. Evans, S. Park, and Campbell and Tullock.

DeAlessi, L., "An Analysis of Aid Administration in Korea," *Southern Economic Journal*, July 1958, pp. 64-73.

Nathan Associates, *An Economic Program for Korean Reconstruction*, 1954.

National Economic Board, U.S. Army Military Government in Korea, *Price Development in Korea*, 1947.

Sung, C., *Studies on the Korean Economy* (Hanguk Kyungje Ron), 1957.

Chapter 7

The Keynesian Model
with the Changing Supply of Money

I. Introduction

While the controversy continues between the Keynesian theory and the quantity theory of money,[1] several attempts have been made to reconcile the two approaches.[2] In Section II, we wish to show that the velocity theory can be interpreted as a special case of the Keynesian multiplier theory; in Section III, we shall present two Keynesian multiplier models: one with a constant supply of money and the other with a changing supply of money;[3] and in Section IV, we attempt to show that an optimal fiscal and monetary mix can be

---

[1]See for the predictability controversy Friedman and Meiselman (1963), Ando and Modigliani (1965),DePrano and Mayer (1965), Hester (1904), Barret and Walters (1966), Mayer (1964), and Tucker (1971).

[2]See Samuelson's criticism on the earlier attempts by several authors (1942, pp. 602-604). For recent attempts see Lutz (1955) and Tsiang (1956).

[3]The conventional investment or government expenditure multiplier model assumes a constant supply of money.

obtained by an introduction of a social welfare function. In Section V, some implications of the above analysis are summarized.

II. The Keynesian Theory and the Quantity Theory

A. The Quantity Theory of Money

We start with the quantity theory of money which can be stated by the following equations.[4]

$$L = kY \qquad (1\text{-}1)$$
$$M = M_0 \qquad (1\text{-}2)$$
$$kY = M \qquad (1\text{-}3)$$

where L is the demand for money which is a constant portion of money income Y, M is an exogenous, fixed supply of money, and k is a constant. Equation (1-3) states the equilibrium condition.

From (1-3) we obtain the equation of income determination in the quantity theory.

$$Y = \frac{1}{k}M \qquad (1\text{-}4)$$

The effect of an increase in the supply of money is given by:

$$\frac{dY}{dM} = \frac{1}{k} \qquad (1\text{-}5)$$

where $1/k$ is the velocity of money.

---

[4]See Ando and Midigliani's summary formulation of the quantity theory (1965).

B. The Keynesian Theory

A Keynesian demand model may be expressed by the following equations:

$$Y = C + I + G + X - H \qquad (2\text{-}1)$$
$$C = C_0 + c(Y - T) \qquad (2\text{-}2)$$
$$T = T_0 + tY \qquad (2\text{-}3)$$
$$G = G_0 + gY \qquad (2\text{-}4)$$
$$I = I_0 - \alpha i + jY \qquad (2\text{-}5)$$
$$M = M_0 \qquad (2\text{-}6)$$
$$L = L_1(Y) + L_2(i) \qquad (2\text{-}7)$$
$$L_1 = kY \qquad (2\text{-}8)$$
$$L_2 = L_0 - \beta i \qquad (2\text{-}9)$$
$$M = kY + L_0 - \beta i \qquad (2\text{-}10)$$
$$X = X_0 + xY \qquad (2\text{-}11)$$
$$H = H_0 + hY \qquad (2\text{-}12)$$

We have twelve equations and twelve variable.[5]

---

[5]where

Y = Income	L_1 = Transactions and precautionary demand for money
C = Consumption	
I = Investment	L_2 = Asset demand for money, or speculative demand for money
T = Taxes	
G = Government expenditure	i = The rate of interest
M = The supply of money	X = Export
L = Demand for money	H = Import

The Constants are: C_0, c, T_0, t, G_0, g, I_0, α, j, M_0, k, L_0, β, X_0, x, H_0, h

The consumption function takes various forms in the post-Keynesian economics:

$C_t = a + b \ Y_t^2/Y_0$ (Duesenberry's relative income hypothesis)

$C_t = k[\beta(w_1Y_t + w_2Y_{t-1} + w_3Y_{t-3}\ldots w_{17}Y_{t-17})]$ (Friedman's permanent income hypothesis)

$\qquad = k[\beta \sum_{i=1}^{17} \lambda^i Y_{t-i}]$

$C_t = a + bY_t + \lambda C_{t-1}$ (Koyck distributed lag model)

The equilibrium income is given by:

$$Y = \frac{\beta(C_0 - cT_0 + G_0 + X_0 - H_0 + I_0) + \alpha(M - L_0)}{\beta(1 - c + ct - g - x + h - j) + \alpha k} \qquad (2\text{-}13)$$

Equation (2-13) may be written as:

$$Y = \text{constant} + \text{coefficient} \times M \qquad (2\text{-}13)'$$

This is very similar to equation (1-4) of the quantity theory. Also from Equation (2-13),

$$Y = \text{constant} + \text{coefficient} \times I_0 \qquad (2\text{-}13)''$$

The investment multiplier is given by:

$$\frac{\partial Y}{\partial I_0} = \frac{\beta}{\beta(1 - c + ct - g - x + h - j) + \alpha k} \qquad (2\text{-}14)$$

The effect of an increase in the supply of money is:

$$\frac{\partial Y}{\partial M} = \frac{\alpha}{\beta(1 - c + ct - g - x + h - j) + \alpha k} \qquad (2\text{-}15)$$

$\partial Y / \partial M$ may be called the monetary income multiplier. From (2-14) and (2-15), we note that,

$$\frac{\partial Y}{\partial I_0} = \frac{\beta}{\alpha} \frac{\partial Y}{\partial M} \qquad (2\text{-}16)[6]$$

---

[6]The reduced forms of the quantity theory and the Keynesian theory by Friedman (1963) are:

$$Y = k_0 + kM \qquad \text{(Quantity theory)}$$
$$Y = k_0' + k'(I + G - T + X - H) \qquad \text{(Keynesian theory)} \qquad (2\text{-}13\text{-a})$$

where k, k_0, k', k_0' are constants.

Friedman's formulation of the Keynesian theory is a special case in which I, G, T, X, H are all autonomous expenditures. Compare with Equation (2-13).

The above equations explain the similarity of the quantity and the multiplier theories,[7] i.e., the quantity theory is a special case of the Keynesian model, where β and L_0 are set zero in Equation (2-13).[8]

If the asset demand for money does not exist, as equation (1-1) of the quantity theory implies, $\beta \to 0$ and equation (2-14) reduces to

$$\frac{\partial Y}{\partial I_0} = 0 \tag{2-17}$$

and equation (2-15) reduces to

$$\frac{\partial Y}{\partial M} = \frac{1}{k} \tag{2-18}$$

We note that equation (2-18) is the same as the velocity equation (1-5).

In quality, however, the difference between the two theories is substantial. The Keynesian investment multiplier explains what happens to income when investment increases, and the Keynesian monetary multiplier explains what happens with income when the supply of money increases. Also the velocity theory explains what happens if the supply of money increases, but it maintains that an increase in autonomous expenditures without an increase in the supply of money does not have any effect on income as is seen in Equation (2-17). In the Keynesian world, money can be substituted for goods and services, stocks

---

[7]Samuelson regards this likeness as purely coincidental (1942, p. 601). For the theoretical preference of the multiplier theory to the velocity theory, see Samuelson (1942, p. 602).

[8]Equation (2-13) reduces to $Y = (1/k)M$ and Equation (1-4) is also $Y = (1/k)M$.

and bonds, savings and time deposits[9] from an individual point of view, even if the supply of money is constant for the economy as a whole. But in the velocity theory, money is substitutable only for goods and services. In the velocity theory, an increase in the supply of money directly and always in constant proportion increases the expenditures on goods and services and the level of prices because the real output and the velocity are constant. But in the Keynesian world, an increase in the supply of money can increase expenditures on bonds causing the rate of interest to fall. If the fall in the rate of interest increases expenditures and income, the rate of interest will rise as the demand for money increases as income rises. However, the final equilibrium rate of interest will be lower than the initial equilibrium rate.[10]

III. Multiplier Effects and the Supply of Money

A. Multiplier Effects with the Constant Supply of Money

The conventional Keynesian system, equations (2-1)—(2-12) may be represented in a more simplified system of equilibrium equations, assuming G, M and T are exogenous policy variables, and that investment is a function of the rate of interest alone.[11]

---

[9]If savings and time deposits are included in the definition of the supply of money in the Keynesian model, the demand for money can be divided into the active money and the idle money demands. This classification seems to be more useful in the Keynesian model. Holding of the idle money in the form of cash may decrease as compared to the forms of savings and time deposits.

[10]See IS-LM curve diagram Ch. 1, p. 17. For a more detailed discussion and empirical results on the Fisherian quantity theory and the Keynesian theory, see Zwick (1971).

[11]This is an Allen's Keynesian model which is represented here to derive the model shown in the following section B. Allen (1967) pp. 140-44.

The equilibrium conditions in the commodity market and the money market are given by

$$I_0 - \alpha i = s(Y-T) + T - G \qquad (3\text{-}1)$$
$$M = k\,Y - \beta i \qquad (3\text{-}2)$$

where

$$Y_d = Y - T$$

$$\frac{\partial S}{\partial Y_d} = s \qquad 0<s<1$$

$$\frac{\partial I}{\partial i} = -\alpha$$

$$\frac{\partial L}{\partial Y} = k \qquad 0<k<1$$

$$\frac{\partial L}{\partial i} = -\beta$$

To see the effects of an increase in government expenditures on income and the rate of interest, differentiating (3-1) with respect to G, holding I_0 and T constant, i.e., $\partial I_0/\partial G = 0$ and $\partial T/\partial G = 0$,

---

The underlying equations are:

$$S = s(Y-T) \qquad \text{Saving function}$$
$$I = I_0 - \alpha i \qquad \text{Investment function}$$
$$L = kY - \beta i \qquad \text{Demand for money}$$
$$M = M_0 \qquad \text{Supply of money}$$
$$T = T_0 \qquad \text{Taxation}$$
$$G = G_0 + X_0 - H_0 \qquad \text{Government expenditures (plus net export surplus), exogenous variables}$$
$$Y-T = Y_d \qquad \text{Disposable income}$$
$$I+G = S + T \qquad \text{Equilibrium condition in the commodity market}$$
$$M = kY - \beta i \qquad \text{Equilibrium condition in the money market}$$

$$-\alpha \cdot \frac{di}{dG} = s \frac{dY}{dG} - 1$$

Rearranging the terms,

$$\frac{dY}{dG} = \frac{1}{s} - \frac{\alpha}{s} \frac{di}{dG} \qquad (3\text{-}3)$$

Differentiating (3-2) with respect to G, holding the supply of money constant, i.e., $dM/dG = 0$,

$$0 = k \cdot \frac{dY}{dG} - \beta \frac{di}{dG} \qquad (3\text{-}4)$$

$$\frac{di}{dG} = \frac{k}{\beta} \cdot \frac{dY}{dG} \qquad (3\text{-}5)$$

Substituting (3-5) in (3-3), and arranging the terms,

$$\frac{dY}{dG} = \frac{1}{s(1 + \frac{\alpha}{s} \cdot \frac{k}{\beta})} > 0 \qquad (3\text{-}6)$$

Equation (3-6) states the multiplier effect of government expenditures. Substituting (3-6) in (3-5),

$$\frac{di}{dG} = \frac{k}{\beta} \frac{1}{s(1 + \frac{\alpha}{s} \cdot \frac{k}{\beta})} > 0 \qquad (3\text{-}7)$$

Equation (3-7) states that the rate of interest will rise if government expenditure increases, holding the supply of money constant. The theory behind Equation (3-7) is that as government expenditure increases, income rises. As income rises, the demand for money increases and the rate of interest rises, if the supply of money is held constant.

The effects of an increase in taxation can be obtained similarly. Differentiating equation (3-1) with respect to T,

$$-\alpha \cdot \frac{di}{dT} = s \frac{dY}{dT} - s + 1 \qquad (4\text{-}1)$$

$$\frac{dY}{dT} = \frac{s-1}{s} - \frac{\alpha}{s} \frac{di}{dT} \qquad (4\text{-}2)$$

Differentiating equation (3-2) with respect to T, holding the supply of money constant, i.e., dM/dT=0,

$$0 = k \cdot \frac{dY}{dT} - \beta \frac{di}{dT}$$

$$\frac{di}{dT} = \frac{k}{\beta} \cdot \frac{dY}{dT} \qquad (4\text{-}3)$$

Substituting (4-3) in (4-2), and rearranging the terms,

$$\frac{dY}{dT} = \frac{s-1}{s(1 + \frac{\alpha}{s} \cdot \frac{k}{\beta})} < 0 \qquad (4\text{-}4)$$
$$1 > s > 0$$

Substituting (4-4) in (4-3)

$$\frac{di}{dT} = \frac{k}{\beta} \frac{s-1}{s(1 + \frac{\alpha}{s} \cdot \frac{k}{\beta})} < 0 \qquad (4\text{-}5)$$

Equations (4-4) and (4-5) state that both income and the rate of interest will fall as tax revenue increases, holding government expenditures and the supply of money constant. The theory behind Equation (4-5) is that as tax increases, income falls. As income falls, the demand for money falls, and the rate of interest decreases, if the supply of money is held constant.

The balanced budget multiplier is given by adding equations (3-6) and (4-4):

$$\frac{dY}{dG} + \frac{dY}{dT} = \frac{1}{s(1+\frac{\alpha}{s} \cdot \frac{k}{\beta})} + \frac{s-1}{s(1+\frac{\alpha}{s} \cdot \frac{k}{\beta})}$$

$$= \frac{1}{(1+\frac{\alpha}{s} \cdot \frac{k}{\beta})} > 0 \qquad (4\text{-}6)$$

If $\alpha = 0$, i.e., $I = I_0$ instead of $I = I_0 - \alpha i$, then equation (4-6) reduces to the "unitary balanced budget theorem," where the balanced budget multiplier is equal to unity, $dY/dG + dY/dT = 1$ The effect of the balanced budget on the rate of interest is given by adding equations (3-7) and (4-5):

$$\frac{di}{dG} + \frac{di}{dT} = \frac{k}{\beta} \frac{1}{s(1+\frac{\alpha}{s} \cdot \frac{k}{\beta})} + \frac{k}{\beta} \frac{s-1}{s(1+\frac{\alpha}{s} \cdot \frac{k}{\beta})}$$

$$= \frac{k}{\beta} \frac{1}{(1+\frac{\alpha}{s} \cdot \frac{k}{\beta})} > 0 \qquad (4\text{-}7)$$

Equation (4-7) states that an increase in the balanced budget will increase the rate of interest. This implies that the positive expenditure effect outweighs the negative tax effect on the rate of interest.

The above conclusions are seen in the usual IS-LM curve diagram. An increase in government expenditures will shift IS curve to the right, but an increase in tax revenue will shift IS curve to the left. The net effect of an increase in both government expenditures and taxation is an increase in the IS curve from IS_1 to IS_2, and the rate of interest and income both rise as shown in Figure 1.[12]

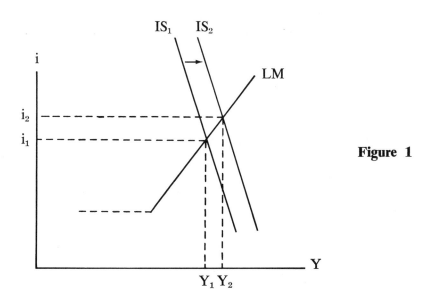

Figure 1

---

[12]For empirical estimates of IS-LM curves, see Scott (1966). His results are estimated from reduced form in accordance with 2SLS estimating techniques:

$$Y = 2019.65 - 1545.33i + 43.94G \qquad R=0.986$$
$$(212.8) \qquad (5.48)$$
$$i = 2.441 + 0.0233Y - 0.0460M \qquad R=0.861$$
$$(0.0073) \qquad (0.0195)$$

M includes time deposits, i is yield on AAA corporate bonds. Quarterly data for 1951-1964 are used. N=56.

B. Multiplier Effects with the Changing Supply of Money

The above model by Allen can be easily modified to see effects of increases in government expenditures and tax revenue with a changing supply of money. To determine the effects of an increase in government expenditures which accompanies an increase in the supply of money, let the equilibrium conditions in the commodity and the money markets be:

$$I_0 - \alpha i = s(Y - T) + T - G \tag{5-1}$$

$$M_0 + mG - nT = kY - \beta i \tag{5-2}$$

where the supply of money is given by

$$M = M_0 + mG - nT$$

If $m = 1$, it implies that the government expenditure is financed entirely by a new supply of money.[13] Differentiating (5-2) with respect to G,

$$m = k \frac{dY}{dG} - \beta \frac{di}{dG}$$

$$\frac{di}{dG} = \frac{k}{\beta} \cdot \frac{dY}{dG} - \frac{m}{\beta} \tag{5-3}$$

Differentiating (5-1) with respect to G,

$$-\alpha \frac{di}{dG} = s \frac{dY}{dG} - 1$$

$$\frac{dY}{dG} = \frac{1}{s} - \frac{\alpha}{s} \frac{di}{dG} \tag{5-4}$$

---

[13]The supply function of money is given by $M = M_0 + mG - nT$, where M_0

Substituting (5-3) in (5-4),

$$\frac{dY}{dG} = \frac{1}{s} - \frac{\alpha}{s} \left(\frac{k}{\beta} \cdot \frac{dY}{dG} - \frac{m}{\beta}\right)$$

$$\frac{dY}{dG} = \frac{1 + \dfrac{\alpha m}{\beta}}{s\left(1 + \dfrac{\alpha}{s} \cdot \dfrac{k}{\beta}\right)} > 0 \qquad (5\text{-}5)$$

Substituting (5-5) in (5-3)

$$\frac{di}{dG} = \frac{1}{\beta} \cdot \frac{\left(\dfrac{k}{s} - m\right)}{\left(1 + \dfrac{\alpha}{s} \cdot \dfrac{k}{\beta}\right)} \geq 0 \qquad (5\text{-}6)$$

provided

$$\frac{k}{s} \geq m \qquad (5\text{-}7)$$

To study the effects of an increase in tax revenue which influences the supply of money, from $M = M_0 + mG - nT$

$$\frac{dM}{dT} = -n \qquad\qquad 0 \leq n \leq 1 \qquad (6\text{-}1)$$

is the exogenous supply of money which does not depend upon the government sector. In this model, the government expenditures play two roles: it increases both the supply of money directly and the demand for money indirectly by increasing the level of income.

If $n=1$, it implies that the increase in tax revenue absorbs an equal amount of the supply of money from the private sector. Differentiating equation (5-2) with respect to T,

$$-n = k \, \frac{dY}{dT} - \beta \, \frac{di}{dT} \qquad\qquad (6\text{-}2)$$

$$\frac{di}{dT} = \frac{k}{\beta} \cdot \frac{dY}{dT} + \frac{n}{\beta} \qquad\qquad (6\text{-}3)$$

Differentiating (5-1) with respect to T,

$$\frac{dY}{dT} = \frac{s-1}{s} - \frac{\alpha}{s} \, \frac{di}{dT} \qquad\qquad (6\text{-}4)$$

Sutstituting (6-3) in (6-4),

$$\frac{dY}{dT} = \frac{-1 + s - \dfrac{\alpha n}{\beta}}{s(1 + \dfrac{\alpha}{s} \cdot \dfrac{k}{\beta})} < 0 \qquad\qquad (6\text{-}5)$$

since

$$-1 + s - \frac{\alpha n}{\beta} < 0$$

Substituting (6-5) in (6-3)

$$\frac{di}{dT} = \frac{ns - k(1-s)}{\beta s(1 + \dfrac{\alpha}{s} \cdot \dfrac{k}{\beta})} \geq 0 \qquad\qquad (6\text{-}6)$$

provided

$$\frac{k(1-s)}{s} \geq n \qquad\qquad (6\text{-}7)$$

The balanced budget multiplier is obtained by adding equations (5-5) and (6-5)

$$\frac{dY}{dG} + \frac{dY}{dT} = \frac{1 + \frac{\alpha m}{\beta}}{s(1 + \frac{\alpha}{s} \cdot \frac{k}{\beta})} + \frac{-1 + s - \alpha \frac{n}{\beta}}{s(1 - \frac{\alpha}{s} \cdot \frac{k}{\beta})}$$

$$= \frac{s + \frac{\alpha}{\beta}(m - n)}{s(1 + \frac{\alpha}{s} \cdot \frac{k}{\beta})} > 0 \qquad (6-8)$$

provided $m > n$

If $m = n$, then equation (6-8) reduces to (4-6). The condition, $m = n$ implies that the supply of money remains constant by the balanced budget. If $\alpha = 0$, then the balanced budget multiplier is equal to unity, $dY/dG + dY/dT = 1$. The condition, $\alpha = 0$ implies that the investment elasticity with respect to the rate of interest approaches zero, i.e.,

as $\alpha \rightarrow 0,$ $\frac{dY}{dG} + \frac{dY}{dT} \rightarrow 1$

In the case of the liquidity trap,

as $\beta \rightarrow \infty,$ $\frac{dY}{dG} + \frac{dY}{dT} \rightarrow 1$

To see if the effect of an increase in the size of the balanced budget on income can be zero, let

$$\frac{dY}{dG} + \frac{dY}{dT} = \frac{s + \frac{\alpha}{\beta}(m - n)}{s(1 + \frac{\alpha}{s} \cdot \frac{k}{\beta})} = 0 \qquad (6-9)$$

This requires,

$$s + \frac{\alpha}{\beta}(m-n) = 0$$

or,

$$\frac{-\beta s}{\alpha} = m - n \qquad (6\text{-}10)$$

If $m=n$, it requires $s = 0$, or $\beta = 0$

Therefore, the sign of $dY/dG + dY/dT$ depends upon whether or not:

$$\frac{-\beta s}{\alpha} \gtrless m - n \qquad (6\text{-}10)$$

The effect of an increase in the size of the balanced budget on the rate of interest is obtained by adding (5-6) and (6-6)

$$\frac{di}{dG} + \frac{di}{dT} = \frac{\frac{k}{s} - m + n - \frac{k}{s}(1-s)}{\beta(1 + \frac{\alpha}{s} \cdot \frac{k}{\beta})}$$

$$= \frac{k - (m-n)}{\beta(1 + \frac{\alpha}{s} \cdot \frac{k}{\beta})} \geq 0 \qquad (6\text{-}11)$$

provided $k \geq (m-n)$

If $m-n=0$, equation (6-11) reduces to (4-7). In the case of the liquidity trap,

as $\beta \rightarrow \infty$, $\quad \frac{di}{dG} + \frac{di}{dT} \rightarrow 0$

To see if the effect of an increase in the size of the balanced budget on the rate of interest can be zero, let

$$\frac{di}{dG} + \frac{di}{dT} = \frac{k - (m-n)}{\beta(1 + \frac{\alpha}{s} \cdot \frac{k}{\beta})} = 0 \qquad (6\text{-}12)$$

This requires,

$$k = m - n$$

Therefore, the sign of $di/dG + di/dT$ depends upon whether or not:

$$k \gtreqless m - n \qquad (6\text{-}13)$$

We can compare these results with equations (4-6) and (4-7) where the effects of an increase in the balanced budget are always to increase income and the rate of interest. The case where increases in both government expenditures and taxation will decrease the rate of interest and will increase the level of output is illustrated in Figure 2.

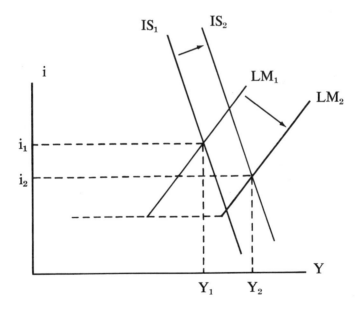

Figure 2

IV. Social Welfare Function and Economic Policy

As long as the increases in the government expenditures and the supply of money, and the decreases in tax revenue increase real output, there is no reason why such a policy should not be pursued. However, in a real economy, it is often true that before full employment is reached the rate of interest and the level of prices tend to rise and these increases may counteract the full employment policies. Then the problem is a choice of an optimal combination of government expenditures, taxation and the supply of money to maintain the optimal rate of inflation, the rate of interest, and the rate of unemployment.

Assume that the net social welfare function W' is given by

$$W' = W(Q) - V(i,P,U) \qquad (7\text{-}1)$$

where

$$
\begin{aligned}
Q &= Q(G, T, M) & (7\text{-}2)\\
V &= V(i, P, U) & (7\text{-}3)\\
i &= i(G, T, M) & (7\text{-}4)\\
P &= P(G, T, M) & (7\text{-}5)\\
U &= U(G, T, M) & (7\text{-}6)
\end{aligned}
$$

where social utility W is an increasing function of real output Q; social disutility V is an increasing function of the rate of interest i, the level of prices P, and the rate of unemployment U. The rate of interest, the level of prices, and the rate of unemployment are all functions of the government expenditures, tax revenue and the supply of money.[14]

---

[14] (1) $\dfrac{\partial W}{\partial G} = \dfrac{\partial W}{\partial Q} \cdot \dfrac{\partial Q}{\partial G} > 0$ (see 5-5) $\dfrac{\partial i}{\partial G} > 0$ (see 5-6) $\dfrac{\partial P}{\partial G} > 0 \quad \dfrac{\partial U}{\partial G} < 0$

In the above model, changes in the government expenditures, taxation and the supply of money influence both social utility and social disutility. The problem is to choose an optimal combination of the above three variables which maximize net social welfare. The first order condition requires:

$$\frac{\partial W'}{\partial G} = \frac{dW}{dQ} \cdot \frac{\partial Q}{\partial G} - \frac{\partial V}{\partial i} \cdot \frac{\partial i}{\partial G} - \frac{\partial V}{\partial P} \cdot \frac{\partial P}{\partial G} - \frac{\partial V}{\partial U} \cdot \frac{\partial U}{\partial G} = 0$$

$$(7\text{-}7)$$

$$\frac{\partial W'}{\partial T} = \frac{dW}{dQ} \cdot \frac{\partial Q}{\partial T} - \frac{\partial V}{\partial i} \cdot \frac{\partial i}{\partial T} - \frac{\partial V}{\partial P} \cdot \frac{\partial P}{\partial T} - \frac{\partial V}{\partial U} \cdot \frac{\partial U}{\partial T} = 0$$

$$(7\text{-}8)$$

$$\frac{\partial W'}{\partial M} = \frac{dW}{dQ} \cdot \frac{\partial Q}{\partial M} - \frac{\partial V}{\partial i} \cdot \frac{\partial i}{\partial M} - \frac{\partial V}{\partial P} \cdot \frac{\partial P}{\partial M} - \frac{\partial V}{\partial U} \cdot \frac{\partial U}{\partial M} = 0$$

$$(7\text{-}9)$$

The marginal condition for taxation and the government expenditures is given by dividing $\partial W'/\partial G$ by $\partial W'/T$. From (7-7) and (7-8),

---

$$(2) \quad \frac{\partial W}{\partial T} = \frac{\partial W}{\partial Q} \cdot \frac{\partial Q}{\partial T} < 0 \text{(see 6-5)} \quad \frac{\partial i}{\partial T} \geq 0 \text{(see 6-6)} \quad \frac{\partial P}{\partial T} < 0 \quad \frac{\partial U}{\partial T} > 0$$

$$(3) \quad \frac{\partial W}{\partial M} = \frac{\partial W}{\partial Q} \cdot \frac{\partial Q}{\partial M} > 0 \quad \frac{\partial i}{\partial M} < 0 \quad \frac{\partial P}{\partial M} > 0 \quad \frac{\partial U}{\partial M} < 0$$

$$(4) \quad \frac{\partial V}{\partial i} > 0 \quad \frac{\partial V}{\partial P} > 0 \quad \frac{\partial V}{\partial U} > 0$$

$$\frac{\partial T}{\partial G} = \frac{\dfrac{\partial V}{\partial i}\cdot\dfrac{\partial i}{\partial G} + \dfrac{\partial V}{\partial P}\cdot\dfrac{\partial P}{\partial G} + \dfrac{\partial V}{\partial U}\cdot\dfrac{\partial U}{\partial G}}{\dfrac{\partial V}{\partial i}\cdot\dfrac{\partial i}{\partial T} + \dfrac{\partial V}{\partial P}\cdot\dfrac{\partial P}{\partial T} + \dfrac{\partial V}{\partial U}\cdot\dfrac{\partial U}{\partial T}} \qquad (7\text{-}10)$$

Equation (7-10) states that the marginal rate of government expenditures and taxation should be equal to the ratio of the marginal disutilities of government expenditures and taxation. Similarly, from (7-7) and (7-9) we obtain the marginal condition for the supply of money and the government expenditures:

$$\frac{\partial M}{\partial G} = \frac{\dfrac{\partial V}{\partial i}\cdot\dfrac{\partial i}{\partial G} + \dfrac{\partial V}{\partial P}\cdot\dfrac{\partial P}{\partial G} + \dfrac{\partial V}{\partial U}\cdot\dfrac{\partial U}{\partial G}}{\dfrac{\partial V}{\partial i}\cdot\dfrac{\partial i}{\partial M} + \dfrac{\partial V}{\partial P}\cdot\dfrac{\partial P}{\partial M} + \dfrac{\partial V}{\partial U}\cdot\dfrac{\partial U}{\partial M}} = m \qquad (7\text{-}11)$$

Equation (7-11) states that the marginal rate of the supply of money and the government expenditures should be equal to the ratio of the marginal disutilities of government expenditures and the supply of money.

The marginal condition for the supply of money and taxation is obtained by dividing (7-11) by (7-10):

$$\frac{\partial M}{\partial T} = \frac{\dfrac{\partial V}{\partial I}\cdot\dfrac{\partial i}{\partial M} + \dfrac{\partial V}{\partial P}\cdot\dfrac{\partial P}{\partial M} + \dfrac{\partial V}{\partial U}\cdot\dfrac{\partial U}{\partial M}}{\dfrac{\partial V}{\partial i}\cdot\dfrac{\partial i}{\partial T} + \dfrac{\partial V}{\partial P}\cdot\dfrac{\partial P}{\partial T} + \dfrac{\partial V}{\partial U}\cdot\dfrac{\partial U}{\partial T}} = -n \qquad (7\text{-}12)$$

Equation (7-12) states that the marginal rate of the supply of money and taxation should be equal to the ratio of the marginal disutilities of the supply of money and taxation.

To eliminate the marginal disutilities, let

$$v_1 \cdot \frac{\partial V}{\partial i} = \frac{\partial V}{\partial P}$$

$$v_2 \cdot \frac{\partial V}{\partial i} = \frac{\partial V}{\partial U}$$

(7-13)

where v_1 and v_2 are nonzero constants which measure the intensities of marginal disutilities in terms of marginal disutility of the rate of interest.

Substituting (7-13) in (7-10, 11, 12),

$$\frac{\partial T}{\partial G} = \frac{\dfrac{\partial U}{\partial i} \dfrac{\partial i}{\partial G} + v_1 \dfrac{\partial P}{\partial G} + v_2 \dfrac{\partial U}{\partial G}}{\dfrac{\partial V}{\partial i} \dfrac{\partial i}{\partial T} + v_1 \dfrac{\partial P}{\partial T} + v_2 \dfrac{\partial U}{\partial T}}$$

$$= \frac{\dfrac{\partial i}{\partial G} + v_1 \dfrac{\partial P}{\partial G} + v_2 \dfrac{\partial U}{\partial G}}{\dfrac{\partial i}{\partial T} + v_1 \dfrac{\partial P}{\partial T} + v_2 \dfrac{\partial U}{\partial T}}$$

(7-14)

$$\frac{\partial M}{\partial G} = \frac{\dfrac{\partial V}{\partial i} \left(\dfrac{\partial i}{\partial G} + v_1 \dfrac{\partial P}{\partial G} + v_2 \dfrac{\partial U}{\partial G} \right)}{\dfrac{\partial V}{\partial i} \left(\dfrac{\partial i}{\partial M} + v_1 \dfrac{\partial P}{\partial M} + v_2 \dfrac{\partial U}{\partial M} \right)}$$

$$= \frac{\dfrac{\partial i}{\partial G} + v_1 \dfrac{\partial P}{\partial G} + v_2 \dfrac{\partial U}{\partial G}}{\dfrac{\partial i}{\partial M} + v_1 \dfrac{\partial P}{\partial M} + v_2 \dfrac{\partial U}{\partial M}} = m$$

(7-15)

$$\frac{\partial M}{\partial T} = \frac{\dfrac{\partial V}{\partial i}\left(\dfrac{\partial i}{\partial T} + v_1 \dfrac{\partial P}{\partial T} + v_2 \dfrac{\partial U}{\partial T}\right)}{\dfrac{\partial V}{\partial i}\left(\dfrac{\partial i}{\partial M} + v_1 \dfrac{\partial P}{\partial M} + v_2 \dfrac{\partial U}{\partial M}\right)}$$

$$= \frac{\dfrac{\partial i}{\partial T} + v_1 \dfrac{\partial P}{\partial T} + v_2 \dfrac{\partial U}{\partial T}}{\dfrac{\partial i}{\partial M} + v_1 \dfrac{\partial P}{\partial M} + v_2 \dfrac{\partial U}{\partial M}} = -n$$

$$(7\text{-}16)$$

In terms of elasticities,

$$\frac{\partial T}{\partial G} = \frac{\dfrac{\partial i}{\partial G}\cdot\dfrac{G}{i}\cdot\dfrac{i}{G} + v_1 \dfrac{\partial P}{\partial G}\cdot\dfrac{G}{P}\cdot\dfrac{P}{G} + v_2 \dfrac{\partial U}{\partial G}\cdot\dfrac{G}{U}\cdot\dfrac{U}{G}}{\dfrac{\partial i}{\partial T}\cdot\dfrac{T}{i}\cdot\dfrac{i}{T} + v_1 \dfrac{\partial P}{\partial T}\cdot\dfrac{T}{P}\cdot\dfrac{P}{T} + v_2 \dfrac{\partial U}{\partial T}\cdot\dfrac{T}{U}\cdot\dfrac{U}{T}}$$

$$= \frac{E_{Gi}\dfrac{i}{G} + v_1 E_{GP}\dfrac{P}{G} + v_2 E_{GU}\dfrac{U}{G}}{E_{Ti}\dfrac{i}{T} + v_1 E_{TP}\dfrac{P}{T} + v_2 E_{TU}\dfrac{U}{T}} \qquad (7\text{-}17)$$

$$\frac{\partial M}{\partial G} = \frac{E_{Gi}\dfrac{i}{G} + v_1 E_{GP}\dfrac{P}{G} + v_2 E_{GU}\dfrac{U}{G}}{E_{Mi}\dfrac{i}{M} + v_1 E_{MP}\dfrac{P}{M} + v_2 E_{MU}\dfrac{U}{M}} = m \quad (7\text{-}18)$$

$$\frac{\partial M}{\partial T} = \frac{E_{Ti}\dfrac{i}{T} + v_1 E_{TP}\dfrac{P}{T} + v_2 E_{TU}\dfrac{U}{T}}{E_{Mi}\dfrac{i}{M} + v_1 E_{MP}\dfrac{P}{M} + v_2 E_{MU}\dfrac{U}{M}} = -n \quad (7\text{-}19)$$

Equations (7-17, 18, 19) imply that optimal values of m and n can be determined, given v_1 and v_2 by the social welfare function.

V. Conclusions

The above analysis may be useful to resolve some existing controversies. First, the continuing predictability controversy between the quantity theory and the Keynesian theory may be said to have been caused by the misleading formulation of the Keynesian model by the quantity theorists ignoring the money market in the Keynesian model. The quantity theorists regarded the empirical results of equation (2-13)′ as the quantity equation of money, and that of equation (2-13)″ as the Keynesian multiplier equation. Both can be interpreted as the Keynesian equations: one investment multiplier equation, the other monetary multiplier equation. If β/α is very close to one, there is little wonder that the two multipliers are very close.[15] The essence of the quantity theory is to maintain that equation (2-17) is true, i.e., a zero investment multiplier. We have shown that equations (2-17) and (2-18) are special cases of the Keynesian investment and monetary multipliers.

Secondly, in this paper the balanced budget theorems have been more generalized. The multiplier effect of a balanced budget can be zero as shown by condition (6-10). The theory behind the mathematical equation is that the aggregate demand increases due to an increase in the government expenditures. But if taxation increases by decreasing the supply of money, both consumption and investment expenditures will decrease so that these decreases will offset the increase in the aggregate

---

[15]See Equation (2-16).

demand which is caused by an increase in the government expenditures.

A third point is that it is possible for the rate of interest to fall, or remain constant when the balanced budget increases, if an increase in the government expenditures accompanies an increase in the supply of money as shown by equation (6-13). These conclusions suggest that fiscal and monetary variables are far more complicated than what many simple economic models suggest.

Finally, when there exist various alternative combinations of government expenditures, taxation, the rate of interest, the rate of unemployment, the level of prices, real output, and the supply of money, it is the social welfare function or an economic policy authority that may determine an optimal solution.[16]

---

[16]If we assume, for instance, $v_1 = 1$, $v_2 = 2$, (7-15), (7-16), and (7-14) will be rewritten as

$$m = \frac{\dfrac{\partial i}{\partial G} + \dfrac{\partial P}{\partial G} + 2\dfrac{\partial U}{\partial G}}{\dfrac{\partial i}{\partial M} + \dfrac{\partial P}{\partial M} + 2\dfrac{\partial U}{\partial M}} \tag{7-15$'$}$$

$$-n = \frac{\dfrac{\partial i}{\partial T} + \dfrac{\partial P}{\partial T} + 2\dfrac{\partial u}{\partial T}}{\dfrac{\partial i}{\partial M} + \dfrac{\partial P}{\partial M} + 2\dfrac{\partial U}{\partial M}} \tag{7-16$'$}$$

$$\frac{\partial T}{\partial G} = \frac{\dfrac{\partial i}{\partial G} + \dfrac{\partial P}{\partial G} + 2\dfrac{\partial U}{\partial G}}{\dfrac{\partial i}{\partial T} + \dfrac{\partial P}{\partial T} + 2\dfrac{\partial U}{\partial T}} \tag{7-14$'$}$$

REFERENCES

Ackley, G., "Liquidity Preference and Loanable Funds Theories of Interest: Comment," *American Economic Review*, Sept, 1957, pp. 662-673; "Reply" by S.G. Tsiang, pp. 673-678.

Allen, R.G.D., *Macro-economic Theory*, 1967, pp. 140-142.

Ando, A., and F. Modigliani, "The Relative Stability of Monetary Velocity and the Investment Multiplier," *American Economic Review*, Sept. 1965, pp. 693-728.

Barrett, C.R., and A.A. Walters, "The Stability of Keynesian and Monetary Multipliers in the United Kingdom," *Review of Economics and Statistics*, Nov. 1966, pp. 395-405.

DePrano, M., and T. Mayer, "Tests of the Relative Importance of Autonomous Expenditures and Money," *American Economic Review*, Sept. 1965, pp. 730-752: "Reply" to Ando and Modigliani and to DePrano and Mayer," by M. Friedman and D. Meiselman, pp. 753-790, "Rejoinder" by DePrano and Mayer, pp. 790-791.

Friedman, M., and D. Meiselman, "The Relative Stability of Monetary Velocity and Investment Multiplier in the United States, 1897-1958," *Stabilization Policies*, ed. by E.C. Brown, et al., A Series of Research Studies Prepared for the Commission on Money and Credit, 1963, pp. 152-268.

Hester, D.D., "Keynes and the Quantity Theory: A Comment on the Friedman-Meiselman CMC Paper," *Review of Economics and Statistics*, Nov. 1964, pp. 364-377, "Reply to Donald Hester" by M. Friedman and Meiselman, D., pp. 369-377. "Rejoinder," by Hester, pp. 376-377.

Lutz, V., "Multiplier and Velocity Analysis: A Marriage," *Economica*, Feb. 1955, pp. 29-44.

Mayer, T., "Multiplier and Velocity Analysis: An Evaluation," *Journal of Political Economy*, Dec. 1964, pp. 563-574.

Ritter, L.S., "Some Monetary Aspects of Multiplier Theory and Fiscal Policy," *Review of Economic Studies*, Nov. 1956, pp. 126-131.

Samuelson, P.A., "Fiscal Policy and Income Determination," *Quarterly Journal of Economics*, Aug. 1942, pp. 575-605.

Scott, R.H., "Estimates of Hicksian IS and LM Curves for the United States," *Journal of Finance*, 21, 1966, pp. 479-487. Rep. in J. Praeger, ed., *Monetary Economics, Controversies in Theory and Policy*, 1971, pp. 216-222.

Tsiang, S.C., "Liquidity Preference and Loanable Funds Theories, Multiplier and Velocity Analysis: A Synthesis," *American Economic Review*, Sept. 1956, pp. 539-564.

Tucker, D.P., "Mayer's Test of Keynesianism: A Correction," *Journal of Political Economy*, Aug. 1965, pp. 394-395.

Zwick, B., "The Adjustment of the Economy to Monetary Changes," *Journal of Political Economy*, Jan. 1971, pp. 77-96.

Chapter 8

The Tax Burden
in the U.S. States

I. Introduction
II. Tax Function and Regression Results
III. Tax Burden Ranking by State
IV. Alternative Methods
V. Conclusions

I. Introduction

A number of studies have appeared to explain that tax burden should have a limit and that tax burden largely depends upon GNP. Earlier, Clark (1945) maintained that if tax increases more than 25% of GNP, the economy will become inflationary. However, Martin and Lewis (1956) found that high per capita GNP countries tend to have a high tax ratio (total tax revenue divided by GNP). Similar observations were made by Oshima (1957) and Williamson (1963), implying that if GNP rises, tax ratio can be further increased. Lewis (1963) and Hinrichs (1966) added the foreign trade ratio (the ratio of total exports and absolute value of imports to GNP) as an additional source of tax capacity in their regression analysis.

Recently, Lots and Morss (1967) presented a measure of international "tax effort" using the tax regression equation where the dependent variable is the tax ratio and the independent variables are per capita GNP and the foreign trade ratio. Their idea is that if the "actual" tax ratio of a country is above the "predicted" tax ratio, predicted by the regression equation, the country's "tax effort" is regarded as high, and if the actual tax ratio is lower than the predicted tax ratio, the country's tax effort is regarded as low. They ranked countries in the descending order of percentage deviations of the actual tax ratio from the predicted tax ratio. Shin (1969) maintained that in measuring the tax capacity some additional variables such as population growth rate, industrial composition and the rate of inflation could be included in the tax ratio function in addition to the per capita GNP and the foreign trade ratio, and presented alternative tax ratio regression equations and tax effort ranking. Similar regression methods were used by Cheliah and other IMF research staff (1973, 1975).

In order to measure the tax efforts of U.S. States, similar regression methods were adopted by Akin (1973) and Morgan (1974). Akin calculated three regression equations, one of which contains 26 tax bases as independent variables, which include federally taxable income, corporate wages and salaries, retail sales, market value of non-farm residential realty, etc. Morgan calculated a log-linear regression equation in which the independent variables were population, per capita income, and seven representative tax rates for 31 U.S. States.

In this paper, we wish to apply a similar regression technique to measure the tax efforts of 50 U.S. States and Washington, D.C. with respect not only to the State and local taxes but also to the Federal personal income tax and the total tax which is defined as the sum of the two taxes. It may be easy to realize the importance of such studies in the current fiscal crises of many State and local governments as well as the Federal government with regard to the mounting public debt.

In the following section II, the effective "standard" U.S. tax system is estimated by the regression equations. The tax burden of the states is ranked in section III using the regression method. In Section IV, alternative methods of measuring the tax burden are presented, and the conclusions are summarized in section V.

II. Tax Function and Regression Results

The first step of the regression method of measuring tax effort is to estimate the effective "standard" U.S. tax system. In the United States, the major federal, state and local tax revenues consist of the following:

Individual income tax, corporate income tax, sales and excise taxes,
Property tax, inheritance, estate, and gift taxes
Social insurance tax, custom duties

If we assume that individual and corporate income taxes, sales and excise taxes, social insurance taxes and custom duties depend upon mainly GNP, and property tax, inheritance, estate, and gift taxes depend upon mainly national wealth, the tax function, either on aggregate basis or per capita basis, may be stated as:

$$T = F(Y, W, u) \qquad (1)$$

where T=per capita or aggregate tax revenue, Y=per capita or aggregate GNP or personal income, W=per capita or aggregate wealth, and u=stochastic term.

By applying the above equation to explain the state-by-state differences in tax revenue, we could assume that they are caused by variations in income and wealth. Since the data on per capita or aggregate wealth are not available for state-by-state, we may use the median value of owner-occupied homes as the proxy of per capita wealth.

Assuming a linear and log-linear forms of tax functions, we wish to test the following tax functions for the federal, state and local, and the total tax revenues:

$$T = a + b\,Y + c\,H \qquad (2)$$
$$\ln T = \ln a + b\,\ln Y + c\,\ln H \qquad (3)$$

We expect that both the per capita income Y and the house value H have positive signs since these variables represent the tax bases. The data were taken from the Bureau of the Census, U.S. Department of Commerce, *The Statistical Abstract of the U.S.*, 1972-73 editions. And the variables are defined below:

FT = Federal individual income tax originating from each state (1970 per capita dollars). 94th ed. (1973), p. 399.

ST = State and local tax revenue originating from each state (1970 per capita dollars) 93rd ed. (1972), p. 418.

TT = Total tax revenue (Federal personal income tax plus State and local taxes) originating from each state (1970, per capita dollars). (The sum of FT and ST)

Y = Per capita personal income of each state (1970 dollars) 94th ed. (1973), p. 326.

H = The median value of owner-occupied homes in each state (1970 dollars) 94th ed. (1973), p. 690.

When the data for the 50 states and Washington, D.C. were used to calculate the linear and the log-linear regression equations by the method of ordinary least squares regression, we have obtained Tables 1 and 2.

In Tables 1 and 2, we note that the regression results are very similar, though $\overline{R}^2$ values are slightly higher in the log-linear regression results. The per capita income is significant at the 1% level in all equations in Tables 1 and 2, but the house value is significant at the 5% level for the state and total tax revenues. These results are consistent with the U.S. tax system that property tax is a major source of tax revenue for the state and local governments.[1]

In the regression results of Tables 1 and 2, the residuals showed extreme deviations for New York and Hawaii. In addition to these two states, we have excluded Washington, D.C. and Alaska for possible unique characteristics of these areas, and calculated the regression equations as summarized in Tables 3 and 4.

As a result of the exclusion of the three states and Washington, D.C., in Tables 3 and 4, we note that the $\overline{R}^2$'s have slightly improved in both arithmetic and logarithmic regression results, and that the standard errors of estimate have been greatly reduced. Also we note that the arithmetic regression equations show slightly higher $\overline{R}^2$'s for the total and the federal tax revenues. The per capita income is again significant at the 1% level for all equations in Tables 3 and 4, but the house value is significant at the 5% level only for the total and the state tax revenues in Table 3, and only for the state tax revenue in Table 4. For these reasons, we may regard the regression equations 1, 2 and 3 in Table 3, as representing the effective "standard" U.S. tax system for year 1970.

A by-product of the above regression results is the estimate of the tax elasticity. The federal income tax elasticity ranged between 1.545 and 1.739, and the state tax elasticity ranged

---

[1]In 1970, the major federal tax revenue sources were individual income tax 46.7%, corporate income tax 16.9%, social insurance tax 23.4%, excise tax 8.1%, custom duties, estate and gift taxes 3.1%. The major state and local government tax revenue sources were property tax 26.6%, sales tax 23.6%, individual income tax 8.4%, and corporate income tax 2.9%. (1972-73 editions).

Table 1. T=a+bY+cH (50 States and Washington, D.C.)

	a	Y	H	R	$\overline{R}^2$	S.E.E.	d
(1) TT	−227.1227	0.2316 (7.57)**	0.0085 (2.11)*	0.9112	0.8232	79.9288	1.929
(2) FT	−237.2425	0.1562 (7.21)**	0.0019 (0.68)	0.8785	0.7623	56.5608	1.562
(3) ST	10.1198	0.0754 (4.06)**	0.0066 (2.69)**	0.8351	0.6848	48.5290	2.057

Note: The regression results are for the 50 states and Washington, D.C. The numbers in parentheses are the t-ratios. **Significant at the 1% level, *Significant at the 5% level.

Table 2. ln T=lna+αlnY+βlnH (T=aY^{α}H^β) (50 States and Washington, D.C.)

	ln a	ln Y	ln H	R	$\overline{R}^2$	S.E.E.	d
(1) ln TT	−4.3791	1.1305 (8.57)**	0.1781 (2.14)*	0.9359	0.8707	0.0845	1.848
(2) ln FT	−7.6438	1.5843 (7.81)**	0.0541 (0.42)	0.9017	0.8052	0.1299	1.635
(3) ln ST	−2.7440	0.7167 (3.88)**	0.2922 (2.51)*	0.8421	0.6971	0.1183	1.896

Note   See Table 1 footnote.

Table 3. T=a+bY+cH (47 States)

	a	Y	H	R	$\overline{R}^2$	S.E.E.	d
(1) TT	-257.7887	0.2426 (9.26)**	0.0079 (2.13)*	0.9549	0.9079	48.0348	2.160
(2) FT	-260.7059	0.1658 (8.25)**	0.0011 (0.39)	0.9229	0.8449	38.4741	1.934
(3) ST	2.9172	0.0767 (3.36)**	0.0067 (2.0)*	0.8214	0.6599	43.7346	1.549

Note: Excludes New York, Alaska, Hawaii, Washington, D.C. The numbers in parentheses are t-ratios.
**Significant at the 1% level, *Significant at the 5% level.

Table 4. lnT=lna+αlnY+βlnH (T=aY$^{\alpha}$·H$^{\beta}$) (47 States)

	ln a	ln Y	ln H	R	$\overline{R}^2$	S.E.E.	d
(1) ln TT	-4.6882	1.1992 (9.95)**	0.1519 (1.90)	0.9510	0.9000	0.0667	2.120
(2) ln FT	-8.0842	1.6926 (8.22)**	0.0078 (0.06)	0.9102	0.8207	0.1139	1.976
(3) ln ST	-2.9343	0.7519 (3.65)**	0.2821 (2.07)*	0.8243	0.6794	0.1140	1.606

Note: See Table 3 footnote.

Table 5. Tax Elasticities (Total, Federal and State Tax Revenues)

		$\frac{dT}{dY}\frac{Y}{T}$ (1)	$\frac{\partial T}{\partial Y}\frac{Y}{T}$ (2)	$\frac{\partial T}{\partial H}\frac{H}{T}$ (3)	$\frac{dT}{dY}\frac{Y}{T}$ (4)	$\frac{\partial T}{\partial Y}\frac{Y}{T}$ (5)	$\frac{\partial T}{\partial H}\frac{H}{T}$ (6)
		(estimated at mean values)			(log regression coefficients)		
(1970 data)							
50 States and D.C.	TT	1.360	1.114	0.179	1.363	1.131	0.178
	FT	1.660	1.545	0.083	1.655	1.584	0.054
	ST	1.077	0.705	0.269	1.098	0.717	0.292
47 States	TT	1.400	1.181	0.164	1.388	1.199	0.152
	FT	1.739	1.673	0.049	1.702	1.693	0.008
	ST	1.083	0.722	0.271	1.103	0.752	0.282
(1968 ACIR data)							
50 States and D.C.	ST	0.995			1.029		
47 States	ST	1.002			1.034		

Table 6. T=a+bY (50 States and Washington, D.C.)

	a	Y	R	$\overline{R}^2$	S.E.E.	d
(1) TT	−279.8467	0.2829 (14.67)**	0.9025	0.8107	82.7074	1.828
(2) FT	−249.1599	0.1678 (12.80)**	0.8773	0.7650	56.2458	1.527
(3) ST	−30.6868	0.1151 (9.57)**	0.8073	0.6446	51.5344	1.998

Table 7. ln T=ln a+αlnY (T=aY$^\alpha$) (50 States and Washington, D.C.)

	ln a	ln Y	R	$\overline{R}^2$	S.E.E.	d
(1) ln TT	−4.5683	1.3632 (17.65)**	0.9295	0.8613	0.0876	1.706
(2) ln FT	−7.7013	1.6550 (14.56)**	0.9013	0.8085	0.1288	1.594
(3) ln ST	−3.0545	1.0984 (9.99)**	0.8192	0.6644	0.1245	1.867

Table 8. T=a+bY (47 States)

	a	Y	R	$\overline{R^2}$	S.E.E.	d
(1) TT	−298.9910	0.2876 (20.45)**	0.9502	0.9007	49.8800	1.903
(2) FT	−266.6840	0.1724 (16.04)**	0.9226	0.8512	38.1084	1.896
(3) ST	−32.3069	0.1152 (9.05)**	0.8032	0.6373	45.1668	1.495

Table 9. ln T=lna+αlnY (T=aY^α) (47 States)

	ln a	ln Y	R	$\overline{R^2}$	S.E.E.	d
(1) ln TT	−4.7721	1.3880 (19.74)**	0.9468	0.8941	0.0686	1.893
(2) ln FT	−8.0885	1.7023 (14.74)**	0.9102	0.8247	0.1126	1.968
(3) ln ST	−3.0900	1.1026 (9.11)**	0.8052	0.6405	0.1180	1.569

between 0.705 and 1.103. The total tax elasticity ranged between 1.114 and 1.400. These values are slightly greater than the previous estimates.[2] However, the results are consistent with the current U.S. tax system in which the federal income tax system is rather progressive, while the state tax system is rather proportional or even regressive.

The tax elasticities calculated in this paper are summarized in Table 5.

III. Tax Burden Ranking by State

In the previous section, we have calculated a number of regression equations to estimate the effective "standard" U.S. tax system. Now the next step to estimate the burden of tax is to compare the predicted tax revenue with the actual tax revenue for each state. As we have seen in Tables 3 and 4, the arithmetic and the logarithmic regression results were very similar, but the arithmetic regression results were slightly better for the total and the federal tax equations. Also the arithmetic regression equations are easier to read. So we have chosen the regression equations (1), (2) and (3) in Table 3 as the effective "standard" U.S. tax system.

---

[2]Previous estimates for the federal individual income tax elasticities are:
 Mishan and Dicks-Mireaux (1958), 1.42483 (1953 data)
 Blackburn (1967), 1.3589-1.5809 (1962 data)
 Waldorf (1967), 1.4111-1.629 (1947-65 annual cross section elasticity)
 Tanzi (1969), 1.36263-1.41581 (1963 data)
Possible reasons for differences in elasticity estimates are: (1) differences in observation period, (2) the use of different types of income such as per capita personal income, per capita adjusted gross income, aggregate income, (3) exclusion of certain states, (4) structural changes in tax system.

Table 10. Tax Effort Ranking in 50 U.S. States and Washington, D.C. (1970 Cross Section Data)

State	Actual total tax ($) (1)	Pre-dicted tax (2)	Total tax effort index (1/2) (3)	Actual federal tax ($) (4)	Pre-dicted tax (5)	Federal tax effort index (4/5) (6)	Actual state-local tax (7)	Pre-dicted tax (8)	State-local tax effort index (7/8) (9)
1. New York	1448 (1)	1068	135.6 (1)	796 (1)	548	145.3 (1)	652 (1)	511	127.6 (1)
2. Vermont	807 (17)	708	114.0 (2)	336 (31)	330	101.8 (28)	471 (11)	378	124.6 (3)
3. Wisconsin	881 (14)	779	113.1 (3)	372 (26)	375	99.2 (32)	509 (6)	404	126.0 (2)
4. Mississippi	497 (50)	460	108.0 (4)	201 (51)	183	109.8 (6)	296 (47)	278	106.5 (13)
5. New Mexico	650 (36)	603	107.8 (5)	291 (39)	233	106.6 (12)	359 (32)	331	108.5 (12)
6. West Virginia	610 (42)	567	107.6 (6)	309 (35)	255	121.2 (2)	301 (45)	312	96.5 (31)
7. Arizona	802 (21)	749	107.1 (7)	377 (24)	358	105.3 (18)	425 (19)	391	108.7 (11)
8. Wyoming	807 (18)	754	107.0 (8)	373 (25)	366	101.9 (27)	434 (18)	388	111.9 (8)
9. Maine	674 (34)	630	107.0 (9)	294 (38)	292	100.7 (31)	380 (29)	338	112.4 (7)
10. Delaware	996 (8)	933	106.8 (10)	546 (4)	481	113.5 (5)	450 (12)	452	99.6 (28)
11. Maryland	981 (10)	930	105.5 (11)	499 (9)	472	105.7 (15)	482 (10)	458	105.2 (15)
12. South Dakota	632 (38)	600	105.3 (12)	234 (49)	277	84.5 (47)	398 (25)	323	123.2 (4)
13. North Dakota	617 (41)	589	104.8 (13)	241 (48)	263	91.6 (42)	376 (30)	326	115.3 (5)
14. Nevada	1065 (3)	1023	104.1 (14)	548 (3)	520	105.4 (17)	517 (5)	503	102.8 (20)
15. Pennsylvania	836 (16)	806	103.7 (15)	435 (15)	409	106.4 (13)	401 (23)	397	101.0 (26)
16. Michigan	907 (13)	883	102.7 (16)	451 (12)	445	101.3 (29)	456 (14)	438	104.1 (18)
17. Montana	703 (31)	688	102.2 (17)	305 (36)	326	93.6 (38)	398 (26)	362	109.9 (10)
18. Illinois	1005 (6)	987	101.8 (18)	518 (6)	506	102.4 (25)	487 (8)	481	101.2 (24)
19. Oregon	778 (24)	766	101.6 (19)	378 (23)	373	101.3 (30)	400 (24)	392	102.0 (23)

20. Massachusetts	971 (11)	958	101.4 (20)	474 (11)	483	98.1 (34)	497 (7)	475	104.6 (17)
21. Utah	665 (35)	656	101.4 (21)	290 (40)	293	99.0 (33)	375 (31)	363	103.3 (19)
22. Tennessee	592 (44)	587	100.9 (22)	313 (33)	264	118.6 (3)	279 (48)	323	86.4 (45)
23. California	1001 (7)	1002	99.9 (23)	442 (14)	503	87.9 (46)	559 (3)	500	111.8 (9)
24. Colorado	804 (20)	808	99.5 (24)	385 (20)	394	97.7 (35)	419 (20)	414	101.2 (25)
25. Washington	850 (15)	855	99.4 (25)	406 (17)	421	96.4 (36)	443 (15)	433	102.3 (22)
26. New Hampshire	744 (27)	750	99.2 (26)	411 (16)	358	114.8 (4)	333 (39)	391	85.2 (48)
27. Florida	741 (28)	749	98.9 (27)	394 (19)	364	108.2 (8)	347 (35)	385	90.1 (38)
28. Kentucky	585 (46)	593	98.7 (28)	286 (41)	268	106.7 (11)	299 (46)	326	91.7 (36)
29. Connecticut	1093 (2)	1112	98.3 (29)	608 (2)	567	107.2 (9)	485 (9)	544	89.2 (39)
30. Minnesota	805 (19)	819	98.3 (30)	363 (28)	399	91.0 (43)	442 (16)	420	105.2 (16)
31. Indiana	753 (25)	770	97.8 (31)	396 (18)	383	103.4 (20)	357 (33)	387	92.2 (34)
32. North Carolina	609 (43)	624	97.6 (32)	298 (37)	288	103.5 (19)	311 (43)	336	92.6 (33)
33. Oklahoma	618 (40)	638	96.9 (33)	312 (34)	305	102.3 (26)	306 (44)	333	91.9 (35)
34. Texas	681 (33)	704	96.7 (34)	365 (27)	346	105.5 (16)	316 (41)	358	88.3 (41)
35. Idaho	623 (39)	645	96.6 (35)	276 (42)	297	92.9 (40)	347 (34)	348	99.7 (27)
36. Missouri	727 (30)	756	96.2 (36)	384 (21)	372	103.2 (21)	343 (36)	385	89.1 (40)
37. Kansas	752 (26)	788	95.4 (37)	357 (29)	403	88.6 (45)	395 (28)	385	102.6 (21)
38. New Jersey	985 (9)	1037	95.0 (38)	538 (5)	525	102.5 (24)	447 (13)	512	87.3 (42)
39. Arkansas	494 (51)	520	95.0 (39)	242 (47)	226	107.1 (10)	252 (51)	293	86.0 (46)
40. Alabama	508 (49)	536	94.8 (40)	250 (44)	230	108.7 (7)	259 (50)	306	84.6 (49)
41. Hawaii	1065 (4)	1125	94.7 (41)	493 (10)	533	92.5 (41)	572 (2)	588	97.3 (30)
42. Rhode Island	790 (22)	836	94.5 (42)	382 (22)	410	93.2 (39)	408 (22)	426	95.8 (32)
43. Georgia	634 (37)	671	94.5 (43)	322 (32)	312	103.2 (22)	312 (42)	359	86.9 (43)
44. Nebraska	740 (29)	788	93.9 (44)	343 (30)	382	89.8 (44)	397 (27)	377	105.3 (14)
45. South Carolina	522 (48)	556	93.9 (45)	248 (45)	241	102.9 (23)	274 (49)	316	86.7 (44)

Table 10. Tax Effort Ranking in 50 U.S. States and Washington, D.C. (1970 Cross Section Data)—Continued

State	Actual total tax ($) (1)	Pre-dicted tax (2)	Total tax effort index (1/2) (3)	Actual federal tax ($) (4)	Pre-dicted tax (5)	Federal tax effort index (4/5) (6)	Actual state-local tax (7)	Pre-dicted tax (8)	State-local tax effort index (7/8) (9)
46. Ohio	789 (23)	846	93.3 (46)	446 (13)	419	106.4 (14)	343 (37)	427	80.3 (50)
47. Louisiana	550 (47)	598	92.0 (47)	219 (50)	262	83.6 (48)	331 (40)	336	98.5 (29)
48. Iowa	691 (32)	761	90.8 (48)	255 (43)	377	67.6 (50)	436 (17)	384	113.5 (6)
49. Alaska	917 (12)	1034	88.7 (49)	500 (8)	525	95.2 (37)	417 (21)	588	70.9 (51)
50. District of Columbia	1026 (5)	1236	83.0 (50)	509 (7)	669	76.1 (49)	517 (4)	565	91.5 (37)
51. Virginia	586 (45)	762	76.9 (51)	246 (46)	364	67.6 (51)	340 (38)	398	85.4 (47)

Note: The numbers in parentheses are rank numbers in descending order for each column. The predicted values are obtained from regression equations (4)–(6) in Table 3, which are calculated with the 47 state data. The predicted values for New York, Alaska, Hawaii, and Washington, D.C. are obtained by substituting the actual values in those regression equations. The basic data for the regression equations are from U.S. Department of Commerce, Bureau of the Census, *The Statistical Abstract of the U.S.*, 1972, 1974 editions.

Using these standard tax equations, the predicted tax revenues and the actual tax revenues are listed and compared in Table 10.

In column (1), the actual per capita total taxes (federal personal income tax plus state-local tax revenue) are listed. The numbers in parentheses are the ranking numbers in the descending order. The per capita total tax was $1,448 for New York. Since the amount is the largest in the 50 U.S. states and Washington, D.C., the rank number 1 is assigned. The per capita total tax of Arkansas is the smallest, so the rank number 51 is assigned.

In column (2) the predicted per capita total taxes are listed. For instance, in New York, the per capita income was $4,731, and the median house value was $22,500. Substituting these values in regression equation (1) in Table 3, we obtain the predicted per capita total tax for New York, $1,068. Dividing the actual tax $1,448 by the predicted tax $1,068, we obtain the tax burden index or the tax effort index, 135.6 for New York $((1448/1068) \times 100)$, and it is listed in column 3. The tax effort index 135.6 indicates that the actual per capita total tax paid by New York residents exceeded the predicted per capita total tax by 1.356 times or 35.6%. Similarly, for Vermont, dividing the actual tax $807 by the predicted tax $708, we obtain the tax effort index 114.0. For Virginia, dividing the actual tax $586 by the predicted tax $762, we obtain the tax effort index 76.9. This index indicates that Virginia's actual per capita total tax was 76.9% of the predicted tax, or the actual tax payment was smaller than the predicted tax by 23.1%. Since the tax effort index was the largest for New York, the rank number 1 is assigned, and the rank number 2 to Vermont, and the rank number 51 to Virginia.

Similarly, column (4) lists the actual per capita federal personal income tax and column (5) lists the predicted per capita federal tax, predicted by regression equation (2) of Table 3. Column (6) lists the tax effort index for the federal tax. Columns (7), (8) and (9) are for the state-local taxes. We note that New York state has the largest tax effort index for the federal, state-local and total taxes. The top five states for the per capita total tax are New York, Vermont, Wisconsin, Mississippi, and New Mexico. It should be noted that the tax effort index obtained by the regression method does not measure the absolute amount of tax burden nor the tax burden relative to the national average. It measures the tax burden relative to the State's own tax capacity which is predicted by the regression equation.

Also we note that some States have a higher tax effort in the Federal tax payment, but not in State-local taxes, and vice versa. For instance, West Virginia is the 2nd in the Federal tax effort, but the 31st in the State-local tax effort. Vermont's State-local tax effort is the 3rd, but it is the 28th in the federal tax effort. It should be useful to examine causes of deviations of actual taxes from the predicted taxes for each State.

IV. Alternative Methods

In the previous section, we have applied "the regression method" to rank the tax efforts of States. The tax effort index was obtained from the actual per capita tax divided by the predicted per capita tax, predicted from the regression equation in which the dependent variable is the per capita tax, and the independent variables are per capita income and the median house value as a proxy of per capita wealth. However, a few alternative methods of measuring tax efforts of State and local governments are available.

(1) Under the "tax/income ratio" method, actual per capita tax is divided by actual per capita income, and States are

ranked in the order of the tax ratio or the average tax rate. However, this method assumes that tax capacity is equal to income, and other determinants of tax capacity are ignored.

(2) Under the "representative family" method or the "statutory tax rate" method we first establish a "representative family" consisting of a husband, a wife, and two dependent children, with the adjusted gross income $9,867 (the median family income of 1970), and a $17,000 house (the median value of owner occupied house in 1970). Next, applying the State and local tax rates, we calculate how much the family should pay in State and local taxes if the family resided in each of the 50 U.S. States and Washington, D.C. The taxes which the representative family should pay may include personal income tax, property tax, sales tax, inheritance, estate, and gift taxes, motor fuel taxes, alcoholic beverage taxes, tobacco taxes, amusement taxes, public utility taxes, motor vehicle and operator's license taxes. Then the States are ranked in the order of the amount of taxes the representative family should pay in each State.[3] One disadvantage of this method is that it measures the statutory tax effort and not the effective tax effort.

(3) Perhaps the most elaborate method of measuring the tax efforts of State and local governments is the "representative tax system" approach or the "national average tax rate" method adopted by the U.S. Advisory Commission on Intergovernmental Relations (1971).[4] Under this method, the following methodology

---

[3]As to the federal and state income taxes, there exists such a study by Melichar (1963). Also the U.S. Advisory Commission on Intergovernmental Relations has published the effective rates of State personal income taxes for selected adjusted gross income levels, married couple, with two dependent children. The selected income levels ranges between $2,500 and $50,000. ACIR (1974). Table 15 shows the State personal income tax burden ranked by the statutory tax rate method calculated by ACIR (1977).

[4]The 1971 research report was carried out by the special project staff of

is involved to estimate the tax capacity: (a) Examine various kinds of State and local taxes to determine which taxes should be handled separately. (b) Locate tax-base data for each tax. In the absence of such data, use some quantitative proxy data that could reasonably be taken to represent the actual base. (c) Obtain a national average tax rate for each tax by dividing its nation-wide yield by the nationwide base or its proxy. (d) Obtain the tax capacity (potential yield) of each tax class for particular areas (States, counties and SMSA's) by applying the national average rate to the base measure for such areas. (e) Add tax capacity figures thus developed for particular taxes in each area to arrive at the area's total tax capacity (ACIR, 1971, p. 7, pp. 49-60).

The ACIR's tax capacities thus obtained for the 50 U.S. States and D.C. for 1968-69 fiscal year are listed in column 2 of Table 11. Dividing the actual per capita tax in column 1 by the ACIR's tax capacity of column 2, we obtain the ACIR's "relative tax effort index" as listed in column 3. For instance, Alabama's actual per capita state-local tax was $227, and the estimated tax capacity was $270. Dividing the actual tax by the tax capacity, we obtain the ACIR's tax effort index 84.1. It indicates that Alabama's actual per capita tax was 84.1% of the potential tax yield which could have been collected if the Alabama's estimated tax base was applied by the national average tax rate. Similarly, Arizona's tax effort index 103.1 indicates that Arizona's actual per capita tax was 3.1% above the tax yield which could have been collected if Arizona's tax base was applied by the national average tax rate. According to this

---

the Commission under the direction of Allen D. Manvel, participated by Donald J. Curran, Raymond J. Kransniewski and others. ACIR (1971). The method was first adopted in 1962 ACIR report. ACIR (1962).

method, New York has the greatest tax effort index, 138.8, and thus the rank number 1 is assigned, while Nevada has the smallest tax effort index 71.0, and thus the rank number 51 is assigned (Table 11, column 3).

In order to compare the ACIR's national average tax rate method with the regression method, we have calculated several regression equations with the ACIR data, and the results are summarized in Tables 13 and 14. The regression equations in Table 13 are calculated with the data for the 50 states and Washington, D.C., and those in Table 14 are calculated with the data for the 47 states excluding New York, Alaska, Hawaii, and Washington, D.C.

The following points may be noted:

First, the 47 State data yielded better regression results than the 50 State and D.C. data did. Secondly, in both tables, the log regression yielded better results than the arithmetic regression. Thirdly, in both tables, per capita income better explained the variations in the State and local taxes for 1968 than the ACIR's tax capacity. Fourthly, the per capita income explained about 52% of the total variation of the tax capacity. However, these statistical results alone do not tell which method is theoretically superior in measuring the tax capacity and tax effort. The ACIR's method measures the tax capacity "as it should be" when a national norm is imposed on the tax base, while the regression equation method regards the predicted tax as the tax capacity under the current tax system.[5]

With the above regression results, alternative measures of tax effort index are possible. First, instead of measuring the tax

---

[5]See Manvel's (1973) reply to detailed criticism by Akin (1973) on ACIR's method. For more detailed explanations on the differences between the two methods, see Appendix Note (p. 232).

Table 11. State-Local Tax Effort Rankings (1968 ACIR Data, 50 States and Washington, D.C.)

	Actual tax (t)	ACIR's tax capacity (K)	ACIR's tax effort index (I) T/K ratio ranking ((1)/(2))100	Pre-dicted tax K'= a+bK 100	ACIR's tax effort index (II) T/K' ratio ranking ((1)/(4))100	Per capita income (Y)	Tax/income ratio (T/Y ratio) ranking ((1)/(6))100	Pre-dicted tax, T'= a+bY	Tax effort index by regression method ((1)/(7))100
	(1)	(2)	(3)	(4)	(5)	(6)	(7)	(8)	(9)
1. Alabama	227 (50)	270 (49)	84.1 (40)	276	82.2 (48)	2337 (49)	9.7 (42)	259	87.6 (42)
2. Alaska	399 (15)	403 (16)	99.0 (20)	369	108.1 (16)	4146 (4)	9.6 (43)	460	86.7 (43)
3. Arizona	393 (19)	381 (27)	103.1 (12)	354	110.0 (13)	3027 (33)	13.0 (5)	336	117.0 (5)
4. Arkansas	222 (51)	299 (47)	74.2 (48)	297	74.7 (51)	2322 (50)	9.6 (44)	258	86.0 (45)
5. California	547 (2)	472 (3)	115.9 (6)	417	131.2 (3)	3968 (6)	13.8 (3)	441	124.0 (3)
6. Colorado	392 (20)	398 (19)	98.5 (22)	365	107.4 (17)	3340 (21)	11.7 (22)	371	105.7 (22)
7. Connecticut	397 (16)	451 (6)	88.0 (33)	402	98.8 (26)	4256 (2)	9.3 (48)	472	84.1 (48)
8. Delaware	377 (22)	465 (5)	81.1 (44)	412	91.5 (35)	3795 (10)	9.9 (38)	421	89.5 (38)
9. D.C.	426 (9)	465 (4)	91.6 (27)	412	103.4 (23)	4464 (1)	9.5 (45)	496	85.9 (46)
10. Florida	338 (31)	419 (10)	80.7 (45)	380	88.9 (38)	3191 (28)	10.6 (30)	356	94.9 (30)
11. Georgia	273 (44)	314 (43)	86.9 (35)	307	88.9 (39)	2781 (39)	9.8 (40)	309	88.3 (41)
12. Hawaii	492 (3)	381 (26)	129.1 (2)	354	139.0 (2)	3513 (15)	14.0 (2)	390	126.2 (1)
13. Idaho	340 (29)	338 (39)	100.6 (18)	324	105.0 (20)	2668 (41)	12.7 (8)	296	114.9 (8)
14. Illinois	376 (23)	431 (7)	87.2 (34)	388	96.9 (28)	3981 (5)	9.4 (47)	442	85.1 (47)
15. Indiana	338 (30)	375 (28)	90.1 (30)	349	96.8 (29)	3412 (18)	9.9 (39)	379	89.2 (39)
16. Iowa	395 (17)	385 (24)	102.6 (13)	356	111.0 (12)	3265 (24)	12.1 (14)	362	109.1 (15)
17. Kansas	351 (27)	405 (14)	86.7 (37)	370	94.9 (32)	3303 (23)	10.6 (29)	367	95.6 (29)
18. Kentucky	278 (43)	312 (44)	89.1 (32)	306	90.8 (36)	2645 (44)	10.5 (32)	293	94.9 (31)

19. Louisiana	301 (40)	364 (31)	82.7 (41)	342	88.0 (42)	2634 (45)	11.4 (24)	292	103.1 (23)
20. Maine	321 (37)	316 (42)	101.6 (15)	308	104.2 (22)	2824 (37)	11.4 (23)	313	102.6 (24)
21. Maryland	416 (10)	398 (18)	104.5 (10)	365	114.0 (9)	3742 (11)	11.1 (25)	415	100.2 (26)
22. Massachusetts	455 (5)	382 (25)	119.1 (4)	354	128.5 (5)	3835 (9)	11.9 (18)	426	106.8 (19)
23. Michigan	439 (7)	404 (15)	108.7 (8)	370	118.6 (8)	3675 (13)	11.9 (19)	408	107.6 (18)
24. Minnesota	413 (11)	367 (30)	112.5 (7)	344	120.1 (7)	3341 (20)	12.4 (9)	371	111.3 (9)
25. Mississippi	245 (48)	252 (51)	97.2 (23)	264	92.8 (34)	2081 (51)	11.8 (21)	231	106.1 (21)
26. Missouri	304 (39)	373 (29)	81.5 (43)	348	87.4 (43)	3257 (26)	9.3 (49)	362	84.0 (49)
27. Montana	356 (25)	391 (21)	91.0 (29)	361	98.6 (27)	2942 (34)	12.1 (15)	326	109.2 (14)
28. Nebraska	361 (24)	416 (12)	86.8 (36)	378	95.5 (31)	3239 (27)	11.1 (26)	360	100.3 (25)
29. Nevada	475 (4)	669 (1)	71.0 (51)	554	85.7 (44)	3957 (7)	12.0 (17)	439	108.2 (17)
30. New Hampshire	325 (34)	422 (9)	77.0 (47)	382	85.1 (46)	3259 (25)	10.0 (36)	362	89.8 (37)
31. New Jersey	411 (13)	410 (13)	100.2 (19)	374	109.9 (15)	3954 (8)	10.4 (33)	439	93.6 (33)
32. New Mexico	324 (35)	355 (34)	91.3 (28)	336	96.4 (30)	2651 (43)	12.2 (13)	294	110.2 (12)
33. New York	580 (1)	418 (11)	138.8 (1)	379	153.0 (1)	4151 (3)	14.0 (1)	461	125.8 (2)
34. North Carolina	267 (46)	308 (45)	86.7 (38)	303	88.1 (41)	2664 (42)	10.0 (37)	296	90.2 (36)
35. North Dakota	333 (33)	352 (35)	94.6 (26)	333	100.0 (25)	2730 (40)	12.2 (12)	303	109.9 (13)
36. Ohio	318 (38)	387 (23)	82.2 (42)	358	88.8 (40)	3509 (16)	9.1 (51)	390	81.5 (51)
37. Oklahoma	290 (41)	392 (20)	74.0 (49)	361	80.3 (49)	2880 (35)	10.1 (35)	320	90.6 (35)
38. Oregon	406 (14)	401 (17)	101.2 (16)	368	110.3 (14)	3317 (22)	12.2 (11)	368	110.3 (10)
39. Pennsylvania	346 (28)	350 (36)	98.9 (21)	332	104.1 (21)	3419 (17)	10.1 (34)	380	91.1 (34)
40. Rhode Island	380 (21)	355 (33)	107.0 (9)	336	113.1 (10)	3549 (14)	10.7 (28)	394	96.4 (28)
41. South Carolina	227 (49)	254 (50)	89.4 (31)	265	85.7 (45)	2380 (48)	9.5 (46)	264	86.0 (44)
42. South Dakota	353 (26)	349 (37)	101.1 (17)	331	106.6 (19)	2876 (36)	12.3 (10)	320	110.3 (11)
43. Tennessee	254 (47)	302 (46)	84.1 (39)	299	84.9 (47)	2579 (46)	9.8 (41)	286	88.8 (40)
44. Texas	280 (42)	388 (22)	72.2 (50)	358	78.2 (50)	3029 (32)	9.2 (50)	336	83.3 (50)

219

	Actual tax (t) (1)	ACIR's tax capacity (K) (2)	ACIR's tax effort index (I) T/K ratio ranking ((1)/(2))100 (3)	Predicted tax K' = a+bK (4)	ACIR's tax effort index (II) T/K' ratio ranking ((1)/(4))100 (5)	Per capita income (Y) (6)	Tax/income ratio (T/Y ratio) ranking ((1)/(6))100 (7)	Predicted tax, T' = a+bY (8)	Tax effort index by regression method ((1)/(7))100 (9)
45. Utah	337 (32)	326 (41)	103.4 (11)	315	107.0 (18)	2790 (38)	12.1 (16)	310	108.7 (16)
46. Vermont	394 (18)	339 (38)	116.2 (5)	324	121.6 (6)	3072 (30)	12.8 (7)	341	115.5 (7)
47. Virginia	323 (36)	337 (40)	95.8 (24)	323	100.0 (24)	3068 (31)	10.5 (31)	341	94.7 (32)
48. Washington	434 (8)	424 (8)	102.4 (14)	384	113.0 (11)	3688 (12)	11.8 (20)	409	106.1 (20)
49. West Virginia	269 (45)	284 (48)	94.7 (25)	286	94.1 (33)	2470 (47)	10.9 (27)	274	98.2 (27)
50. Wisconsin	441 (6)	358 (32)	123.2 (3)	338	130.5 (4)	3363 (19)	13.1 (4)	373	118.2 (4)
51. Wyoming	413 (12)	530 (2)	77.9 (46)	457	90.4 (37)	3190 (29)	12.9 (6)	354	116.7 (6)

Note: 1. The numbers in parentheses are rank numbers in descending order for each column. Actual tax, tax capacity, per capita income are from Advisory Commission on Intergovernmental Relations, *Measuring the Fiscal Capacity and Effort of State and Local Area*, Information Report, M-58, March 1971, p. 209.

2. Column (4)=The predicted tax capacity is given by regression equation (1) of Table 6:

$$K' = 88.2861 + 0.6964 \ K$$

Column (7)=The predicted tax is given by regression equation (2) of Table 6:

$$T' = -0.7556 + 0.1112 \ Y$$

Table 12. States with Inconsistent Rankings with Respect to Below-or-Above Average State-Local Tax Effort

	1970 tax effort index from Table 4, column 9. $T/(T'=a+bY+cH)$ ranking (1)	1968 tax effort indexes from Table 7 ACIR's T/K ranking (2)	ACIR's T/K' ranking (3)	T/Y ranking (4)	$T/(T'=a+bY)$ ranking (5)
1. Alaska	70.9 (51)	99.0 (20)	108.1 (16)**	9.6 (43)	86.7 (43)
2. Colorado	101.2 (25)	98.5 (22)*	107.4 (17)	11.7 (22)	105.7 (22)
3. D.C.	91.5 (37)	91.6 (27)	103.4 (23)**	9.5 (45)	85.9 (46)
4. Hawaii	97.3 (30)*	129.1 (2)	139.0 (2)	14.0 (2)	126.2 (1)
5. Idaho	99.7 (27)*	100.6 (18)	105.0 (20)	12.7 (8)	114.9 (8)
6. Illinois	101.2 (24)**	87.2 (34)	96.9 (28)	9.4 (47)	85.1 (47)
7. Kansas	102.6 (21)**	86.7 (37)	94.9 (32)	10.6 (29)	95.6 (29)
8. Montana	109.9 (10)	91.0 (29)*	98.6 (27)*	12.1 (15)	109.2 (14)
9. Mississippi	106.5 (13)	97.2 (23)*	92.8 (34)*	11.8 (21)	106.1 (21)
10. Nebraska	105.3 (14)	86.8 (36)*	95.5 (31)*	11.1 (26)	100.3 (23)
11. Nevada	102.8 (20)	71.0 (51)*	85.7 (44)*	12.0 (17)	108.2 (12)
12. New Jersey	87.3 (42)	100.2 (19)**	109.9 (15)**	10.4 (33)	93.6 (33)
13. New Mexico	108.5 (12)	91.3 (28)*	96.4 (30)*	12.2 (13)	110.2 (12)
14. North Dakota	115.3 (5)	94.6 (26)*	100.0 (25)	12.2 (12)	109.9 (13)
15. Louisiana	98.5 (32)	82.7 (41)	88.0 (42)	11.4 (24)**	103.1 (23)**
16. Pennsylvania	101.0 (26)	98.9 (21)*	104.2 (21)	10.1 (34)	91.1 (34)
17. Rhode Island	95.8 (32)	107.0 (9)**	113.1 (10)**	10.7 (28)	96.4 (28)
18. Wyoming	111.9 (8)	77.9 (46)*	90.4 (37)*	12.9 (6)	116.7 (6)

Note: *Underestimate of tax effort compared with rankings by their majority criteria. **Overestimate compared with rankings by other criteria.
The "Majority ranking" is not intended to imply a true or standard ranking.
Virginia is excluded from the above table because the index 100 in column (5) in Table 7 is regarded as consistent with the majority ranking.

Table 13. Regression Results (1968 ACIR Data, 50 States and Washington, D.C.)

	R	$\bar{R}^2$	S.E.E.	d
(1) ST=80.4619+0.7369 K 　　　　　　　(6.17)**	0.6613	0.4259	59.2418	2.041
(2) ST=1.7223+0.1110 Y 　　　　　　(9.25)**	0.7976	0.6287	47.6444	1.979
(3) ST=−15.1120+0.1942 K+0.0934 Y 　　　　　　　(1.41)　　　　(5.41)**	0.8065	0.6359	47.1774	1.918
(4) K=86.6744+0.0123 Y 　　　　　　(7.83)**	0.7258	0.5171	48.7645	1.548
(5) ln ST=0.48669+0.9077 ln K 　　　　　　　　(7.53)**	0.7324	0.5364	0.1507	1.961
(6) ln ST=−2.4361+1.0291 ln Y 　　　　　　　(10.44)**	0.8305	0.6834	0.1233	2.067
(7) ln ST=−2.3215+0.2486 ln K+0.8323 ln Y 　　　　　　　(1.56)　　　　　(5.23)**	0.8395	0.6924	0.1215	1.984
(8) ln K=−0.4608+0.7916 ln Y 　　　　　　(9.07)**	0.7917	0.6192	0.1091	1.552

Note: The numbers in parentheses are t-ratios. **Significant at the 1% level. The basic data are from Advisory Commission on Intergovernmental Relations, *Measuring the Fiscal Capacity and Effort of State and Local Areas*, Information Report, M-58, March 1971, p. 209.

222

Table 14. Regression Results (1968 ACIR Data, 47 States)

	R	$\overline{R}^2$	S.E.E.	d
(1) ST=88.2861+0.6964 K (6.70)**	0.7069	0.4885	50.4988	1.855
(2) ST=−0.7556+0.1112 Y (9.33)**	0.8119	0.6516	41.6799	2.149
(3) ST=−12.8368+0.2324 K+0.0874 Y (1.88)　　(5.08)**	0.8273	0.6701	40.5571	2.047
(4) K=51.9837+0.1027 Y (7.35)**	0.7368	0.5354	48.8494	1.519
(5) ln ST=0.7134+0.8666 ln K (7.77)**	0.7568	0.5633	0.1362	1.8478
(6) ln ST=−2.4770+1.0338 ln Y (10.17)**	0.8348	0.6902	0.1147	2.3207
(7) ln ST=−2.1829+0.2850 ln K+0.7877 ln Y (1.88)　　(4.80)**	0.8482	0.7067	0.1117	2.182
(8) ln K=−1.0318+0.8635 ln Y (8.90)**	0.7985	0.6295	0.1096	1.534

Note: Does not include New York, Hawaii, Alaska, and Washington, D.C.
The numbers in parentheses are t-ratios. **Significant at the 1% level. See footnote to Table 13.

Table 15. State Income Taxes by the Standard Tax Rates (1974, A Family of 4)

	Per capita income	Tax on income $10,000	Tax on income $17,500	Tax on income $25,000	Sales tax rate (1974)	Sales tax rate (1976)
1. Alabama	4198 (48)	147 (25)	239 (23)	593 (26)	0.04	0.04*
2. Alaska	7023 (1)	182 (16)	369 (21)	668 (24)	0	0
3. Arizona	4989 (30)	148 (23)	314 (28)	646 (25)	0.04	0.04*
4. Arkansas	4280 (45)	163 (18)	387 (19)	771 (20)	0.03	0.03*
5. California	5997 (8)	64 (34)	293 (30)	688 (23)	0.0475	0.0475*
6. Colorado	5343 (20)	157 (19)	382 (20)	785 (19)	0.03	0.03*
7. Connecticut	6471 (2)	0	0	0	0.06	0.07
8. Delaware	6227 (6)	236 (11)	652 (3)	1238 (3)	0	0
9. Florida	5235 (25)	0	0	0	0.04	0.04
10. Georgia	4662 (35)	83 (33)	319 (27)	714 (22)	0.03	0.03*
11. Hawaii	5882 (10)	212 (13)	611 (6)	1133 (6)	0.04	0.04
12. Idaho	4934 (31)	138 (27)	474 (14)	973 (10)	0.03	0.03
13. Illinois	6337 (4)	150 (21)	338 (25)	525 (27)	0.04	0.04*
14. Indiana	5263 (24)	150 (22)	300 (26)	450 (26)	0.04	0.04
15. Iowa	5302 (21)	295 (3)	528 (10)	884 (14)	0.03	0.03
16. Kansas	5406 (18)	126 (28)	297 (29)	560 (30)	0.03	0.03*
17. Kentucky	4470 (40)	243 (9)	444 (17)	750 (21)	0.05	0.05
18. Louisiana	4310 (44)	48 (38)	125 (40)	227 (40)	0.03	0.03*
19. Maine	4439 (42)	60 (35)	160 (38)	359 (38)	0.05	0.05
20. Maryland	5881 (11)	255 (7)	479 (13)	812 (18)	0.014	0.04
21. Massachusetts	5731 (12)	277 (5)	641 (4)	1013 (7)	0.03	0.05
22. Michigan	5928 (9)	− 59 (41)	103 (41)	221 (41)	0.04	0.04

23. Minnesota	5450 (17)	543 (1)	1016 (1)	1724 (1)	0.04	0.04*
24. Mississippi	3764 (50)	38 (39)	218 (35)	473 (35)	0.05	0.05
25. Missouri	5056 (29)	109 (32)	268 (33)	567 (29)	0.03	0.03
26. Montana	4776 (34)	279 (4)	499 (12)	947 (11)	0	0
27. Nebraska	4887 (32)	35 (40)	158 (39)	330 (39)	0.025	0.03*
28. Nevada	6074 (7)	0	0	0	0.03	0.03*
29. New Hampshire	5143 (28)	0	0	0	0	0
30. New Jersey	6384 (3)	0	0	0	0.05	0.05
31. New Mexico	4137 (49)	84 (32)	238 (34)	527 (30)	0.04	0.04
32. New York	6244 (5)	206 (14)	550 (8)	1174 (5)	0.04	0.04*
33. North Carolina	4612 (36)	258 (6)	535 (9)	1000 (9)	0.03	0.03*
34. North Dakota	5547 (15)	105 (31)	338 (24)	822 (16)	0.04	0.04
35. Ohio	5549 (14)	55 (36)	188 (37)	390 (37)	0.04	0.04*
36. Oklahoma	4566 (38)	50 (37)	196 (36)	517 (33)	0.02	0.02*
37. Oregon	5270 (22)	238 (10)	633 (5)	1184 (4)	0	0
38. Pennsylvania	5490 (16)	200 (15)	350 (22)	500 (28)	0.06	0.06*
39. Rhode Island	5376 (19)	119 (29)	286 (31)	521 (32)	0.05	0.06
40. South Carolina	4258 (46)	157 (20)	420 (18)	885 (13)	0.04	0.04
41. South Dakota	4218 (47)	0	0	0	0.04	0.04*
42. Tennessee	4484 (39)	0	0	0	0.035	0.045*
43. Texas	4790 (33)	0	0	0	0.04	0.04*
44. Utah	4452 (41)	148 (24)	452 (15)	821 (17)	0.04	0.04*
45. Vermont	4588 (37)	216 (12)	520 (11)	946 (12)	0.03	0.03*
46. Virginia	5265 (23)	175 (17)	449 (16)	829 (15)	0.03	0.03*
47. Washington	5651 (13)	0	0	0	0.045	0.046*
48. West Virginia	4390 (43)	144 (26)	276 (32)	494 (34)	0.03	0.03*
49. Wisconsin	5210 (26)	365 (2)	801 (2)	1488 (2)	0.04	0.04*
50. Wyoming	5156 (27)	0	0	0	0.03	0.03
51. Washington D.C.		250 (8)	579 (7)	1107 (8)	0.05	0.05

(Footnote to Table 15)

Note: The numbers in parentheses are the rank numbers in the descending order. No rank number was assigned to the states without the state income tax. New Jersey enacted the state income tax in 1976. The taxes were calculated on the following assumptions: All income is from wages and salaries earned by one spouse. A family of a married couple with two children. At income $10,000, 15% deduction is used. At income $17,500, itemized deduction of $3,520 is used. At income $25,000, itemized deduction of $4,365 is used. For states that allow for a deduction for federal income taxes, deductions were used: $791 at $10,000; $1908 at ⁺17,500, and $3,470 at $25,000. Figures for Michigan are based only on taxes for Detroit homeowners.

Source: The state income taxes at three levels of income were calculated by the U.S. Advisory Commission on Intergovernmental Relations, as reprinted in *U.S. News and World Report*, April 4, 1977, p. 72. The state sales tax rates were collected by Tax Foundation, Inc. as reprinted in *The World Almanac*, annual. Also see Commerce Clearing House, Inc., *State Tax Guide*, 1977.

For more detailed and extensive data, see U.S. Advisory Commission on Intergovernmental Relations, *Significant Features of Fiscal Federalism, 1976-77 edition*, Vol. II, Revenue and Debt, M-110, March 1977.

226

effort index by the T/K ratio, we could measure it by the T/K′ ratio, where K′ is the predicted ACIR's tax capacity by regression equation (1) of Table 14, $ST = K' = 80.4619 + 0.7369$ K. The predicted tax capacity K′ is listed in column 4 of Table 11, and the tax effort index measured by the T/K′ ratio is listed in column 5. In column 6, the per capita income is listed. Dividing the actual per capita tax by the actual per capita personal income we obtain another tax effort index in terms of the tax/income ratio, or the T/Y ratio which is listed in column 7. The predicted tax in column 8 is obtained from regression equation (2) of Table 14, $ST = T' = -0.7556 + 0.1112$ Y. Dividing the actual per capita tax of column (1) of Table 11 by the predicted tax of column 8, we obtain the tax effort index measured by the regression method. In effect we have shown four measures of state-local tax effort in Table 11, namely, T/K ratio, T/K′ ratio, T/Y ratio, and T/T′ ratio. It should be noted that the two tax effort measures of columns (7) and (8) yielded practically the same ranking of the States due to the fact that regression equation (2) of Table 14 includes only one independent variable, namely, the per capita income.

From Tables 10 and 11, we have selected the States which are inconsistently ranked by the tax effort measures discussed in this paper, with respect to only one simple criterion, namely, below-or-above average classification, and they are summarized in Table 12. A total of 18 States are listed. But we note that column (1) is for the 1970 data, for which the tax effort index was measured by the $T/(T' = a + bY + cH)$ ratio, while other columns are measured by the T/K ratio, the $T/(K' = a + bK)$ ratio, the T/Y ratio, and the $T/(T' = a + bY)$ ratio for the 1968 data. Nevertheless, when we compare the 1970 T/T′ ratio index and the 1968 T/T′ ratio index, only 6 States are inconsistent. Among the 1968 rankings, there are 10 inconsistent States between the T/K ratio ranking (column 2) and the T/K′ ratio

ranking (column 5), and 12 inconsistent States between T/K'
ratio ranking (column 3) and the T/T' ratio ranking (column 5).

These results suggest that the different methods of measuring the tax efforts of States need not be always mutually exclu-
sive for some broad policy purposes and for further analytical
studies. In other words, if alternative measures reach a con-
census as to the tax effort status of a State, we are more sure
about the tax effort status of the State. If the alternative methods
do not agree, we may reexamine whether the differences are
caused by the real reasons or by errors of calculation, omission
and estimation of tax bases and other variables.

V. Conclusions

Some policy implications of the tax effort index may be
briefly discussed. First, the tax effort index may be used as a
guideline for State and local governments to evaluate the burden
of State, local and Federal taxes of the residents. A State with
a higher tax effort index relative to national average may wish
to reduce the tax burden of the residents, and a State with a
lower tax effort index may wish to increase the tax burden by
increasing the tax rate, or by expanding the existing tax base or
by creating a new tax base, if the state wishes to provide better
or more public goods and services.

Secondly, the tax effort index may be utilized in the Federal
revenue sharing program. The current shared revenue is distributed on the basis of population of a State weighted by the
revenue/personal income ratio, as a measure of the tax effort or
revenue effort. In place of the simple tax/income ratio or the
revenue/income ratio, the tax effort index as discussed in this
paper may be used.[6] The use of a refined tax effort index in

---

[6]The current Federal shared revenue formula is:

the revenue sharing program will have the following advantages: First, if a State with a higher tax effort index receives a larger shared revenue, the residents of the State would be receiving more or better public goods and services, and thus the net tax burden, as defined as gross tax burden minus the value of public goods and services received, will decrease. Then the tax burden of residents in the States tends to be equalized in terms of the net tax burden due to the redistribution effect of public goods and services by the revenue sharing program. Secondly, if the State has a higher tax effort index and receives a larger shared revenue, it would not encourage the State to use the shared revenue to reduce the State and local taxes, since if the

---

$$S_i = \frac{N_i R_i / Y_i}{\sum\limits_{i=1}^{50} N_i R_i / Y_i} \; F$$

In terms of per capita basis,

$$S_i / N_i = \frac{N_i R_i / Y_i}{\sum\limits_{i=1}^{50} N_i R_i / Y_i} \; F / N_i$$

where

S_i = Shared revenue to State i
N_i = Population of State i
R_i = General revenues from own sources of State and local governments
Y_i = Aggregate personal income of State i
F = Total Federal fund to be shared by 50 States

In the above formulas, instead of the simple R/Y ratio, a more refined revenue effort index or tax effort index may be used. Also instead of the state and local tax effort index, the "total" (federal, state and local) tax effort index may be used.

State reduces the State and local taxes, the tax effort index will fall and the shared revenue will decrease.[7]

In applications of the concepts of tax effort and revenue efforts indexes,[8] the following points should be kept in mind:

First, the tax effort index does not measure the net tax burden, the efficiency of taxation and expenditures, nor the benefit-cost relationship. The net tax burden should be measured by the gross tax payment minus the value of public goods and services received directly and indirectly. The efficiency of tax collection is the tax revenue per tax collection cost. The efficiency or the productivity of tax dollars is the value of public goods and services received directly and indirectly divided by the amount of tax payment, i.e., the benefit-cost ratio. The tax effort index measures the tax payment relative to the potential tax payment with respect to their ability to pay under a given norm.

Secondly, the tax effort index itself does not tell whether a State with a higher tax effort index is better or not. For instance, the residents of a State may wish to pay a higher tax for better highways, public educational facilities, and a beter protection from crimes, fire, and injustice. But the residents of another State may prefer a lower tax and will tolerate poor public services. The residents of the both States may obtain the same level of indifference curve.

The question of whether the residents should have more and better public goods and services or more and better private goods and services in order to increase their welfare may be

----

[7]See Due and Friedlaender (1973), p. 498.

[8]The "tax capacity" and the "tax effort index" are concerned with "tax" revenue, while the "revenue capacity" and the "revenue effort index" are concerned with both tax and non-tax revenues of a State, local or Federal government. Some authors used the words, "fiscal capacity" and "fiscal effort index" as a general term which covers both.

answered in the welfare economics. Furthermore, it does not necessarily follow that an increase in public expenditures and a decrease in private expenditures imply that the residents of the State are shifting their consumption from one good to another different type of good. One good example is the garbage collection service. One local government may charge a higher tax to provide the public collection of garbage, while another local government may charge a less tax, but the household will have to pay the cost of garbage collection as a private expenditure. In either case, the welfare of the residents are the same, if the costs and the quality of the services are equal. In this example, the tax effort index of the State which collects the garbage publicly is higher than the tax effort of another State which does not provide the public garbage collection, and yet the welfare of the residents will be the same. However, if the public garbage collection provides a lower cost and a better quality of service, a higher tax effort State may be said to be better than the lower tax effort state for the residents.[9]

Finally, the above tax effort index as presented in this paper has some limitations in practical applications. For instance, we have calculated the tax effort index only for one year cross section data. However, a State might have a lower tax effort index in one year, but a higher tax effort index in another. To mitigate such a situation, the tax effort index may be calculated annually, and, say, for 3 year average cross-section data. Also a better estimating equation may be used with more refined data. Also other variables may be included in the regression equations to estimate the effective standard tax system. Such variables may include the rate of unemployment, the rate of population growth, the

---

[9]Pier, Vernon and Wicks (1974) found the public garbage collection costs less and is more efficient in general in Montana municipalities.

industrial structure, the degree of urbanization, the age structure of the population, the rate of interest, the rate of migration, tangible and intangible assets, security holdings, and other unique characteristics of the State and local areas. Also the tax burden may be calculated in the real terms by adjusting the regional differences in the level of prices.

Appendix Note

The national average tax rate method (ACIR's method) implicitly maintains that a proportional tax system is fair, while the regression method implicitly maintains that the current (progressive or any other) tax system is fair for the system of tax burden. To illustrate the point, assume four states A, B, C, and D. Their incomes are 100, 200, 300, and 400 dollars respectively. Their actual taxes are 20, 60, 120 and 200 dollars. Then, their effective tax rates are 20, 30, 40 and 50 percents respectively, and the national average tax is 35%.

The national average tax rate method maintains that each state should pay the same tax rate for the same tax base...a proportional tax rate system. When the 35% is applied, the required taxes will be 35, 70, 105, and 140 dollars for the four states respectively. Comparing these required taxes and the actual taxes, we note that States A and B will be regarded as the low-tax effort states since the required taxes are greater than the actual taxes.

Under the regression method, from the above hypothetical income and tax data, we obtain the following regression equation:

$$T = -50 + 0.6\,Y \qquad\qquad r = 0.99$$

We note that the above regression equation implies a progressive income tax system in the sense that as the taxable income rises, the average tax rate $(T/Y = 0.6 - 50/Y)$ rises. Substituting the actual state taxable income in the regression equation, we obtain the predicted or required taxes: 10, 70, 130 and 190 dollars. Comparing these required taxes with the actual taxes, we note that States B and C will be regarded as the low tax effort states.

REFERENCES

Advisory Commission on Intergovernmental Relations, *Measuring the Fiscal Capacity and Effort of State and Local Areas*, Information Report, M-58, March 1971.

———, *Federal-State-Local Finances: Significant Features of Fiscal Federalism*, M-79, February 1974.

Akin, J.S., "Fiscal Capacity and the Estimation Methods of the Advisory Commission on Intergovernmental Relations," *National Tax Journal*, June, 1973, pp. 275-291.

Blackburn, J.O., "Implicit Tax Rate Reductions with Growth, Progressive Taxes, Constant Progressivity, and a Fixed Public Share," *American Economic Review*, March 1967, pp. 162-169.

Cheliah, R.J., "Trends in Taxation in Developing Countries," *IMF Staff Papers*, July 1971, pp. 254-331.

Cheliah, R.J., Baas, H.J., and Kelly, M.R., "Tax Ratios and Tax Effort in Developing Countries, 1969-71," *IMF Staff Papers*, March 1975, pp. 187-205.

Clark, C., "Public Finance and Changes in the Value of Money," *Economic Journal*, Dec. 1945, pp. 371-389.

Dresch, S.P., "An 'Alternative' View of the Nixon Revenue Sharing," *National Tax Journal*, June 1971, pp. 131-142.

Due, J.F., and Friedlaender, A.F., *Government Finance: Economics of Public Sector*, 1973, ch. 19.

Hinrichs, H.H., *A General Theory of Tax Structure Change during Economic Development*, 1966.

Lotz, J.R., and Morss, E.R., "Measuring 'Tax Effort' in Developing Countries," *IMF Staff Papers*, Nov. 1967, pp. 478-497.

Manvel, A.D., "Differences in Fiscal Capacity and Effort: Their Significance for a Federal Revenue-Sharing System," *National Tax Journal*, June 1971, pp. 193-204.

———, "Tax Capacity versus Tax Performance: A Comment," *National Tax Journal*, June 1973, pp. 293-294.

Martin, A. and Lewis, W.A., "Patterns of Public Revenue and Expenditures," *The Manchester School of Economic and Social Studies*, Sept. 1956, pp. 203-244.

Melichar, E., *State Individual Income Taxes: Impact of Alternative Provisions on Burden, Progression and Yields*, University of Connecticut, 1963.

Mishan, E.J., and Dicks-Mireaux, L.A., "Progressive Taxation in an Inflationary Economy," *American Economic Review*, June 1958, pp. 590-606.

234   Ch. 8—Tax Burden in the U.S.

Morgan, W.D., "An Alternative Measure of Fiscal Capacity," *National Tax Journal*, June 1974, pp. 361-365.

Oshima, H.T., "Shares of Government in Gross National Product for Various Countries, *American Economic Review*, June 1957, pp. 381-390.

Pier, W.J., Vernon, R.B., and Wicks, H.H., "An Empirical Comparison of Government and Private Production Efficiency," *National Tax Journal*, Dec. 1974, pp. 653-656.

Shin, K., "International Difference in Tax Ratio," *Review of Economics and Statistics*, May 1969, pp. 213-220.

Tanzi, V., "Measuring the Sensitivity of the Federal Income Tax from Cross-Section Data: A New Approach," *Review of Economics and Statistics*, May 1969, pp. 206-209.

U.S. Bureau of the Census, *The Statistical Abstract of the U.S.*, 1972-74 eds.

Waldorf, W.W., "The Responsiveness of Federal Personal Income Taxes to Income Change," *Survey of Current Business*, Dec. 1967, pp. 32-45.

Williamson, J.G., "Public Expenditures and Revenue: An International Comparison," *The Manchester School of Social Studies*, Jan. 1961, pp. 43-56.

Chapter 9

The Housing Cost
and Home-Ownership Rate
in the U.S. States and Cities

I. Introduction

The question is, in which States (or cities) do residents pay higher housing costs? One simple method of answering the question may be first to select a typical representative house for a middle income family of four, and then compare the market value of the house in each State. The representative house may be defined as a house with three bedrooms, one bathroom, one kitchen, one living room, one family room, one-car garage, 1/4 acre of front and 1/4 acre of back yards, similar building materials, similar environmental surroundings, and so forth. However, selecting such a typical or representative house in each State may not be an easy task.

Another method may be to compare the mean or the median value of housing costs, such as the median value of owner-occupied or the renter occupied homes. Indeed such census data are available for States and SMSA cities. However, the above two methods would not answer the question, in which States do residents pay higher housing costs relative to their income? In this paper, we wish to answer this very question. In the following section, we will explain the methodology used in this paper, and in section III, the statistical measures of the relative housing cost in the U.S. States and cities are presented (Tables 5 and 6). In the final section, conclusions are summarized.

II. The Demand Functions for Housing Services

One method of measuring the housing cost relative to income may be to take the ratio of housing expenditures to income, or the H/Y ratio. Under this method, a state which has a higher H/Y ratio will be regarded as an expensive state with regard to the housing cost. However, this method assumes that income is the only determinant of the demand function for housing services and it is given by:

$$H = b\,Y \qquad\qquad (1)$$

In this paper, we will present the regression method of measuring the burden of housing cost. The demand function for housing services may be expressed by:

$$H = f_1(Y, i, \Delta i, N, W, u) \qquad\qquad (2)$$

where

H=the median value of housing expenditures, such as annual housing expenditures on owner occupied homes or renter occupied homes. Instead of the median housing cost, per capita housing cost may be used. Also instead of annual housing expenditures, the house stock value may be used for owner occupied homes.

Y=per capita personal or family income.

i=the rate of interest or the mortgage rate.

Δi = the interest rate differential between the mortgage rate and the rate of return on an alternative investment, such as the rate of interest on bonds or savings deposits.

N = the family size if H stands for the median value of housing cost.

W = wealth.

u = stochastic and other variables omitted. The other variables may include: the marital and sex status of the head of a household, occupation, race, education, age, property tax, insurance costs, fuel cost, the population density or the degree of urbanization in the area, etc.

Since the per capita income is the only available data for our study, we shall assume the following simple demand function for the housing services:

$$H = f_2(Y, u) \tag{3}$$

Equation (3) states the assumption that if all other conditions are the same, the desired housing expenditures are determined by the size of per capita income.

Under the regression method of comparing the cost of housing relative to income in States (or cities), we first estimate the "standard" or "normal" demand function for the housing services using the State cross section data, and then compare the actual housing cost of a State with the predicted housing cost of the State. If the actual housing cost is greater than the predicted cost, predicted from the "standard" demand function, then we assume that the residents of the State is paying a higher housing cost than the income of the residents can "normally" bear. If the actual housing cost is smaller than the predicted cost, we may assume that the residents are paying a lower housing cost than they can "normally" afford to pay out of their income. The factors which can cause a greater actual cost than the predicted cost may include: high mortgage rate, high land price, housing shortage, high building material cost, large family size, large wealth, expensive housing structure due to cold or warm weather, regional monopolistic elements, etc.

In order to estimate the "standard" demand function for housing services, rewriting Equation (3) for specific types of demand for housing services, we have:

$$HV = F_1 (Y, u)$$
$$AR = F_2 (Y, u) \tag{4}$$
$$HO = F_3 (Y/H, u)$$

where

HV = the median house value of owner-occupied homes in a State or city, 1970 ($). (All the data are from: Bureau of the Census, *The Statistical Abstract of the U.S.*, 95th ed., Oct. 1974).

AR = the median annual rent value of the renter occupied homes or apartment rents (1970, $).

HO = the rate of home ownership (%); the percentage of owner-occupied homes in total occupied homes, 1970.

Y = per capita personal income of a State or a city, 1970 ($). For the city data, 1969 per capita income was used because 1970 data were not available.

Y/H = the ratio of per capita income to the median house value of owner-occupied home, 1970 (%).

The regression parameters are obtained by the method of ordinary least squares using the 1970 data. Tables 1 and 2 are for the State data, and Tables 3 and 4 are for the city data in linear and log-linear forms. Since some States and cities showed extreme deviations in the table of residuals, and the results of linear and log-linear forms were very similar, we have selected the following equations as the "standard" demand functions for the housing services:[1]

38 States $HV = -5538.9608 + 5.8151Y$ $R^2 = 0.8270$
                        $(13.90)**$

              $AR = -492.1665 + 0.3981 Y$ $R^2 = 0.7870$ (5)
                        $(11.21)**$

              $HO = 45.2479 + 0.0750 Y/H$ $R^2 = 0.2686$
                        $(3.39)**$

25 Cities $HV = -16674.1152 + 8.6587Y$ $R^2 = 0.7942$
                        $(9.42)**$

              $AR = -644.1919 + 0.4374 Y$ $R^2 = 0.6862$ (6)
                        $(7.09)**$

              $HO = 45.4884 + 0.7441 Y/H$ $R^2 = 0.2328$
                        $(2.64)*$

The numbers in the parentheses are the t-ratios. We note that the above regression equations explain about 79-83% of the State variations and 69-79% of the city variations of the house value and the apartment rent. The performance for the rate of home ownership is less satisfactory, explaining only 27% of the State variations and 23% of the city variations. However, we note that per capita income is significant at the 1% level for the house value and rent value variations in both State and city data. The Y/H ratio is significant at the 1% level for the State data and at the 5% level for the city data.

---

[1]We have also tested the simple three year average income and the weighted three year average income. The results were very similar to the results obtained in this paper. If the housing cost data were available for 1969 and 1968, we could have tested the three year average income on the three year average housing expenditures.

Table 1. State Regression Results

	Intercept	Y	R	R²	S.E.E.	$\overline{R}^2$	F
(1) HV	-6562.2716	6.1113 (9.26)**	0.7976	0.6362	2808.32	0.6288	85.70
(2) AR	-388.0307	0.3689 (9.71)**	0.8111	0.6580	161.63	0.6510	94.25
(3) HO (%)	43.6932	0.8669 Y/H (2.93)**	0.3864	0.1493	7.27	0.1320	8.60
(4) HV	-5099.9444	5.6503 (10.49)**	0.8424	0.7096	1930.64	0.7032	109.98
(5) AR	-346.3096	0.3550 (11.11)**	0.8560	0.7327	114.54	0.7268	123.35
(6) HO (%)	52.3108	0.5709 Y/H (3.21)**	0.4311	0.1859	3.84	0.1678	10.27
(7) HV	-5538.9608	5.8151 (13.90)**	0.9181	0.8429	1281.74	0.8385	193.10
(8) AR	-492.1665	0.3981 (11.21)**	0.8816	0.7772	108.82	0.7710	125.58
(9) HO (%)	45.2479	0.8750 Y/H (3.39)**	0.5072	0.2572	3.63	0.2366	12.47

(50 States and D.C.: rows 1–3; 47 States: rows 4–6; 38 States: rows 7–9)

Note: **Significant at the 1% level. The numbers in parentheses are the t-ratios. The 47 States do not include New York, Hawaii, Alaska, and D.C. The 38 States do not include New York, Hawaii, Alaska, D.C., Vermont, Connecticut, Pennsylvania, Nebraska, Kansas, Delaware, Texas, Utah, and California.

Table 2. State Regression Results (Log)

	ln a	ln Y	R	R²	S.E.E.	$\overline{R}^2$	F
50 States and D.C.							
(1) ln HV	-1.1691	1.3189 (10.34)**	0.8280	0.6856	0.14	0.6792	106.84
(2) ln AR	-4.7584	1.4150 (11.60)**	0.8562	0.7331	0.14	0.7276	134.55
(3) ln HO (%)	3.0894	0.3372ln(Y/H) (2.54)**	0.3410	0.1163	0.14	0.0982	6.45
47 States							
(4) ln HV	-0.5198	1.2385 (9.81)**	0.8255	0.6815	0.12	0.6744	96.27
(5) ln AR	-4.6660	1.4032 (11.53)**	0.8643	0.7470	0.12	0.7414	132.85
(6) ln HO (%)	3.4700	0.2265ln(Y/H) (3.38)**	0.4503	0.2027	0.06	0.1850	11.44
38 States							
(7) ln HV	-1.0878	1.3093 (13.12)**	0.9094	0.8270	0.09	0.8222	172.04
(8) ln AR	-5.8876	1.5534 (11.53)**	0.8871	0.7870	0.12	0.7811	133.01
(9) ln HO (%)	3.1423	0.3307 ln(Y/H) (3.64)**	0.5183	0.2686	(3.64)** 0.06	0.2483	13.22

Note: See footnote of Table 1.

241

Table 3. City Regression Results

	intercept	Y	R	R²	S.E.E.	R̄²	F
(1) HV	16779.2719	8.6946 (9.70)**	0.8674	0.7523	2260.30	0.7444	94.17
(2) AR	−322.6592	0.3532 (7.44)**	0.8006	0.6410	119.79	0.6294	55.34
(3) HO (%)	24.6486	1.6185Y/H (4.85)**	0.6568	0.4314	5.93	0.4130	23.52
31 Cities							
(4) HV	−17511.4465	8.8062 (10.04)**	0.8812	0.7765	2000.25	0.7688	100.75
(5) AR	−490.3202	0.3967 (8.32)**	0.8395	0.7048	108.70	0.6947	69.25
(6) HO (%)	36.5549	1.1239Y/H (4.25)**	0.6196	0.3839	4.31	0.3627	18.07
25 Cities							
(7) HV	−16674.1152	8.6587 (9.42)**	0.8912	0.7942	1609.57	0.7853	88.78
(8) AR	−644.1919	0.4374 (7.09)**	0.8284	0.6862	108.01	0.6726	50.30
(9) HO (%)	45.4885	0.7441Y/H (2.64)*	0.4825	0.2328	3.60	0.1995	6.98

Note: **Significant at the 1% level. *Significant at the 5% level. For the list of 33 cities see Table 6. The 31 cities do not include: New York, New Orleans. The 25 cities do not include: New York, New Orleans, Detroit, Indianapolis, Los Angeles, Newark, Philadelphia, and San Francisco. The numbers in parentheses are the t-ratios. It should be noted that per capita income is 1969 value since 1970 value was not available. All other variables are 1970 data.

242

Table 4. City Regression Results (Log)

		ln a	ln Y	R	R^2	S.E.E.	$\bar{R}^2$	F
	(1) ln HV	-4.9862	1.7812 (9.10)**	0.8530	0.7277	0.12	0.7189	82.84
33 Cities	(2) ln AR	-3.9222	1.3152 (7.64)**	0.8081	0.6530	0.10	0.6418	58.34
	(3) ln HO (%)	1.9780	0.6847ln(Y/H) (4.68)**	0.6437	0.4144	0.11	0.3955	21.94
	(4) ln HV	-5.6130	1.8549 (9.78)**	0.8760	0.7674	0.10	0.7593	95.65
31 Cities	(5) ln AR	-4.9048	1.4345 (8.14)**	0.8341	0.6958	0.10	0.6853	66.32
	(6) ln HO (%)	2.8027	0.4245ln(Y/H) (4.39)**	0.6320	0.3995	0.07	0.3787	19.29
	(7) ln HV	-5.5823	1.8530 (9.05)**	0.8835	0.7806	0.09	0.7711	81.84
25 Cities	(8) ln AR	-6.0328	1.5714 (6.89)**	0.8209	0.6739	0.10	0.6597	47.53
	(9) ln HO (%)	3.2524	0.2820ln(Y/H) (2.75)*	0.4975	0.2475	0.06	0.2148	7.56

Note: See Footnote of Table 3.

The income elasticities obtained from the regression results which are presented in Tables 1-4 range between 1.239-1.402 for the house value and 1.364-1.553 for the apartment rent for the State data, as summarized in Table 7. We note that the elasticity values are in general greater than one for the house value and apartment rent, and less than one for the rate of home ownership. These results are in accordance with the early elasticity studies which show that cross section group average data tend to produce elasticity values greater than one, and the individual budget data tend to produce elasticity values less than one.[2]

III. The Relative Housing Cost in States and Cities

The actual housing costs and the predicted housing costs, predicted from the above six regression equations, are listed in Tables 5 and 6 for the State and city data respectively. For instance, in column 1 of Table 5, the actual house values, and in column 2 the predicted house values are listed for the State

---

[2]The researchers are divided into three groups: (1) those who found the elasticity greater than one, (2) those who found it less than one, and (3) those who found it about equal to one. The less-than-one group includes: Morton (1955), Winnick (1955), Grebler-Blank-Winnick (1956), Crocket-Friend (1960), Maisel-Winnick (1960), Lee (1963, 1964, 1967, 1968), Morgan (1965), Malone (1966), Maisel-Burnham-Austin (1971), and Carliner (1973). The greater-than-one group includes: Reid (1962), Muth (1960), and Laidler (1963). The about-equal-to-one group includes Leeuw (1971) and Winger (1968).

Previous studies on the determinants of the rate of home-ownership include: Maisel (1966), Kain-Quigley (1972), Morgan (1965), Carliner (1974) and Struyk-Marshall (1975). These studies have shown that the probability of home ownership depends upon many factors such as income, family size, age, education, sex of the household head, marital status, race, etc.

data. Dividing the actual house value by the predicted house value, we obtain the "house value index" in column 3. For Hawaii, for instance, dividing the actual house value, $35,100 by the predicted house value, $20,990, we obtain the house value index, 167.2, which indicates that the house value in Hawaii is 67.2% higher than the predicted value. Since the index is the highest in the 50 States and Washington, D.C., rank number 1 is assigned. Kansas has the lowest index, 72.0. Similarly, as to the apartment rent for Alaska, dividing the actual rent, $2,052 in column 4 by the predicted rent, $1,340 in column 6, we obtain the "apartment rent index," 153.1, which indicates that the apartment rent in Alaska is 53.1% higher than the predicted rent. Since the index is the highest in the 50 States and Washington, D.C., rank number 1 is assigned. Rhode Island has the lowest index, 72.4.

Similarly, as to the rate of home-ownership for Washington, D.C., dividing the actual rate of home-ownership, 28.2% in column 7 by the predicted rate, 67.1% in column 8, we obtain the "home-ownership rate index," 42.0, which indicates that the rate of home-ownership is 42.0% of the predictd rate. Since this index is the lowest in the United States, rank number 51 is assigned. Detroit has the highest home-ownership rate index, 114.4.

In column 10, per capita income is listed. Dividing the house value in column 1 and apartment rent in column 4 by per capita income, we obtain the HV/Y ratio and the AR/Y ratio in columns 11 and 12 respectively, which are listed for the purpose of comparison of the regression method ranking and the H/Y ratio method ranking. We note that the regression method and the H/Y ratio method do not necessarily produce very similar rankings.

In Table 6, in the same way, the house value index, the apartment rent index and the home-ownership rate index are

Table 5. Ranking of Housing Expenditures (50 States and Washington, D.C.)

	House value (HV) (1)	Predicted (HV') (2)	House value index (HV/HV') (3)	Apartment rent (AR) (4)	Predicted (AR') (5)	Apartment rent index (AR/AR') (6)	Home owner-ship (HO) (7)	Predicted (HO') (8)	Home Owner-ship index (HO/HO') (9)	Per capita income (Y) (10)	HV/Y ($) (11)	AR/Y (%) (12)
1. Alabama	12200	11400	107.0 (12)	576	667	86.4 (45)	66.7	66.2	100.8 (20)	2913	4.2 (28)	19.8 (51)
2. Alaska*	22700	21228	106.9 (13)	2052	1340	153.1 (1)	50.3	56.5	88.9 (46)	4603	4.9 (8)	44.6 (1)
3. Arizona	16300	15576	104.6 (18)	1080	953	113.3 (8)	65.3	64.8	100.8 (19)	3631	4.5 (18)	29.7 (10)
4. Arkansas	10500	11145	94.2 (36)	636	650	97.8 (29)	66.7	69.1	96.5 (36)	2869	3.7 (45)	22.2 (45)
5. California*	23100	20437	113.0 (6)	1356	1286	105.4 (17)	54.9	62.1	88.4 (47)	4467	5.2 (4)	30.4 (6)
6. Colorado	17300	16785	103.1 (24)	1164	1036	112.4 (10)	63.4	62.3	101.8 (15)	3839	4.5 (7)	30.3 (7)
7. Connecti.*	25500	22786	111.9 (7)	1260	1447	87.1 (41)	62.5	62.0	100.8 (18)	4871	5.2 (2)	25.9 (23)
8. Delaware*	17100	20530	83.3 (46)	1068	1293	82.6 (47)	68.0	68.2	99.7 (26)	4483	3.8 (41)	23.8 (38)
9. D.C.*	21300	25473	83.6 (45)	1320	1631	80.9 (50)	28.2	67.1	42.0 (51)	5333	4.0 (37)	24.8 (29)
10. Florida	15000	15930	94.2 (37)	1104	978	112.9 (9)	68.6	66.8	102.7 (14)	3692	4.1 (32)	29.9 (9)
11. Georgia	14600	13756	106.1 (15)	780	829	94.1 (33)	61.1	65.1	93.9 (39)	3318	4.4 (21)	23.5 (40)
12. Hawaii*	35100	20990	167.2 (1)	1440	1324	108.8 (14)	46.9	56.6	82.9 (49)	4562	7.7 (1)	31.6 (3)
13. Idaho	14100	13535	104.2 (20)	840	814	103.2 (18)	70.1	65.6	106.9 (6)	3280	4.3 (26)	25.6 (24)
14. Illinois	19800	20582	96.2 (33)	1284	1296	99.1 (25)	59.4	67.7	87.7 (48)	4492	4.4 (20)	28.6 (15)
15. Indiana	13800	16279	84.8 (44)	984	1001	98.3 (27)	71.7	69.0	103.9 (11)	3752	3.7 (44)	26.2 (22)
16. Iowa	13900	16262	85.5 (43)	924	1000	92.4 (34)	71.7	68.9	104.1 (8)	3749	3.7 (43)	24.6 (30)
17. Kansas*	12100	16797	72.0 (51)	900	1037	86.8 (42)	69.1	73.0	94.7 (38)	3841	3.2 (51)	23.4 (41)

246

18. Kentucky	12600	12511	100.7 (28)	756	743	101.8 (22)	66.9	66.8	100.2 (23)	3104	4.1 (33)	24.4 (33)
19. Louisiana	14600	12302	118.7 (4)	744	729	102.1 (20)	63.1	63.6	99.2 (29)	3068	4.8 (10)	24.3 (35)
20. Maine	12800	13488	94.9 (34)	828	810	102.2 (19)	70.1	67.6	103.7 (12)	3272	3.9 (39)	25.3 (27)
21. Maryland	18700	19355	96.6 (31)	1320	1212	108.9 (13)	58.8	65.3	90.0 (45)	4281	4.4 (24)	30.8 (5)
22. Massachu.	20600	19699	104.6 (19)	1068	1235	86.5 (44)	57.5	63.7	90.3 (43)	4340	4.7 (11)	24.6 (31)
23. Michigan	17500	18629	93.9 (38)	1116	1162	96.0 (30)	74.4	66.0	112.7 (1)	4156	4.2 (27)	26.9 (20)
24. Minnesota	18000	16838	106.9 (14)	1212	1040	116.5 (4)	71.5	64.0	111.7 (2)	3848	4.7 (13)	31.5 (4)
25. Mississippi	11200	9557	117.2 (5)	552	541	102.0 (21)	66.3	65.5	101.2 (17)	2596	4.3 (25)	21.3 (47)
26. Missouri	14400	16372	88.0 (42)	888	1008	88.1 (39)	67.2	68.2	98.5 (30)	3768	3.8 (40)	23.6 (39)
27. Montana	14000	14802	94.6 (35)	852	900	94.7 (32)	65.7	67.1	97.9 (31)	3498	4.0 (36)	24.4 (32)
28. Nebraska*	12400	16524	75.0 (50)	924	1018	90.8 (37)	66.4	72.0	92.2 (41)	3794	3.3 (50)	24.4 (34)
29. Nevada	22400	20350	110.1 (9)	1476	1280	115.3 (6)	58.5	62.7	93.3 (40)	4452	5.0 (6)	33.2 (2)
30. New Ham.	16400	16239	101.1 (26)	948	999	94.9 (31)	68.2	65.2	104.6 (7)	3745	4.4 (23)	25.3 (26)
31. New Jersey	23400	21414	109.3 (10)	1332	1353	98.4 (26)	60.9	62.6	97.3 (34)	4635	5.0 (5)	28.7 (14)
32. New Mexi.	13000	12587	103.3 (22)	864	749	115.4 (5)	66.4	66.2	100.3 (22)	3117	4.2 (29)	27.7 (18)
33. New York*	22500	21873	102.9 (25)	1140	1384	82.4 (48)	47.3	63.6	74.4 (50)	4714	4.8 (9)	24.2 (36)
34. North Caro.	12800	13174	97.2 (30)	708	789	89.7 (38)	65.4	67.2	97.3 (33)	3218	4.0 (38)	22.0 (46)
35. North Dako.	13000	12604	103.1 (23)	924	750	123.2 (2)	68.4	66.2	103.3 (13)	3120	4.2 (31)	29.6 (12)
36. Ohio	17600	17675	99.6 (29)	996	1097	90.8 (36)	67.7	65.1	104.0 (10)	3992	4.4 (19)	24.9 (28)
37. Oklahoma	11100	13942	79.6 (47)	768	841	91.3 (35)	69.2	71.7	96.5 (49)	3350	3.3 (49)	22.9 (42)
38. Oregon	15400	15942	96.6 (32)	1032	978	105.5 (16)	66.1	66.2	99.8 (25)	3694	4.2 (30)	27.9 (17)
39. Pennsyl.*	13600	17390	78.2 (49)	876	1078	81.3 (49)	68.8	70.6	97.5 (32)	3943	3.4 (47)	22.2 (44)
40. Rhode Is.	18200	17378	104.7 (16)	780	1077	72.4 (51)	57.9	64.2	90.2 (44)	3941	4.6 (14)	19.8 (50)
41. South Caro.	13000	11691	111.2 (8)	600	687	87.3 (40)	66.1	65.2	101.4 (16)	2963	4.4 (22)	20.2 (49)
42. South Dako.	11400	12627	90.3 (41)	828	751	110.3 (12)	69.6	69.2	100.6 (21)	3124	3.6 (46)	26.5 (21)

Table 5. Ranking of Housing Expenditures (50 States and Washinton, D.C.)—Continued

	House value (HV) (1)	Predicted (HV') (2)	House value index (HV/HV') (3)	Apartment rent (AR) (4)	Predicted (AR') (5)	Apartment rent index (AR/AR') (6)	Home ownership (HO) (7)	Predicted (HO') (8)	Home Owner-ship index (HO/HO') (9)	Per capita income (Y) (10)	HV/Y ($) (11)	AR/Y (%) (12)
43. Tennessee	12500	12383	100.9 (27)	744	735	101.2 (24)	66.7	66.9	99.7 (27)	3082	4.1 (34)	24.1 (37)
44. Texas*	12000	15256	78.7 (48)	912	931	98.0 (28)	64.7	71.3	90.7 (42)	3576	3.4 (48)	25.5 (25)
45. Utah*	16800	13232	127.0 (2)	960	793	121.1 (3)	69.3	62.7	110.5 (3)	3228	5.2 (3)	29.7 (11)
46. Vermont*	16400	13715	119.6 (3)	912	826	110.4 (11)	69.1	62.9	109.9 (4)	3311	5.0 (7)	27.5 (19)
47. Virginia	17100	15704	108.9 (11)	1104	962	114.8 (7)	62.0	64.0	96.9 (35)	3653	4.7 (12)	30.2 (8)
48. Washing.	18500	17849	103.6 (21)	1128	1109	101.7 (23)	66.8	64.2	104.1 (9)	4022	4.6 (15)	28.0 (16)
49. West Vir.	11300	12180	92.8 (39)	624	721	86.5 (43)	68.9	68.9	100.1 (24)	3047	3.7 (42)	20.5 (48)
50. Wisconsin	17300	16524	104.7 (17)	1092	1018	107.3 (15)	69.1	64.4	107.3 (5)	3794	4.6 (16)	28.8 (13)
51. Wyoming	15300	16535	92.5 (40)	864	1019	84.8 (46)	66.4	66.9	99.3 (28)	3796	4.0 (35)	22.8 (43)

Note: The numbers in parentheses are rank numbers in the descending order.
The predicted values are obtained by the following equations from the 38 State cross section data.

$HV' = -5538.9608 + 5.8151 \, Y$ (Equation 7 of Table 1)
$AR' = -492.1665 + 0.3981 \, Y$ (Equation 8 of Table 1)
$HO' = 45.2479 + 0.8750 \, Y/H$ (Equation 9 of Table 1)

*States with asterisk were excluded from the data in calculating the regression equations. The predicted values were obtained by substituting the data in the above regression equations.

248

calculated for the 33 cities. We note that New Orleans has the top house value index of 140, Denver has the top apartment rent index, and New York has the lowest home-ownership rate index.

IV. Conclusions

The above analysis does not give any solution for housing problems, but it merely indicates which States and cities have housing problems. If the goals of housing policies are to reduce the house value and apartment rents relative to income and to increase the rate of home-ownership, then the States and cities with high house value and apartment rent indexes, and low home-ownership rate indexes should be selected first.

Then each "problem state" or city should be examined as to the possible causes of high housing expenditures and a low rate of home-ownership. Such causes may include: high degree of urbanization and high land value as in New York City and Washington, D.C., high interest rate and tight mortgage terms, housing shortages, high building costs due to high material costs and wages, monopolistic elements in regional housing industry, lack of incentives in building industry due to decreasing population, high rate of migration or decaying regional economy, a high property tax rate, lack of building site, etc.

If some policy variables are identified in each "problem State" and city, the housing authorities may set up extensive long-run housing goals and policies which may include: changing the zoning regulations, providing easier mortgage terms, providing more mortgage funds, building more low rental apartments or low priced houses, slum area rehabilitation projects, establishing home and apartment clearing centers, reducing property

Table 6. Ranking of Housing Expenditures Relative to Income (33 Cities)

	House value (HV) (1)	Pre-dicted (HV') (2)	House value index (HV/HV') (3)	Apart-ment rent (AR) (4)	Pre-dicted (AR') (5)	Apart-ment rent index (AR/AR') (6)	Home owner ship (HO) (7)	Pre-dicted (HO') (8)	Home Owner-ship index (HO/HO') (9)	Per capita income (Y) (10)	HV/Y ($) (11)	AR/Y (%) (12)
1. Atlanta	19200	17900	107.3 (9)	1140	1102	103.4 (11)	59.1	61.0	96.9 (22)	3993	4.8 (14)	28.6 (14)
2. Baltimore	15200	16714	90.9 (28)	1152	1042	110.6 (4)	58.2	64.4	90.4 (28)	3856	3.9 (27)	29.9 (8)
3. Boston	23600	20394	115.7 (4)	1272	1228	103.6 (10)	53.7	59.0	91.0 (27)	4281	5.5 (4)	29.7 (11)
4. Buffalo	17900	16420	109.0 (7)	924	1027	102.4 (11)	62.9	61.4	102.4 (11)	3822	4.7 (16)	24.2 (26)
5. Charlotte	15200	16411	92.6 (25)	852	1027	83.0 (31)	62.7	64.2	97.7 (21)	3821	4.0 (25)	22.3 (33)
6. Chicago	24300	23831	102.0 (13)	1392	1401	99.4 (17)	52.9	59.8	88.5 (29)	4678	5.2 (7)	29.8 (10)
7. Cincinnati	17800	17311	102.8 (12)	972	1073	90.6 (25)	61.0	61.9	98.5 (20)	3925	4.5 (17)	24.8 (25)
8. Cleveland	22800	21364	106.7 (11)	1140	1277	89.3 (28)	62.4	59.8	104.3 (8)	4393	5.2 (8)	26.0 (20)
9. Dallas	15300	18411	83.1 (30)	1236	1128	109.6 (5)	62.5	65.2	95.9 (23)	4052	3.8 (30)	30.5 (6)
10. Denver	19100	17000	112.4 (5)	1260	1057	119.2 (1)	61.6	60.4	102.0 (14)	3889	4.9 (11)	32.4 (2)
11. Detroit*	19400	23823	81.4 (32)	1128	1402	80.5 (32)	72.5	63.4	114.4 (1)	4677	4.1 (22)	24.1 (28)
12. Hartford	24800	24498	101.2 (14)	1404	1435	97.8 (19)	60.4	59.8	101.0 (16)	4755	5.2 (6)	29.5 (12)
13. Houston	14600	15138	96.4 (21)	1128	963	117.1 (2)	60.1	64.2	93.6 (25)	3674	4.0 (26)	30.7 (4)
14. Indian.	14900	18428	80.9 (33)	1140	1129	101.0 (13)	65.4	65.7	99.5 (17)	4054	3.7 (33)	28.1 (16)
15. Kansas C.	15900	18506	85.9 (29)	1068	1133	94.3 (21)	65.9	64.5	102.2 (12)	4063	3.9 (28)	26.3 (19)
16. Los Ang.*	24300	24264	100.1 (16)	1320	1424	92.7 (23)	48.5	64.5	75.2 (32)	4728	5.1 (9)	27.9 (17)
17. Louisville	14900	16333	91.2 (27)	912	1023	89.1 (29)	66.6	64.5	103.3 (9)	3812	3.9 (29)	23.9 (30)
18. Memphis	14200	11631	122.1 (2)	828	786	105.3 (8)	57.7	62.6	92.2 (26)	3269	4.3 (18)	25.3 (24)
19. Milwaukee	21500	19822	108.5 (8)	1200	1199	100.1 (15)	59.8	60.1	99.5 (18)	4215	5.1 (10)	28.5 (15)

20. Minneapol.	21300	21589	98.7 (18)	1440	1289	111.7 (3)	66.3	60.9	108.9 (3)	4419	4.8 (12)	32.6 (1)
21. Nashville	15200	14212	107.0 (10)	912	916	99.6 (16)	63.8	63.0	101.3 (15)	3567	4.3 (21)	25.6 (22)
22. New Or.*	20000	14272	140.1 (1)	864	919	94.0 (22)	51.3	58.8	87.2 (30)	3574	5.6 (3)	24.2 (27)
23. Newark*	28400	24498	115.9 (3)	1416	1436	98.6 (18)	55.1	57.9	95.2 (24)	4755	6.0 (1)	29.8 (9)
24. New York*	29900	27096	110.3 (6)	1176	1567	75.0 (33)	30.5	61.0	50.0 (33)	5055	5.9 (2)	23.3 (32)
25. Oakland	13100	13389	97.8 (20)	900	874	103.0 (12)	68.1	65.2	104.4 (7)	3472	3.8 (31)	25.9 (21)
26. Philadel.*	14900	18203	81.9 (31)	1068	1118	95.5 (20)	67.1	64.0	104.8 (6)	4028	3.7 (32)	26.5 (18)
27. Pittsburgh	15300	16290	93.9 (24)	912	1021	89.3 (27)	67.8	64.0	105.9 (5)	3807	4.0 (24)	24.0 (29)
28. Portland	16900	17649	95.8 (22)	1164	1090	106.8 (6)	65.0	63.0	103.2 (10)	3964	4.3 (20)	29.4 (13)
29. Richmond	17300	18402	94.0 (23)	1032	1128	91.5 (24)	62.0	62.9	98.6 (19)	4051	4.3 (19)	25.5 (23)
30. Rochester	20300	20515	99.0 (17)	1308	1234	106.0 (7)	67.3	61.3	109.8 (2)	4295	4.7 (15)	30.5 (7)
31. St. Louis	16400	17900	91.6 (26)	948	1102	86.0 (30)	64.9	63.6	102.0 (13)	3993	4.1 (23)	23.7 (31)
32. San Fran.*	26900	26697	100.8 (15)	1560	1547	100.8 (14)	51.6	59.3	87.0 (31)	5009	5.4 (5)	31.3 (3)
33. Seattle	21500	21970	97.9 (19)	1368	1308	104.6 (9)	64.9	61.0	106.4 (4)	4463	4.8 (13)	30.7 (5)

Note: The numbers in parentheses are the rank numbers in the descending order.
The predicted values are obtained from the following regression equations obtained from the 25 city cross section data:

HV' = −16674.1152 + 8.6587 Y   (Equation 7 of Table 3)
AR' = −644.1919 + 0.4374 Y   (Equation 8 of Table 3)
HO' = 45.4885 + 0.7441 Y/H   (Equation 9 of Table 3)

*The cities with asterisk were those excluded from the data in calculating the regression equations. The predicted values of the excluded cities were obtained by substituting the data in the above regression equations.

251

tax rate or exemption of such taxes for early years of home occupancy, the land development, etc.[3]

Particularly, changes in the zoning regulations may be urgently needed in the suburban area. Under the zoning regulations, a single family house is accompanied with an unreasonably large vacant idle land, and neither low cost housing nor multiple family housing structures are permitted. As a result, the majority of low and middle income families are confined to either a slum area or an area in which the housing cost is unreasonably expensive relative to their income. As long as the zoning regulations are determined by the small community, no change is possible since they are self-preserving.[4]

---

[3]Problems in the housing market include: (1) racial discrimination in the housing market. See Rapkin (1966), Bailey (1966), Haugen-Heins (1969), Lapham (1971), Kain-Quigley (1972), Cicarelli-Landers (1972), and Walzer-Singer (1974). These articles discuss whether or not the black population pays more than the white population for the same quality of housing services; (2) Taxation on housing. See Morton (1955), Goode (1960), White-White (1965), Oldman-Aaron (1965), Netzer (1966), Laidler (1969), Tinney (1969), Aaron (1970), and Curry-Gensch (1975). These papers discuss whether or not the taxation on housing is regressive and discourages housing construction, or whether the home owners are favorably taxed than renters.

[4]The other housing policies may include: abolition or reduction of security deposits in apartment renting, specification of minimum apartment room sizes, prohibition of application fees for apartments, prohibition of fees charged by real estate agents for showing the houses and apartments, changes in property taxes on apartment buildings, etc. Most of all, the major reliance of the housing market on the private sector is clearly sustaining an extraordinarily high burden of housing cost in an average household budget. It takes not only 25 years for a home buyer to payoff the mortgage loan, but also it takes several years of savings for the downpayment. An apartment renter will have to pay about 25% of his income for the rent. In the areas where the housing cost, including the heating and cooling costs, is extremely high, the public housing projects are most urgently needed.

Table 7. Estimated Income Elasticities for Housing Services

		From mean values (Tables 1 and 3)	From log reg. coefficients (Tables 2 and 4)
HV $\frac{dHV}{dY} \cdot \frac{Y}{HV}$	50 States and D.C.	1.402	1.319
	47 States	1.328	1.239
	38 States	1.362	1.309
AR $\frac{dAR}{dY} \cdot \frac{Y}{AR}$	50 States and D.C.	1.381	1.415
	47 States	1.364	1.403
	38 States	1.527	1.553
HO $\frac{dHO}{dY/H} \cdot \frac{Y/H}{HO}$	50 States and D.C.	0.320	0.337
	47 States	0.208	0.227
	38 States	0.315	0.331
HV $\frac{dHV}{dY} \cdot \frac{Y}{HV}$	33 Cities	1.876	1.781
	31 Cities	1.932	1.855
	25 Cities	1.919	1.853
AR $\frac{dAR}{dY} \cdot \frac{Y}{AR}$	33 Cities	1.284	1.315
	31 Cities	1.428	1.435
	25 Cities	1.578	1.571
HO $\frac{dHO}{dY/H} \cdot \frac{Y/H}{HO}$	33 Cities	0.593	0.685
	31 Cities	0.409	0.425
	25 Cities	0.270	0.282

Note: It should be noted that the per capita income (Y) and the Y/H ratio have one year of time lag for the regression equations for the city data.

REFERENCES

Aaron, H., "Income Taxes and Housing," *American Economic Review*, Dec. 1970, pp. 789-806.

Bailey, M.J., "Effects of Race and Other Demographic Factors on the Value of Single Family Homes," *Land Economics*, May 1966, pp. 215-220.

Carliner, G., "Income Elasticity of Housing Demand," *Review of Economics and Statistics*, Nov. 1973, pp. 528-532.

Carliner, G., "Determinants of Home Ownership," *Land Economics*, May 1974, pp. 109-119.

Cicarelli, J., and C. Landers, "The Cost of Housing for the Poor: A Case Study," *Land Economics*, Nov. 1972, pp. 53-57.

Crocket, J., and I. Friend, "A Complete Set of Consumer Demand Relationships," in I. Friend and R. Jones, eds., *Study of Consumer Expenditures, Incomes and Savings: Proceedings of the Conference on consumption and Saving*, Vol. I, University of Pennsylvania, 1960, pp. 1-92.

Curry, C.F., and D.H. Gensch, "Feasibility of Rent Tax Incentives for Renovation in Older Residential Neighborhoods," *Management Science*, April 1975, pp. 883-896.

Duesenberry, J.S., and H. Kisten, "The Role of Demand in the Economic Structure," in W. Leontief, ed., *Studies in the Structure of the American Economy*, 1953.

Eisenmenger, R.W. and others, "Needed: A New Tax Structure for Massachusetts," *New England Economic Review*, Federal Reserve Bank of Boston, May/June 1975, pp. 3-24.

Eisner, R., "The Permanent Income Hypothesis: Comment," *American Economic Review*, Dec. 1958, pp. 972-990.

Goode, R., "Imputed Rent of Owner Occupied Dwellings under the Income Tax," *Journal of Finance*, Dec. 1960, pp. 504-530.

Grebler, L., D. M. Blank, and L. Winnick, *Capital Formation in Residential Real Estate: Trends and Prospects*, NBER, 1956, Chapter 8, pp. 124-133.

Grebler, L., D.M. Blank, and L. Winnick, "Once More: Capital Formation in Residential Real Estate," *Journal of Political Economy*, Dec. 1959, pp. 612-627.

Haugen, R.A., and A.J. Heins, "A Market Separation Theory of Rent Differentials in Metropolitan Areas," *Quarterly Journal of Economics*, Nov. 1968, pp. 660-672.

Heilbrun, J., "Reforming the Real Estate Tax to Encourage Housing Maintenance and Rehabilitation," in A.P. Becker, *Land and Building Taxes: Their Effect on Economic Development*, 1969, Chapter 3.

Herzog, J.P. and Earley, J.S., *Home Mortgage Delinquency and Foreclosure*, NBER, 1970. Chapter 1, pp. 1-25 and Introduction.

Houthakker, H.S., and L.D. Taylor, *Consumer Demand in the United States*, 1966, Ch. 4, pp. 56-77.

Kain, J.F., and J.M. Quigley, "Housing Discrimination, Home-ownership, and Savings Behavior," *American Economic Review*, June 1972, pp. 263-277.

Kain, J.F., and J.M. Quigley, "Measuring the Value of Housing Quality," *Journal of American Statistical Association*, June 1970, pp. 532-548.

Kish, L., and J.B. Lansing, "Response Errors in Estimating the Value of Homes," *Journal of the American Statistical Association*, Sept. 1954, pp. 520-538.

Laidler, D., "Income Tax Incentives for Owner Occupied Housing," in A. Harberger, ed., *Taxation of Income from Capital*, 1969, pp. 50-76.

Lapham, V., "Do Blacks Pay More for Housing?", *Journal of Political Economy*, Nov./Dec. 1971, pp. 1244-57.

Lee, T.H., "Demand for Housing: Cross Section Analysis," *Review of Economics and Statistics*, May 1963, pp. 190-196.

Lee, T.H., "The Stock Demand Elasticities of Non-Farm Housing," *Review of Economics and Statistics*, Feb. 1964, pp. 82-89.

Lee, T.H., "More on the Stock Demand Elasticities of Non-Farm Housing," *Review of Economics and Statistics*, Nov. 1967, pp. 640-642.

Lee, T.H., "Housing and Permanent Income: Tests Based on a Three-Year Reinterview Survey," *Review of Economics and Statistics*, Nov. 1968, pp. 480-490.

Leeuw, F. de, "The Demand for Housing: A Review of Cross Section Evidence," *Review of Economics and Statistics*, Feb. 1971, pp. 1-10.

Maisel, S., "Rates of Ownership, Mobility and Purchase," in *Essays in Urban Land Economics, in Honor of Sixty-Five Birthday of Leo Grebler*, 1966, pp. 76-108.

Maisel, S., J. Burnham, and J.S. Austin, "The Demand for Housing: A Comment," *Review of Economics and Statistics*, Now. 1971, pp. 410-413.

Maisel, S., and L. Winnick, "Family Housing Expenditures: Elusive Laws and Intrusive Variances," Friend, I. and R. Jones, eds., *Study of Consumer Expenditures, Incomes and Savings: Proceedings of the Conference on Consumption and Saving*, Vol. I, University of Pennsylvania, 1960, pp. 359-435.

Malone, J.R., "The Capital Expenditure for Owner-Occupied Housing: A Study of Determinants," *Journal of Business*, July 1966, pp. 359-365.

Morgan, J.N., "Housing and Ability to Pay," *Econometrica*, April 1965, pp. 289-306.

Morton, W.A., *Housing Taxation*, 1955, Chapter 3, pp. 41-59, Chapter 9, pp. 144-151.

Muth, R.F., "The Demand for Non-Farm Housing," in A. Harberger, ed., *The Demand for Durable Goods*, 1960, pp. 29-96.

Muth, R.F., "The Stock Demand Elasticities of Non-Farm Housing: Comment," *Review of Economics and Statistics*, Nov. 1965, pp. 447-449.

Netzer, D., *Economics of the Property Tax*, 1966.

Oksanen, E.H., "Housing Demand in Canada, 1947-62," *Canadian Journal of Economics*, August 1966, pp. 302-318.

Oldman, O., and H. Aaron, "Assessment—Sales Ratios under the Boston Property Tax," *National Tax Journal*, March 1965, pp. 36-49.

Ramathan, R., "Measuring the Permanent Income of a Household: An Experiment in Methodology," *Journal of Political Economy*, Jan. 1971, pp. 177-185.

Rapkin, C., "Price Discrimination Against Negroes in the Rental Housing Market," in Essays in *Urban Land Economics, in Honor of Sixty-Five Birthday of Leo Grebler*, 1966, pp. 333-345.

Reid, M.G., "Capital Formation in Residential Real Estate," *Journal of Political Economy*, April 1958, pp. 131-135.

Reid, M.G., *Housing and Income*, 1962, Chapters 7 and 8, pp. 162-207.

Ridker, R.G., and J.A. Hennings, "The Determinants of Residential Property Values with Special Reference to Air Pollution," *Review of Economics and Statistics*, May 1967, pp. 246-257.

Shelton, J.P., "The Cost of Renting Versus Owning a Home," *Land Economics*, Feb. 1968, pp. 59-72.

Struyk, R. and S.A. Marshall, "Income and Urban Home Ownership," *Review of Economics and Statistics*, Feb. 1975, pp. 19-26.

Tinney, R.W., "Taxing Rental Income on Owner-Occupied Homes," in A.B. Wills, ed., *Studies in Substantive Tax Reform*, 1969, pp. 125-137.

U.S. Bureau of the Census, *The Statistical Abstract of the U.S.*, 1971-75 editions (91-95 editions).

Walzer, N., and D. Singer, "Housing Expenditures in Urban Low-Income Areas," *Land Economics*, Aug. 1974, pp. 224-231.

Weaver, M.F., and E.R. Fry, "Bank Rates on Business Loans: Revised Series," *Federal Reserve Bulletin*, June, 1971, pp. 468-477.

White, M., and J. White, "Horizontal Inequality in the Federal Income Tax Treatment of Homeowners and Tenants," *National Tax Journal*, Sept. 1965, pp. 225-239.

Winger, A.R., "An Approach to Measuring Potential Upgrading Demand in the Housing Market," *Review of Economics and Statistics*, Aug. 1963, pp. 239-244.

Winger, A.R., "Housing and Income," *Western Economic Journal*, June 1968, pp. 226-232.

Winnick, L., "Housing: Has There Been a Downward Shift in Consumer Preferences?", *Quarterly Journal of Economics*, Feb. 1955, pp. 85-98.

Chapter 10

The Cumulative Voting Formula: Derivation and Extension

I. Introduction

Most finance textbooks give the cumulative voting formula and explain how the formula can be applied, but none of the available textbooks provides the proof or explanations as to how the formula has been derived.[1] In this brief note, we wish to show how the formula has been derived, and we wish to extend the basic formula to a more general case in connection with the game theory.[2]

The conventional cumulative voting formula is given by:

---

[1]For instance, see some of the most popular finance textbooks such as: Weston, J.F., and E.F. Brigham, *Managerial Finance*, 5th ed., 1975, p. 420; J.C. Van Horn, *Financial Management and Policy*, 3rd ed., 1974, p. 323; E.E. Nemmers, and A.E. Grunewald, *Basic Financial Management*, 2nd ed., 1975, p. 539.

[2]J. von Neuman and O. Morgenstern, *Theory of Games and Economic Behavior*, 1944.

$$R = n\ \frac{V}{D+1} + 1 \qquad\qquad (1)$$

where

> R = the minimum number of votes required to elect a desired number of directors (n)
>
> n = the desired number of directors a group wishes to elect
>
> D = the total number of directors to be elected by all groups
>
> V = the total number of votes held by all groups

In the cumulative voting, the number of votes given to a person who holds S_i shares is equal to

$$V_i = S_i \cdot D$$

The person who holds V_i votes may vote all the votes for one director or may divide the votes for a number of directors.

II. 2-Independent Groups (All opposition groups can make a collusion)

Assume that there are two independent groups: group A and group B, which may be one independent opposition group or a collusion of all opposition groups. The total number of directors to be elected is four, and there are five candidates, four from group A and one from group B. The total number of votes is 100. Then for the five candidates to be tied, each must get 20 votes:

1	2	3	4	5
20 votes	20	20	20	20

Figure 1   Tied for all 5 candidates

4 candidates for group A

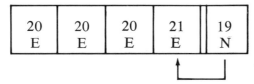

Figure 2   Tie broken for 4 candidates from group A

3 candidates for Group A

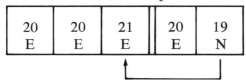

Figure 3   Tie broken for 3 candidates from group A

2 candidates for group A

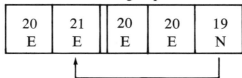

Figure 4   Tie broken for 2 candidates from group A

1 candidate for group A

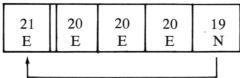

Figure 5   Tie broken for 1 candidate from group A

$$\frac{\text{Total No.}}{\text{Total No.}} = \frac{\text{Total No.}}{\text{Total No. of}} = \frac{V}{D+1} = \frac{100}{4+1} = 20 \qquad (1)$$
$$\frac{\text{of votes}}{\text{of candidates}} = \frac{\text{of votes}}{\text{directors} +} \text{Extra candidates}$$

Assume that group A wishes to elect four directors, and so no director may be elected from group B. How many votes does group A need? Not 100 votes, but only 81 votes! In other words, to be tied, each candidate needs 20 votes. So for four candidates, group A needs $4 \times 20 = 80$ votes. To break a tie, group A can take away "one" vote from group B's candidate. Then group B is left with 19 votes for its one candidate, and group B has 81 votes: three candidates have 20 votes each and the fourth candidate has 21 votes.

Or in a formula form, it is obtained by:

$$[4 \times 20] + 1 = 81 \qquad (2)$$

The above equation is equivalent with the following:

$$\begin{pmatrix} \text{No. of} \\ \text{directors} \\ \text{desired (n)} \end{pmatrix} \times \begin{pmatrix} \text{Tied votes} \\ \text{for each} \\ \text{candidate} \end{pmatrix} + \begin{pmatrix} \text{No. of votes} \\ \text{needed to} \\ \text{break a tie} \end{pmatrix} = \begin{pmatrix} \text{Total required} \\ \text{votes to elect} \\ \text{n directors} \end{pmatrix}$$

$$n \, \frac{V}{D+1} + 1 = R \qquad (3)$$

To elect four directors,

$$4 \, \frac{100}{4+1} + 1 = 81$$

To elect three directors,

$$3 \, \frac{100}{4+1} + 1 = 61$$

To elect two directors,

$$2 \; \frac{100}{4+1} \; + \; 1 = 41$$

To elect one director,

$$1 \; \frac{100}{4+1} \; + \; 1 = 21$$

The extra vote need not be exercised. It may be used for abstention or may be simply discarded.

The above reasoning is also illustrated in Figures 1-5. Equation (3) may be rewritten to obtain the number of directors group A can elect, given the number of votes held by the group.

$$n = (R-1) \; \frac{(D+1)}{V} \tag{4}$$

where

  n = the number of directors a group can elect with a given number of votes held (R)
  R = the given number of votes held by the group
  D = the total number of directors to be elected by all groups
  V = the total number of votes held by all groups

Also it should be noted that the cumulative voting system does not guarantee that at least one minority candidate will always be elected. That is, if the minority vote holding is smaller than the required votes, $R = n[V/(D+1)]+1$, then no minority candidate will be elected. However, if the total number of directors to be elected by all groups increases, the required number of votes will decrease for each candidate to be elected. Thus given the minority vote holding, R, and given the desired number of directors the minotiry group wishes to elect, n, the total number of directors should be increased to[3]

$$D = \frac{n\ V - R + 1}{R + 1} \tag{5}$$

III. N-Independent Groups (The opposition groups can not make collusions, and the opposition groups' vote holdings are equally distributed)

In this section, we wish to show the cumulative voting formula for the case where there are N-independent groups and the opposition groups' vote holdings are equal and known. For instance, assume there are three groups, A, B, and C. The total number of directors to be elected is four, and there are six candidates. The total number of votes is 102. For the six candidates to be tied, each must get 17 votes:

$$\frac{\text{Total No. of votes}}{\text{Total No. of candidates}} = \frac{\text{Total No. of votes}}{\text{Total No. of directors} + \text{extra candidates}} = \frac{V}{D+2} = \frac{102}{4+2} = 17 \tag{6}$$

---

[3]Differentiating Equation (3) with respect to D, we see that:

$$\frac{\partial R}{\partial D} = \frac{-n\ V}{(D+1)^2} < 0$$

In the above example, to elect one director, group A needs 21 votes. If group A holds only 15 votes, group A can maintain that the total number of directors should be increased to six from four so that one director may be elected by group A with 15 votes. Substituting n=1, V=100, and R=15 in Equation (5), we obtain D=5.38=6 directors.

1	2	3	4	5	6
17 votes	17	17	17	17	17

Figure 6   Tied for all 6 candidates

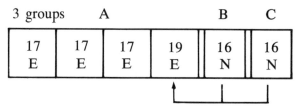

Figure 7   Tie broken for 4 candidates from group A

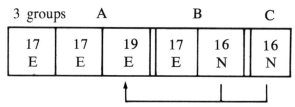

Figure 8   Tie broken for 3 candidates from group A

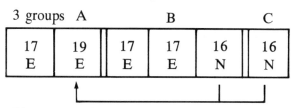

Figure 9   Tie broken for 2 candidates from group A

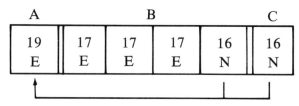

Figure 10   Tie broken for 1 candidate from group A

Assume that group A wishes to elect four directors from its own group, and so no director may be elected from groups B and C. How many votes does group A need to elect four directors? For each of the six candidates, 17 votes are necessary for a tie. In addition to these 17 votes for each candidate, to break a tie, group A must take away "one" vote from group B and another vote from group C. That is, group A must take away two votes in total from groups B and C, and the two votes should be added to any of the group A's candidates.[4] So the required number of votes to elect four directors is given by:

$$4 \ \frac{102}{4+2} \ + \ 2 = 70$$

To elect three directors,

$$3 \ \frac{102}{4+2} \ + \ 2 = 53$$

To elect two directors,

$$2 \ \frac{102}{4+2} \ + \ 2 = 36$$

To elect one director,

$$1 \ \frac{102}{4+2} \ + \ 2 = 19$$

The above reasoning is illustrated in Figures 6-10.[5] It should be noted that the underlying assumption in this model is that

---

[4]The two votes may be divided and added to two candidates of group A, each receiving one extra vote, or the two votes may be discarded or abstained.

[5]Note that we have changed the number of total votes in each example to

the two opposition groups are equally distributed in vote holdings. In such a case, the cumulative voting formula may be stated as:

$$\left(\begin{array}{c}\text{No. of}\\\text{directors}\\\text{desired (n)}\end{array}\right) \times \left(\begin{array}{c}\text{Tied votes}\\\text{for each}\\\text{candidate}\end{array}\right) + \left(\begin{array}{c}\text{No. of votes}\\\text{needed to}\\\text{break a tie}\end{array}\right) = \left(\begin{array}{c}\text{Total required}\\\text{votes to elect}\\\text{n directors}\end{array}\right)$$

$$n \ \frac{V}{D+E} \ + \ E = R \qquad\qquad (7)$$

---

simplify the calculation. If decimal numbers are obtained, the required votes should be rounded up: For the previous example, if the total number of votes is 100 instead of 102,

$$4 \ \frac{100}{4+2} + 2 = 68.7 \quad \text{(69 votes)}$$

$$3 \ \frac{100}{4+2} + 2 = 52.0 \quad \text{(52)}$$

$$2 \ \frac{100}{4+2} + 2 = 35.3 \quad \text{(36)}$$

$$1 \ \frac{100}{4+2} + 2 = 18.7 \quad \text{(19)}$$

Similarly, when there are 4 groups, A, B, C and D, and 7 candidates,

$$4 \ \frac{100}{4+3} + 3 = 60.1 \quad \text{(62)}$$

$$3 \ \frac{100}{4+3} + 3 = 45.9 \quad \text{(46)}$$

$$2 \ \frac{100}{4+3} + 3 = 31.6 \quad \text{(32)}$$

$$1 \ \frac{100}{4+3} + 3 = 17.3 \quad \text{(18)}$$

where

　　　$n=$ the number of directors a group wishes to elect
　　　$V=$ the total number of votes held by all groups
　　　$D=$ the number of directors to be elected by all groups
　　　$E=$ the number of "extra" candidates, or the number of
　　　　　votes to break a tie
　　　$R=$ the number of required votes to elect n directors

From Equation (7), we may derive the following:

$$n = \frac{(R-E)\,(D-E)}{V} \tag{8}$$

$$D = \frac{E(R+E)+n\,V}{E-R} \tag{9}$$

　　　It should be noted that the required number of votes to elect a desired number of directors varies with the number of "extra" candidates.[6] Thus, given a number of votes held, an optimal number of extra candidates E may be set up as "paper tigers" in certain political manipulations:[7]

$$E = \frac{-(D-R) \pm \sqrt{(D-R)^2 - 4(nV - RD)}}{2} \tag{10}$$

---

[6]Differentiating Equation (7) with respect to E, we see that:

$$\frac{\partial R}{\partial E} = \frac{-n\,V+(D+E)^2}{(D+E)^2} \quad \begin{array}{l} < 0 \quad \text{if } n\,V > (D+E)^2 \\ > 0 \quad \text{if } n\,V < (D+E)^2 \end{array}$$

[7]If the number of votes held by group A is 50, and there are seven candidates, then group A can elect only three directors, as shown in footnote 5. However, by setting up either 5 or 42 extra candidates, group A can elect

IV. N-Independent Groups (The opposition groups' vote holdings are unequally distributed and unknown)

The example of the previous section was based on the following assumptions: The total number of votes is 102. The total number of directors to be elected is four. There are six candidates. To elect four directors, group A needed 70 votes. However, it should hold true only when the opposition groups' vote holdings are known and they are equally distributed. However, when the vote holdings are unknown, and they are unequally distributed, the 70 votes would not guarantee four directors. For instance, if opposition group B holds 20 votes and opposition group C holds 12 votes, group A will be able to elect only three directors instead of four, with 70 votes. In an extreme case, group B may be holding 32 votes, and Group C may be holding no vote. (Figures 12-14.)

In such uncertain cases, group A will have to assume that only one opposition group holds all the remaining votes for the worst case. Thus to assure that four directors are elected from group A, the

---

all 4 directors: Substitute in Equation (10): $R=50$, $D=4$, $n=4$, $V=100$, and obtain $E=4.9$ (5) or 41.1 (42).

$$4 \; \frac{100}{4+5} \; + 5 = 49.44$$

$$4 \; \frac{100}{4+42} \; + 42 = 50.70$$

This technique holds true only when the opposition votes are equally distributed among the opposition groups' extra candidates, and there is no collusion among them.

For a positive solution to exist in Equation (10), the necessary condition is:

$$\sqrt{(D-R)^2 - 4\,(nV - RD)} > 0$$

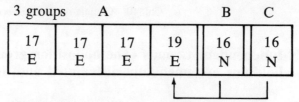

3 groups   A   B   C

17	17	17	19	16	16
E	E	E	E	N	N

Figure 11   **Votes are equally distributed between groups B and C**

       A   B   C

17	17	17	19	20	12
N	E	E	E	E	N

Figure 12   **Votes are unequally distributed between groups B and C**

       A   B   C

17	17	17	19	32	0
N	E	E	E	E	N

Figure 13   **Votes are unequally distributed between groups B and C**

       A   B   C

20	20	20	23	19	0
E	E	E	E	N	N

Figure 14   **Votes are unequally distributed between groups B and C**

E . . Elected.   N . . Not elected

270

required number of votes should be determined by the conventional cumulative voting formula (1):

$$4 \ \frac{102}{4+1} \ + \ 1 \ = \ 82.6 \ (83)$$

To elect 3, 2, and 1 directors, the required numbers of votes that will guarantee the desired numbers of directors under uncertainty are 62.2 (63), 41.8 (42), and 21.4 (22) votes respectively.

V. Summary and Conclusions

In the previous sections, we have shown how the basic cumulative voting formula has been derived and how it can be extended further to the cases where there are n-independent groups. The practical applications of the formula is currently limited to the simple case of corporate elections. However, the principle behind the cumulative voting formula, particularly in the cases of n-independent groups, is often in operation even in the current political voting system of "one person one vote." The cumulative voting system may be seriously studied in comparison with other alternative methods of representing the fair share of the minority candidates in the congress. In the face of increasing difficulties of social choice[8] by the conventional methods, a cumulative voting system may deserve serious studies.

---

[8]K.J. Arrow, *Social Choice and Individual Values*, 1951.

REFERENCES

Arrow, K., *Social Choice and Individual Values*, 1951.

Nemmers, E.E., and Grunewald, A.E., *Basic Financial Management*, 2nd ed., 1975, p. 539.

Neuman, J. von, and Morgenstern, O., *Theory of Games and Economic Behavior*, 1944.

Van Horn, J.C., *Financial Management and Policy*, 4th ed., 1977.

Weston, J.F., and Brigham, E.F., *Managerial Finance*, 5th ed., 1975.

Chapter 11

The Cost of Human Capital

I. Introduction

The practical classifications of personal saving and consumption have not been in accordance with the theoretical definitions. Recently a group of economists have argued for reclassification of personal saving and consumption. According to one extreme argument, personal saving should include not only expenditures on financial assets, residential houses and consumer durable goods, but also medical and educational expenditures and the cost of rearing children.

The primary objective of this paper is to present an estimate of the cost of rearing children as a component of total personal saving. In Section II, we shall review some past definitions of personal saving and consumption in comparison with the new definition. In Section III, the cost of rearing children is defined and a method of estimating the rearing cost is presented. Also the statistical results of the estimate are presented. In Section IV, regression equations are calculated to compare the newly defined total personal saving with the conventional personal

---

*The writer is indebted to John W. Kendrick for very useful suggestions on an earlier draft.

saving and the conventional gross saving. In Section V, a summary and conclusions are presented.

II. Definitions of Personal Saving and Consumption

According to the official government statistical classification, personal consumption is the household expenditures on goods and services, and personal saving is the household expenditures on new residential houses and financial assets. A simplified classification is as follows:

Current Practical Classification [1]

Personal saving   Financial assets [2]
                           New residential houses

Personal consumption   Foods (perishables)
                           Clothings (semi-durables)
                           Rental payments

---

[1] For more detailed components of personal saving and consumption, see U.S. Department of Commerce, Bureau of the Census, *The Statistical Abstract of the U.S.*, Annual, 1974 (94th ed.), pp. 450, 322; U.S. Department of Commerce, Office of Business Economics, *Survey of Current Business*, Monthly. Also, see Friend and Schor (1959, p. 219).

In a simplified form, personal saving = Expenditures on new residential houses − depreciation of homes + increases in financial assets − increases in debt to corporations and financial intermediaries. (U.S. Department of Commerce, *U.S. Income and Output*, 1958, p. 194.

In another form, personal saving = personal disposable income − personal consumption − consumer interest payment − consumer transfer payments to foreigners.

In general simple macroeconomic models, personal saving = personal disposable income − personal consumption.

[2] Financial assets include stocks, bonds, savings account, checking account, and cash holding at hand.

Consumer durable goods
Educational expenditures
Medical expenditures
Cost of rearing children
Other expenditures

In the above classification, we note that the household expenditures on new residential houses are included in personal saving rather than in personal consumption. This is considered as the only exception to the theoretical definition that the household expenditures on goods and services are personal consumption.[3]

In the Keynesian model, personal consumption is the household expenditures on goods and services. The rest of the household income is defined as personal saving. It may be spent to purchase financial assets, or it may be simply hoarded, without purchasing anything. Thus it should be noted that personal saving is a leakage only from the flow of the household expenditures on goods and services. Under this definition, the household expenditures on new residential houses should be included in personal consumption:[4]

---

[3]See Ruggles and Ruggles (1956, p. 77) and Shapiro (1966, p. 110). Some justifications for including the household expenditures on new residential houses in personal saving and business investment are: (1) the expenditure is the largest household expenditure, (2) the house has a very long durability, (3) the household expenditures on residential houses is highly elastic with respect to the rate of interest, and behave in a similar way as the business investment expenditures, (4) the distinction between the commercial residential buildings and the non-commercial residential buildings is not clear, etc. None of these arguments, however, is theoretically satisfactory since many consumer durable goods have the similar characteristics as the residential houses.

[4]Keynes defines: "saving means the excess of income over expenditure on consumption." "Expenditure on consumption during any period must mean the value of goods sold to consumers during that period, which throws us

The Keynesian Classification

Personal saving   Financial assets

Personal consumption   New residential houses
                                  Foods
                                  Clothings
                                  Rental payment
                                  Consumer durable goods
                                  Educational expenditures
                                  Medical expenditures
                                  Cost of rearing children
                                  Other expenditures

The Keynesian definition is useful to explain the determination of equilibrium income. In a simple Keynesian model, saving is undertaken entirely by the household sector, and investment is initiated entirely by the business sector, and equilibrium income or the equilibrium level of production of goods and services is determined at the equilibrium of saving and

---

back to the question of what is meant by a consumer-purchaser. Any reasonable definition of the line between consumer purchasers and investor purchasers will serve us equally well, provided that it is consistently applied. Such problem as there is, e.g., whether it is right to regard the purchase of a motor-car as a consumer-purchase and the purchaser of a house as an investor-purchase, has been frequently discussed and I have nothing material to add to the discussion." (Keynes, 1936, p. 61). Thus Keynes himself did not care whether the expenditures on residential houses be included in saving or consumption. However, if .we follow the "leakage approach," expenditures on residential houses should be included in consumption, and for the Keynesian econometric model, the following revisions may be made: Keynesian investment=conventional investment−expenditures on new residential houses, Keynesian saving=conventional saving−new residential houses, Keynesian consumption=conventional consumption+new residential houses.

investment, where the aggregate supply is equal to the aggregate demand.

According to the Classical abstinence theory, personal consumption is expenditures on goods and services from which the household aims to derive utilities during the current period, and personal saving is expenditures from which the household aims to derive utilities during the future period.[5] This definition is

---

[5]Senior (1836, 1951) prefers the term abstinence and avoids the term capital: "But although Human Labour, and the Agency of Nature, independently of that of man, are the primary productive Powers, they require the concurrence of a Third Productive Principle to give them complete efficiency.... To the Third Principle, or Instrument of Production, without which the two others are inefficient, we shall give the name of Abstinence: a term by which we express the conduct of a person who either abstains from the unproductive use of what can command, or designedly prefers the production of remote to that of immediate results" (1951 ed., p. 58). "By the word Abstinence, we wish to express that agent, distinct from labor and the agency of nature, the concurrence of which is necessary to the existence of capital, and which stands in the same relation to Profit as Labour does to Wages" (p. 59).

Marshall (1890, 1960) prefers the term waiting to abstinence and calls the reward of waiting interest. "The sacrifice of present pleasure for the sake of future, has been called *abstinence* by economists. But this term has been misunderstood: for the greatest accumulators of wealth are very rich persons, some of whom live in luxury, and certainly do not practice abstinence in that sense of the term in which it is convertible with abstemiousness. What economists meant was that, when a person abstained from consuming anything which he had the power of consuming, with the purpose of increasing his resources in the future, his abstinence from that particular act of consumption increased the accumulation of wealth. Since, however, the term is liable to be misunderstood, we may with advantage avoid its use, and say that the accumulation of wealth is generally the result of a postponement of enjoyment, or of a *waiting* for it. Or, in other words again, it is dependent on man's *prospectiveness*; that is, his faculty of realizing the future." (1962 ed., p. 193). Marshall adds footnote: "The argument that it is Waiting rather than Abstinence, which is rewarded by Interest and is a factor of production, was given by Macvane in the Harvard *Journal of Economics* for July, 1887."

useful to explain the determination of the rate of interest. According to the abstinence theory, interest payment is the reward to the household for abstaining from current consumption which is preferred to future consumption.

However, this definition faces a difficulty in practical classification of goods and services. For instance, are expenditures from which the household can derive utilities or pleasures during both the current period and the future period personal consumption or personal saving? The household is neither abstaining from, postponing current consumption nor waiting for future consumption, when the household purchases new residential houses or consumer durable goods. The Classical school, therefore, would include expenditures on new residential houses in personal consumption. Then to be consistent, the Classical personal consumption should be defined as expenditures from which the household aims to derive utilities during both current and future periods, and personal saving is expenditures from which the household aims to derive utilities only during the future period. Then the Classical definition is the same as the Keynesian definition:[6]

---

[6]The Classical definition assumes that the household does not enjoy watching its savings account grow and the stock prices soar to the sky. On the same token, a picture hung on the wall gives pleasure but a stock certificate or being a share-holder does not give any pleasure.

Also in the Classical theory, the proportion of hoarding (cash at hand and checking account) in financial asset will be kept at a minimum for transaction and precautionary purposes only, since idle balances will not receive any reward or interest.

The Classical Classification

Personal saving	Financial assets
Personal consumption	New residential houses
	Foods
	Clothings
	Rental payments
	Consumer durable goods
	Educational expenditures
	Medical expenditures
	Cost of rearing children
	Other expenditures

Recently, a group of economists have argued for revisions of definitions of personal saving and consumption. According to one argument, which may be called "the durable goods approach," personal expenditures from which the household aims to derive utilities during both current period and the future period should be regarded as personal saving, and expenditures from which the household aims to derive utilities only during the current period should be defined as personal consumption. Since the household can derive utilities during both current period and the future period from the consumer durable goods, they are included in personal saving:[7]

---

[7]When the consumer durable goods are included in personal saving, the imputed values of services generated from the durable goods will be included in personal consumption. However, no clear theoretical reasons are given for including consumer durable goods in personal saving. For proponents, for example, see Friedman (1957, p. 20ff), David and Scadding (1974).

Durable Goods Approach Classification

Personal saving   Financial assets
New residential houses
Consumer durable goods

Personal consumption   Foods
Clothings
Rental payments
Educational expenditures
Medical expenditures
Cost of rearing children
Other expenditures

However, the above classification is not strictly in accordance with the theoretical definition. For instance, educational and medical expenditures will increase utilities not only during the current period but also during the future period. Then these expenditures should be included in the personal saving. So is the cost of rearing children, since children are "expected" to give pleasure to parents, who make the expenditures, not only during the current period but also during the future period. According to this argument, which may be called the "human capital approach," we have the following classification:[8]

---

[8]For proponents see Kendrick (1965). And articles by Schultz, Becker, Mincer, Sjaastad, Weisbrod, Denison and Muskin in Schultz, ed. (1962).

Human Capital Approach Classification

Personal saving

Financial assets
New residential houses
Consumer durable goods
Educational expenditures
Medical expenditures
Cost of rearing children

Personal consumption

Foods
Clothings
Rental payments
Other expenditures

The above two classifications are not necessarily without criticisms as to justifications and usefulness. First, as to justifications, why, for instance, are consumer durable goods included in the personal saving? If they are regarded as personal saving because they produce utilities during both the current period and the future period, why not expenditures on trips, food, and clothings? Today's expenditures on beautiful scenic drives, delicious food, and the fancy dresses one wears would certainly increase utilities in the future when one recalls the happy old days.

So if we discard the utility criterion, what can be an alternative criterion? One alternative criterion is the capital stock theory or productivity theory which maintains that any expenditure which is aimed to increase the capital stock or to increase the productivity of the economy should be regarded as saving and investment. Accepting this definition, consumer durable goods are certainly not part of the capital stock, though they are components of wealth. It is not clear how the consumer durable goods, such as jewels, diamonds, and gold rings, can increase the productivity of an economy.[9] Nor is it always true that medical expenditures on, say, a retired 99-year-old man or woman are intended to increase the productivity of the economy.

Secondly, the purposes of the new definitions in the durable goods and human capital approaches are not clear. We cannot see any imperative necessity for the new definitions as we can in the Keynesian and the Classical theories. In other words, the Keynesian definition of saving as a leakage from the flow of goods and services is useful to explain the determination of equilibrium income, and the Classical definition of saving as abstinence or waiting is useful to explain the determination of the equilibrium rate of interest. However, the durable goods and the human capital approach have not presented any such fundamental theories in which the new definitions must play a necessary role. (See Figures 1 and 2.)

However, this does not imply that the new approaches are completely useless games of semantics economists play. For

---

[9]Marshall states: "In purely abstract, and especially in mathematical, reasoning the terms Capital and Wealth are used as synonymous almost perforce, except that 'land' proper may for some purposes be omitted from Capital. But there is a clear tradition that we should speak of Capital when considering things as agents of production; and that we should speak of Wealth when considering them as results of production, as subjects of consumption and as yielding pleasures of possession. Thus the chief *demand* for capital arises from its productiveness, from the services which it renders, for instance, in enabling wool to be spun and woven more easily than by the unaided hand, or in causing water to flow freely wherever it is wanted instead of being carried laboriously in pails; (though there are other uses of capital, as for instance when it is lent to a spendthrift, which cannot easily be brought under this head). On the other hand the *supply* of capital is controlled by the fact that, in order to accumulate it, men must act prospectively: they must 'wait' and 'save,' they must sacrifice the present to the future." (1962 ed., pp. 68-69).

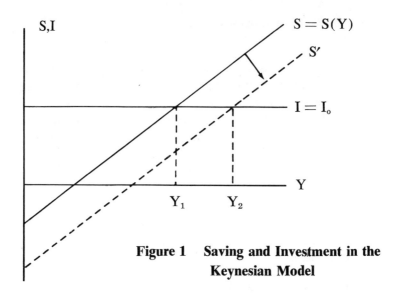

Figure 1   Saving and Investment in the Keynesian Model

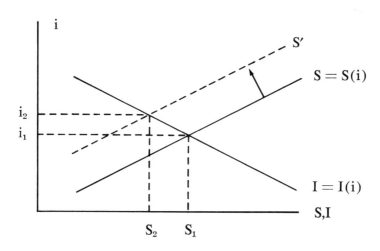

Figure 2   Saving and Investment in the Classical Model

283

instance, regarding educational expenditure as investment, sources of productivity increase or economic growth may be more clearly explained.[10]

Finally, in the following Tables A and B, two national income accounts are presented; one under the conventional classification, and the other under the new classification:

We note the following differences in the two classifications:

Conventional	New
1. Personal consumption	1. Personal consumption
Food	Food
Clothings	Clothings
Rental payments	Rental payments
Consumer durables	2. Personal saving
Educational, medical and	Financial assets
Research expenditures	New residential houses
Rearing cost	Consumer durables
2. Personal saving	Educational, medical and
Financial asset	Research expenditures
New residential houses	Rearing cost
	3. Personal investment
3. Personal investment	New residential houses
None	Consumer durables
	Educational, medical and
	Research expenditures
	Rearing cost

---

[10]Denison (1962) attempts to estimate the contribution of education to economic growth. He estimates that education accounted for 0.67 percentage point of growth per year or 23% of the total economic growth during 1929-57.

David and Scadding (1974) found that the gross private saving including the consumer durable goods is a stable function of GNP including the imputed gross rental flow, and concluded that the interest elasticity of saving must be very low, and that fiscal policies can neither affect aggregate expenditures nor alter the ratio of investment to consumption under full employment.

A. National Income Account in Conventional Classification

Sources (C + S + T)	Uses (C + I + G + X − M)
1. Personal consumption (C) Food Clothings Rental payments Consumer durable goods Educational, medical and Research expenditures Rearing cost	1. Personal consumption (C) Food Clothings Rental payments Consumer durable goods Educational, medical and Research expenditures Rearing cost
2. Personal saving (S^P) Financial assets New residential houses	2. Business investment (I) New residential houses Business structures Producer's durable goods Change in inventories
3. Business savings (S^B) Undistributed profits Depreciation	3. Government expenditures (consumption) (G) Government structures Research expenditures
4. Government taxes (T) (Federal, state, local) Personal taxes Corporate profit taxes Indirect taxes Social security taxes from individuals from buxiness from governments	4. Net exports of goods and and services (X − M) Exports (+) Imports (−)

Note: S^P = conventional personal saving. S^B = business saving.
$S = S^P + S^B$. In equilibrium, $C + S + T = C + I + G + X - M$.

B. National Income Account in New Classification

Sources $(C + S + T)$	Uses $(C + I + G + X - M)$

1. Personal consumption (C)
    Food
    Clothings
    Rental payments
	1. Personal consumption (C^P)
	    Food
	    Clothings
	    Rental payments

2. Personal saving (S^P)
    Financial assets
    New residential houses
    Consumer durable goods
    Educational, research and
    Medical expenditures
    Rearing cost
	2. Government consumption (C^G)
	    Non-durable goods and
	    Services

3. Business saving (S^B)
    Undistributed profits
    Depreciation
	3. Personal investment (I^P)
	    New residential houses
	    Consumer durable goods
	    Education, research and
	    Medical expenditures
	    Rearing cost

4. Government taxes (T)
    (Federal, state, local)
        Personal taxes
        Corporate profit taxes
        Indirect taxes
        Social security taxes
            from individuals
            from business
            from governments
	4. Business investment (I^B)
	
	    Business structures
	    Producer's durable goods
	    Research expenditures
	    Change in inventories

	5. Government investment (I^G)
	    Government structures
	    Educational and research
	    expenditures

	6. Net exports of goods
	    and services $(X - M)$
	        Exports $(+)$
	        Imports $(-)$

Note: $C = C^P + C^G$ $S = S^P + S^B$ $I = I^P + I^B + I^G$.
      In equilibrium $C + S + T = C + I + G + X - M$.

III. The Estimate of the Rearing Cost

Given the definition of the total personal saving as the sum of household expenditures on financial assets, new residential houses, consumer durable goods, medical, research and educational expenditures and the cost of rearing children, a question is how to estimate the total personal saving. Since all other statistical data are available except for the cost of rearing children, in this section we will present a method of estimating the actual cost of rearing children.

First of all, the "rearing cost" should be defined. The rearing cost or the cost of rearing a population may be defined as the amount of household expenditures to rear population up to labor force.[11] The "rearing population" is defined as the population

---

[11]The rearing cost excludes expenditures on consumer durable goods, new residential houses, medical and educational expenditures which are already estimated in each category. If the rearing cost is to be estimated for its own purpose, some portions of these expenditures for the rearing population should be included in the rearing cost. Since the purpose of estimating the rearing cost is to obtain the total personal saving, to avoid double accounting, we have excluded the above expenditures.

Also, the rearing cost should include not only the household expenditures, but also business and government expenditures. However, in this study, we include only the household expenditures for the same reason given above.

If the rearing cost is to be estimated independently for its own purpose, the following cost may be included:
- (1) the cost of child birth
- (2) food, clothing, room costs
- (3) costs of furniture, toys, musical instruments, and books
- (4) medical, educational and recreational costs
- (5) explicit and implicit child care costs
- (6) birth day celebration costs, gifts and presents to the child

For each of the above items, a standard or an average cost may be calculated for a child in each age group, and may be summed up to obtain a standard rearing cost from birth up to a certain age. Alternatively, the aggregate expenditures for the above items by the children may be obtained for each year.

which is going to enter the labor force. More specifically, the population group in ages 0-13, and the student group in ages 14-35, are regarded as the rearing population. The reasons for this definition may be explained below. First, all the persons who are under age 14 are regarded as persons who are preparing to enter the labor force. Some persons within this group may be unable to enter the labor force permanently due to illness or other reasons. However, expenditures to rear such persons may be interpreted as analogous to the business investment expenditures on defective capital goods.

After age 14, a person faces a few alternatives in his career. First, he may be working, or unemployed and seeking a job. In either case no longer is he regarded as a person who belongs to the rearing population because he has already entered the labor force. Secondly, he may be still at school. Since students are preparing to enter the labor force, as long as they are students, they may be regarded as part of the rearing population. Into this student group, part-time students as well as full-time students are included, because it does not matter whether a student attends school at daytime or evening, whether they attend school three times or four times a week. It is true that the majority of part-time students are already working during daytime and thus are already in the labor force. However, depending upon the point of view, the day-time job may be regarded as the part-time job, and so a part-time student is also included in the rearing population.

But a question is: should a person who is still at school at age 60 to 70 be included in the rearing population? Theoretically, yes, if they intend to enter the labor force. But for practical reasons, we may set an age limit for the rearing population. For this reason, we include into the rearing population the students under age 35. Practically, the number of students over age 35 is negligible. In short, the rearing population is defined as all the population in ages 0-13 and the students in ages 14-35:

$$N^R = N^{0-13} + N^S$$

where

N^R =the rearing population
N^{0-13}=the population in ages 0-13
N^S =the students in ages 14-35

Now the rearing cost can be more specifically defined as the expenditures which are generally required for rearing these population groups.

Now the question is how we can estimate expenditures required for rearing these population groups. Note that our purpose is not to estimate how much it would cost for a person to grow and finish school, nor to estimate a standard rearing cost for an average person in ages 0-13 or during his student life. The objective is to estimate how much these groups as a whole have actually spent. That is, from a given historical data we wish to estimate those expenditures which were actually spent by the rearing population.

For example, the total consumption expenditure by the entire population in the U.S. was $77.2 billion in 1929. The question is: how much was spent by the age group 0-13 and the student group in ages 14-35? The following examples may be useful to explain the method of estimation.

If we assume each person consumes equally, then consumption by the age group 0-13 is,

$$C^T \times \frac{N^{0-13}}{N^T} = C^{0-13}$$

and the consumption by student group is,

$$C^T \times \frac{N^S}{N^T} = C^S$$

where

C^T = consumption by the total population
N^{0-13} = the number of population in ages 0-13
N^S = the number of students in ages 14-35
N^T = total population

A difficulty arises because all persons do not consume equally. Depending upon age and sex, for example, the amount of consumption is different. For simplicity, assume that there are two age groups, and that a person in age group 0-13 consumes 1/3 of a person who belongs to the other age group. Then the consumption of the age group 0-13 can be estimated as,

$$C^T \times \frac{(1/3)N^{0-13}}{N^T} = C^{0-13}$$

Now assume that there are three age groups A, B, and C, and that a person who belongs to Group A consumes 40% of the consumption of a person who belongs to group B and a person who belongs to C consumes 50% of the consumption of a person who belongs to Group B, when a person who belongs to Group B consumes one unit of consumer goods. Further assume that group A contains five persons; group B, three persons; and group C, two persons. The question is, how much did each group consume if the total consumption was $200? The following table summarizes the above problem and the answer.

Distribution of Consumption (Hypothetical Example)

Group	A	B	C	Total Consumption
Weight	0.4	1.0	0.5	
Population of each group	5	3	2	
Consumption by each group	$66.67	$100.00	$33.33	$200.00

The numbers 0.4, 1.0, and 0.5 are weight values of consumption for the three groups. The numbers 5, 3, and 2 are the numbers of the group members. Given these weights, members, and the total consumption, the last row shows the consumption by each group. They are obtained from the following calculations:

$$C^A = 200 \times \frac{0.4 \times 5}{(0.4 \times 5) + (1.0 \times 3) + (0.5 \times 2)}$$

$$= 66.67 \quad \text{(consumption by Group A)}$$

$$C^B = 200 \times \frac{1.0 \times 3}{(0.4 \times 5) + (1.0 \times 3) + (0.5 \times 2)}$$

$$= 100.00 \quad \text{(consumption by Group B)}$$

$$C^C = 200 \times \frac{0.5 \times 2}{(0.4 \times 5) + (1.0 \times 3) + (0.5 \times 2)}$$

$$= 33.33 \quad \text{(consumption by Group C)}$$

Suppose now that all persons in group A are in age group 0-13, and one person in group B is a student. The consumption by the student is:

$$C^S = C^B \times \frac{N^S}{N^B} = 100 \times \frac{1}{3}$$

$$= 33.33 \qquad \text{(consumption by student group S)}$$

where

C^S = consumption by the student group
N^B = the number of members of group B
N^S = the number of students in group B

The number of the rearing population is:

$$N^R = 5 + 1 = 6$$

and the rearing cost or consumption by group A and the student who belongs to group B is:

$$C^A + C^S = C^R$$

where

C^A = consumption by group A
C^S = consumption by the student
C^R = the rearing cost

If we have six groups, letting

N_i = the number of persons in group i, (i=1, 2,...6)
W_{ij} = the weight value for i th group's expenditure on j th good (j=1, 2,...n)
C_j = total expenditure on jth good by the total population
C_{ij} = ith group's expenditure on jth good

Given jth good, the consumption by ith group is,

$$C_{ij} = C_j \times \frac{W_{ij}\ N_i}{\sum\limits_{i=1}^{6} W_{ij}\ N_i}$$

If we have 16 types of goods, the consumption by ith group is,

$$\sum\limits_{j=1}^{16} C_{ij} = \sum\limits_{j=1}^{16} C_j \times \frac{W_{ij}\ N_i}{\sum\limits_{i=1}^{6} W_{ij}\ N_i}$$

where $\sum C_{ij} =$ expenditures on all types of goods by i th group.

If a portion of ith group is the student group, then the students' total consumption is:

$$\sum\limits_{j=1}^{16} C_{ij} \times \frac{N_1^S}{N_i} = \sum\limits_{j=1}^{16} C_{ij}^S$$

where

$$\sum\limits_{j=1}^{16} C_{ij}^S = \text{expenditures on all types of goods by the students}$$
of i th group

If the rearing cost is defined as the expenditures of the first two age groups and students who belong to the next two groups, and if there are 16 types of expenditures, then the rearing cost is:

$$\sum\limits_{j=1}^{16} C_{1j}\ \frac{W_{1j}\ N_1}{\sum\limits_{i=1}^{6} W_{ij}\ N_i} + \sum\limits_{j=1}^{16} C_{2j}\ \frac{W_{2j}\ N_2}{\sum\limits_{i=1}^{6} W_{ij}\ N_i}$$

$$+ \sum_{j=1}^{16} C_{3j} \frac{W_{3j} \ N_3}{\sum\limits_{i=1}^{6} W_{ij} \ N_i} \cdot \frac{N_3^S}{N_3}$$

$$+ \sum_{j=1}^{16} C_{4j} \frac{W_{4j} \ N_4}{\sum\limits_{i=1}^{6} W_{ij} \ N_i} \cdot \frac{N_4^S}{N_4} = R \qquad (1)$$

or

$$\sum_{j=1}^{16} \sum_{i=1}^{2} C_{ij} \frac{W_{ij}N_i}{\sum\limits_{i=1}^{6} W_{ij}N_i} + \sum_{j=1}^{16} \sum_{i=3}^{4} C_{ij} \frac{W_{ij}N_i^S}{\sum\limits_{i=1}^{6} W_{ij}N_i} = R$$

where R=the total rearing cost

In this paper we divided the total population into six groups, and the total consumption into 16 categories, and applying formula (1), we have calculated the rearing cost which is shown in Table 1.

Before we discuss the results, we have to explain (1) why the population is divided into six groups, (2) how the weights are assigned, and (3) why the expenditures are divided into 16 categories and what specific types of expenditures are included in the rearing cost.

For the first question, strictly speaking at every level of age, activities and thus the amount of expenditures may be different. However, as a matter of convenience, we can divide the total population into six age groups: 0-4, 5-13, 14-19, 20-34, 35-64, 65- (See Table 2). The sex difference is disregarded because the difference due to sex is assumed not to be significant. The characteristics of these groups may be summarized:

Age group   0-4   infant group, stays at home
Age group   5-13   attends kindergarten and elementary school
Age group   14-19   attends the secondary school, physical and
                     mental activities grow. The period of
                     adolescence
Age group   20-34   the most active period of one's life in
                     physical activities. Most students finish
                     college and graduate schools during this
                     age period.
Age group   35-64   during this age period, a person may be
                     established as an independent consumer
                     and as the head of a household.
Age group   65-   the period of retirement, rest and medita-
                     tion. This period represents the final stage
                     of one's life.

The second question is whether we should include all types of expenditures into the category of rearing cost. First, the statistical data for personal consumption expenditures are taken from the *Survey of Current Business* and then the following expenditures are excluded: medical expenditures, education and research expenditures. It is because the purpose of this paper is to estimate the rearing cost as a component of the total personal investment expenditures, and the data for the medical, educational and research expenditures are separately available directly from the U.S. Department of Commerce except the rearing cost. Secondly, we exclude expenditures on food furnished to government and commercial employees because these expenditures are not directly concerned with the rearing population.

Now we have to explain how the weight values are assigned to the above six age groups. The weights are distributed in terms of the "adult male unit" which takes the expenditures of a 20-year-old as a base weight, 1.00. If weight value is 0.49 for the age group, 0-4, it means that a person who belongs to

Table 1. Consumption by Age Group (million $)

	(1) Age 0-4	(2) 5-13	(3) 14-19	(4) 20	(5) 34	(6) 65-
1929	2182	6145	5045	16289	20477	3434
1930	2033	6274	5462	16543	21076	3557
1931	1740	5418	4740	14613	18754	3220
1932	1329	4178	3613	11629	14980	2025
1933	1191	3828	3350	10973	14159	2524
1934	1246	4125	3725	12391	16029	2899
1935	1312	4364	4027	13317	17275	3169
1936	1402	4681	4435	14605	19021	3540
1937	1482	4873	4732	15635	20466	3868
1938	1455	4606	4588	15258	20095	3860
1939	1515	4583	4666	15474	20489	3996
1940	1608	4714	4855	16192	21453	4266
1941	1853	5568	5046	17845	24669	4940
1942	2203	6116	5910	20391	28518	5742
1943	2225	5689	5887	20744	29550	6115
1944	3005	7369	7288	23676	36145	7598
1945	3433	8228	7895	25044	40587	8718
1946	3987	9497	8949	32914	46350	9975
1947	4773	10603	9814	36202	50992	11158
1948	5318	11853	10401	38600	54938	12202
1949	5501	12072	10022	38596	55565	12547
1950	6032	12935	10272	40372	58832	13514
1951	7075	14590	11146	43158	64587	15143
1952	7204	15966	11643	44531	68264	16343
1953	7577	17241	12157	45752	71553	17482
1954	7936	17235	11841	44565	71165	17734
1955	7891	18543	12431	46365	74968	19028
1956	8430	20102	13353	48257	79548	20480
1957	8971	21276	14483	49557	83486	21813
1958	9374	22752	15576	51730	88850	23500
1959	8678	21356	14584	49158	86123	23120
1960	8971	22637	15379	50662	89829	24375
1961	9282	23157	16776	51653	92405	25305
1962	9627	24311	17807	54192	96424	26571
1963	9843	25296	18826	56643	100127	27729

296

Table 1. Consumption by Age Group (million $) —Continued

	(7) S_3 14-19	(8) S_4 20-34	(9) R (1)+(2) +(7)+(8)	(10) R/Y (%)
1929	2867	598	11792	14.19
1930	3130	612	12049	16.20
1931	2739	545	10442	16.36
1932	2105	437	8049	16.54
1933	1968	416	7402	16.18
1934	2206	473	8050	15.49
1935	2404	513	8593	14.73
1936	2669	567	9320	14.07
1937	2870	611	9837	13.86
1938	2805	601	9468	14.41
1939	2876	614	9589	13.61
1940	3015	648	9984	13.12
1941	3134	714	11269	12.12
1942	3670	816	12806	10.90
1943	3656	830	12400	9.29
1944	4520	947	15847	10.80
1945	4966	1002	17628	11.72
1946	5531	1343	20357	12.68
1947	6281	1488	23146	13.61
1948	6595	1598	25364	13.40
1949	6324	1609	25507	13.45
1950	6749	1696	27412	13.20
1951	7490	1640	30795	13.54
1952	7929	1781	32879	13.77
1953	8437	2150	35404	14.02
1954	8336	2273	35240	13.72
1955	8751	2411	37596	13.70
1956	9694	2992	41218	14.07
1957	10703	3320	44270	14.34
1958	11620	3466	47211	14.85
1959	10938	3195	44167	13.10
1960	11534	3344	46485	13.29
1961	12666	3409	48513	13.30
1962	13818	4227	51983	13.52
1963	14816	4815	54770	13.61

Note: R=Rearing cost, defined as consumption by age groups 0-4, 5-13, and student groups, 14-19, 20-34.

R/Y=Rearing cost ratio (ratio of rearing cost to disposable income).

S_3=Consumption by students aged 14-19.

S_4=Consumption by students aged 20-34.

Table 2. Weight Values for Distribution of Personal Consumption Expenditures by Age Group[4-5]

Items[1]	Age 0-4	5-13	14-19	20-34	35-64	65 up
1. Food & tobacco						
1, 2, 4 (exc. alco.)[2]	.49	.76	1.00	.89	.83	.79
5 and alcohol beverage 3 excluded	.00	.00	.13	1.00	1.00	1.00
2. Clothing, accessories						
1, 2, 3, 5, 6, 8[3] 4, 7 excluded	.32	.62	1.14	1.28	1.28	1.20
3. Personal care, all items (1,2)	.32	.62	1.14	1.28	1.28	1.28
4. Housing, all items (1-4)	.33	.33	.33	1.00	1.00	1.00
5. Household operation						
5, 6, 7, 8, 10, 11 1, 2, 3, 4, 9 exc.	.33	.33	.33	1.00	1.00	1.00
6. Medical care (See Addendum)						
7. Personal business						
3,	.00	.00	.50	1.00	1.00	1.00
4	1.00	1.00	1.00	1.00	1.00	1.00
1, 2, 5, 6, 7, exc.						
8. Transportation						
1, (c,d)	.00	.33	.67	1.00	1.00	1.00
2	.00	.50	1.00	1.00	1.00	1.00
3	.00	.25	.50	1.00	1.00	1.00
1 (a, b, e, f) exc.						
9. Recreation						
half of 3	1.00	1.00	1.00	1.00	1.00	1.00
6, 8, 9	.00	.50	1.00	1.00	1.00	1.00
10, 11, 12 exc.						
10. Private education & research excluded						

Table 2. Weight Values for Distribution of Personal Consumption Expenditures by Age Group[4-5] —Continued

Items[1]	Age 0-4	5-13	14-19	20	35-64	65 up
10. Private education & research excluded						
11. Religious & welfare activities	.00	1.00	1.00	1.00	1.00	1.00
12. Foreign travel & remitt.						
1,2	.00	.25	.50	1.00	1.00	1.00
3,4 excluded						
Addendum						
6. Medical care & death exp.[4]						
1-7	.79	.96	.99	1.90	1.83	2.13
8 excluded						

Notes:

[1]The item numbers correspond to the classification number of the "Personal Consumption Expenditures by Types of Product," Department of Commerce, *Survey of Current Business*, July 1964, p. 16.

[2]Computed from U.S. Department of Agriculture, *Family Economics Review*, April 1964, p. 17. The moderate food plan has been chosen as the data.

[3]Computed by J.D. Tarver (and used in his estimate of "Costs of Rearing and Educating Farm Children," *Journal of Consumer Purchase Study*, Misc. Pub. No. 465, U.S. Department of Agriculture, 1941, pp. 182-193.

[4]Computed from the data, H. Hollingsworth, M.C. Klem and A.M. Brady, *Social Security Administrative Medical Care and Costs in Relation to Family Income, A Statistical Source Book*, Federal Security Agency, Bureau Memorandum, No. 51, May, 1947, p. 177. The data are the average medical costs for all income groups and communities in a 12-month period, 1928-31, 1938; 450 persons in 8,638 families were surveyed.

[5]All other weights have been estimated on the theoretical basis since no survey data have been available.

[6]All values are averages of the adult male units for males and females in each age class.

[7]For reasons why specific expenditures have been excluded see the text.

Table 3. Explanations for Weight Assignment

1. Good and Tobacco

1, 2, 4,

These weights are based on both theoretical and survey data of the Department of Agriculture and thus we may to a certain degree rely upon them.

5 and alcohol

We have assumed that persons who will do it, generally start smoking and drinking at age 18 or in the freshman year of college, and reach a full unit at age 20. Thus the following weights have been assigned to age group 14-19. Since some will start smoking and drinking early, while others will not even after age 18, it is hoped that the deviations will average out.

14—0.00	17—0.13	19—0.50
15—0.00	18—0.13	20—1.00
16—0.00		

2. Clothing and Accessories

1, 2, 3, 4, 5, 6, 8

These weights are based upon sample surveys of the Department of Agriculture, except for age 30 and over.

3. Personal Care

All items

The weights followed the above pattern except over age 65.

4. Housing

All items

All persons under age 20 are assumed to share rooms and furniture in an average family with three children. Thus 1/3 of the adult male unit has been assigned to age groups 0-4, 5-13, 14-19.

5. Household Operation

5, 6, 7, 8, 10, 11

These weights follow the above pattern for its similarities.

6. Medical care and death expenditures

1-7

These weights are based on a sample survey of the Federal Security Agency.

7. Personal Business

3

Services furnished without payment by financial intermediaries except insurance companies are assumed not to give benefits to age group 0-13, while starting age 14, benefits are assumed to be given to them, but half of the adult male unit.

4

The benefits of the life insurance are assumed to be given to all age groups equally even to the young children.

Table 3. Explanations for Weight Assignment—Continued

8. Transportation

1 (c,d) The costs of automobile repair, gasoline, and other costs are not directly concerned with younger children. However, 1/3 was assigned to age groups 5-13, and 2/3 to age group 14-19, and a full unit to 20 and over.

2 The cost of the local transportation is assumed to be half of the adult for age group 5-13.

3 For the purchased inter-city transportation, half of the above corresponding weights have been assigned to age groups 5-13 and 14-19, because the younger children do not travel as much as the adults except the college students.

9. Recreation

3 Half of the nondurable toys and sport supplies are assumed to be spent entirely by age group 0-13, while half of them are assumed to be spent by all groups equally.

6, 8, 9, For expenditures on radio, television and movies half of the cost of the adults for age group 5-13, and none to 0-4 were given. The rationale is that the latter age group generally does not enjoy them, while the former group pays half of the adult costs.

11. Religious and Welfare

All items The age group 0-4 is assumed not to participate in any religious and welfare activities, while persons above age 5 are assumed to participate equally through school, church and other institutions.

12. Foreign Travel and Remittances

1, 2 For the foreign travel and expenditures abroad by United States government personnel, 1/2 of the adult weight was given to age group 5-13 and age group 14-19 respectively, following the transportation pattern 8.3.

Note: See Table 2.

301

that age group spends 49% of a person who belongs to the age group 20-34. The weight distribution for all age groups by the types of expenditures is shown in Table 2, and the explanations for the weight distribution are given in Table 3.

Finally, as to the third question, the total consumption expenditure is divided into 16 categories as is classified in *Survey of Current Business*. A classification of consumption is necessary, because depending upon the type of consumption, the weights for each group must be different.   Putting aside the question whether these weights are accurate or not, given the weight values, the task is to accomplish the calculation by applying formula (1).[12]

The results of calculations of consumption by age group are presented in Table 1. The rearing cost which is defined as the sum of expenditures of age groups, 0-4, 9-13, and students in age groups 14-19 and 20-34, is shown in column (9). The ratio of the rearing cost to disposable personal income is shown

---

[12]An alternative method of estimating the rearing cost is: First, estimate the "standard" cost of living for a typical child of a specific age in a family with a median income living in a selected city. Then multiply the standard rearing cost by the number of the rearing population in that specific age group. If there are m age groups, the total rearing cost R is given by:

$$\sum_{i=1}^{m} (C_i \cdot N_i) = R$$

where

m = the number of age groups, $i = 1, \ldots, m$
C_i = the standard cost of a child in age group i
N_i = the number of rearing population in age group i

This method may yield an over-estimate or an under-estimate since there is no restriction given for the actual amount spent on the total rearing population. The "standard" rearing cost calculated in this way may be compared with the "allocated" rearing cost calculated in this paper.

in column (10). It shows that between 9-16% of the disposable income has been spent as the rearing cost. When the total personal saving is defined as the sum of the rearing cost, medical expenditures, educational and research expenditures, expenditures on the durable goods and the conventional personal saving (financial assets + new residential houses), we see that between 27-41% of the conventional disposable income has been spent on the total personal saving during 1929-63, as shown in Table 5.

IV. Total Personal Saving, Conventional Personal Saving and Gross Investment Ratios: Regression Results

For the purpose of comparison, the newly defined total personal saving ratio, the conventional personal saving ratio and the conventional gross investment ratio are drawn in Figure 3 together with the rearing cost ratio for the period 1929-63.[13] The following points may be summarized:

First, we note that the rearing cost ratio was very stable during the overall period except for a slight dip during the World War II years. In contrast with the slight dip in the rearing cost ratio,

---

[13]The conventional personal saving ratio is the ratio of the conventional saving to conventional personal disposable income; the conventional gross investment ratio is the ratio of conventional gross domestic investment to conventional GNP. Then, the newly defined total personal saving should be defined as the ratio of the newly defined total personal saving to newly defined personal disposable income which should include the imputed personal returns on consumer durable goods, medical and educational expenditures and the rearing cost, if such returns are accurately estimated. In this paper, the total personal saving ratio is the ratio of expenditures on financial assets, consumer durable goods, medical and educational expenditures and the rearing cost to the conventional personal disposable income.

Table 4. Eight Types of Saving Ratios

	(1) I/GNP (%)	(2) S^P/Y (%)	(3) R/Y (%)	(4) E/Y (%)	(5) M_e/Y (%)	(6) C_d/Y (%)	(7) S'/Y (%)	(8) S^T/Y (%)
1929	15.71	5.0	14.19	0.80	3.5	11.1	20.40	34.6
1930	11.39	4.6	16.20	0.92	3.8	9.6	18.92	35.1
1931	7.38	3.9	16.36	1.04	4.0	8.6	17.54	33.9
1932	1.72	−1.3	16.54	1.17	4.4	7.5	11.77	28.3
1933	2.51	−1.4	16.18	1.05	4.3	7.6	11.55	27.8
1934	5.06	0.2	15.49	0.93	4.2	8.1	13.43	28.9
1935	8.86	3.5	14.73	0.87	3.9	8.8	17.07	31.8
1936	10.30	5.4	14.07	0.82	3.8	9.5	19.52	33.6
1937	13.05	5.3	13.86	0.85	3.8	9.8	19.75	33.5
1938	7.67	1.6	14.41	0.94	4.1	8.7	15.34	29.7
1939	10.27	4.1	13.61	0.89	4.0	9.5	18.49	32.1
1940	13.13	5.5	13.12	0.84	4.0	10.2	20.54	33.6
1941	14.37	11.9	12.12	0.75	3.3	10.4	26.35	38.5
1942	6.20	23.6	10.90	0.69	3.2	5.9	33.39	44.3
1943	2.97	24.7	9.29	2.72	3.1	4.9	33.42	42.7
1944	3.37	25.2	10.80	0.66	3.2	4.6	33.66	44.5
1945	5.00	19.1	11.72	0.65	3.4	5.4	28.55	40.3
1946	14.67	8.4	12.68	0.72	3.8	9.9	22.82	35.5
1947	14.69	2.8	13.61	0.83	4.0	12.1	27.20	40.8

Year	I/GNP	SP/Y	R/Y	E/Y	Me/Y	Cd/Y	S'/Y	ST/Y
1948	17.85	5.8	13.40	0.82	4.1	12.0	22.72	36.1
1949	13.91	4.5	13.45	0.89	4.2	12.4	21.99	35.5
1950	18.99	6.1	13.20	0.87	4.2	14.6	25.77	39.0
1951	18.05	7.8	13.54	0.86	4.1	13.0	25.76	39.3
1952	15.02	7.9	13.77	0.88	4.3	12.2	25.28	39.1
1953	14.42	7.9	14.02	0.89	4.4	13.0	26.19	40.2
1954	14.17	7.4	13.72	0.93	4.6	12.6	25.53	39.2
1955	16.93	6.4	13.70	0.95	4.7	14.4	26.45	40.2
1956	16.69	7.9	14.07	0.99	4.8	13.2	26.89	41.0
1957	15.37	7.7	14.34	1.05	5.0	13.4	27.15	41.5
1958	13.61	7.8	14.85	1.13	5.2	11.7	25.83	40.7
1959	15.56	7.0	13.10	1.21	5.4	12.9	26.51	39.5
1960	14.85	6.2	13.29	1.27	5.6	12.8	25.87	39.2
1961	13.78	7.5	13.30	1.30	5.7	12.0	26.50	39.8
1962	14.81	7.2	13.52	1.35	5.8	12.6	26.95	40.4
1963	14.75	6.8	13.61	1.41	5.9	12.9	27.01	40.6

Note: (1) I/GNP=Gross domestic investment ratio
(2) SP/Y = Personal saving ratio (conventional personal saving to disposable personal income)
(3) R/Y = Rearing cost ratio (of the household to disposable income)
(4) E/Y = Educational expenditure ratio (of the household to disposable income)
(5) M_e/Y = Medical expenditure ratio (of the household to disposable income)
(6) C_d/Y = Consumer durable goods ratio (to disposable income)
(7) S'/Y = Personal saving ratio excluding the rearing cost $(2+4+5+6)$(to disposable income)
(8) S^T/Y = Total personal saving ratio $(2+3+4+5+6)$(to disposable income)

Table 5. Population by Age Group (Thousand)

	(1) Age 0-4 N_1	(2) 5-13 N_2	(3) 14-19 N_3	(4) 20-34 N_4	(5) 35-64 N_5
1929	11735	22128	13801	29638	37993
1930	11372	22267	13936	29954	38843
1931	11179	22264	13981	30245	39443
1932	10903	22238	14014	30561	39977
1933	10612	22130	14070	30902	40502
1934	10331	21964	14162	31260	41075
1935	10170	21730	14925	31592	41659
1936	10044	21434	14441	31880	42227
1937	10009	21082	14559	32134	42783
1938	10176	20668	14679	32406	43388
1939	10418	20253	14749	32695	44001
1940	10579	11942	14742	33009	44651
1941	10850	20838	13481	32278	45386
1942	11301	20043	13897	32668	46518
1943	12016	19374	14020	32308	46660
1944	12524	19303	13460	30316	47135
1945	12979	19382	13049	28889	47688
1946	13244	10661	13076	34171	49074
1947	14406	20093	13206	34692	49864
1948	14919	20947	13127	34886	50676
1949	15607	21631	12865	35097	51544
1950	16328	22268	12756	35226	52353
1951	17248	22784	12639	34770	53114
1952	17211	24280	12746	34413	53836
1953	17527	25451	12960	34166	54507
1954	17941	26645	13179	34008	55304
1955	18448	27718	13393	34091	56109
1956	18869	28775	13789	33946	56949
1957	19361	29541	14549	33712	57792
1958	19744	30560	15079	33542	58594
1959	20031	31683	15530	33450	59370
1960	20364	32985	16074	33590	60311
1961	20660	33276	17349	33702	61043
1962	20746	33889	17889	34267	61724
1963	20722	34515	18513	34856	62358

Note: Continued to the next page.

Table 5. Population by Age Group (Thousand)—Continued

	(6) Age 65- N_6	(7) S_3/N_3 (%)	(8) S_4/N_4 (%)
1929	6475	56.82	3.67
1930	6705	57.30	3.70
1931	6928	57.78	3.73
1932	7147	58.26	3.76
1933	7363	58.74	3.79
1934	7582	59.22	3.82
1935	7804	59.70	3.85
1936	8027	60.18	3.88
1937	8258	60.66	3.91
1938	8508	61.14	3.94
1939	8764	61.62	3.97
1940	9031	62.1	4.00
1941	9288	62.1	4.00
1942	9583	62.1	4.00
1943	9867	62.1	4.00
1944	10147	62.1	4.00
1945	10494	62.9	4.00
1946	10828	61.8	4.08
1947	11185	64.0	4.11
1948	11538	63.4	4.14
1949	11921	63.1	4.17
1950	12310	65.7	4.20
1951	12752	67.2	3.8
1952	13194	68.1	4.0
1953	13624	69.4	4.7
1954	14084	70.4	5.1
1955	14550	70.4	5.2
1956	14982	72.6	6.2
1957	15420	73.9	6.7
1958	15813	74.6	6.7
1959	16232	75.0	6.5
1960	16659	75.0	6.6
1961	17013	75.5	6.6
1962	17308	75.5	6.6
1963	17567	78.7	8.5

Source: 1)Rearranged from the data, Bureau of the Census, *Current Population Reports*, Series P-25, Nos. 98, 265, 293.
2) Student ratios: estimated from U.S. Department of Commerce, *The Statistical Abstract of the U.S.*, each year.
S_4/N_4=For 1929-49 extrapolated.
S_3/N_3=For 1929-44 extrapolated except 1930 and 1940;
For 1930, 1940 Bureau of the Census, *1950 Census of Population*.

Table 6. The Basic Data for Regression Analysis

	(1) GNP_t/I_0 (Ratio)	(2) M/GNP (%)	(3) Y_t/C_0 (%)	(4) M/Y (%)	(5) $(\Delta N/N)_{t-1}$ (%)	(6) i_{t-1} (%)
1929	5.04	53.1	105.3	65.9	1.1	4.73
1930	4.54	59.8	98.3	72.7	1.1	4.73
1931	4.19	69.2	94.7	82.1	1.1	4.55
1932	3.57	77.6	81.6	92.5	0.8	4.58
1933	3.50	73.4	79.6	89.3	0.6	5.01
1934	3.82	67.9	85.2	85.1	0.6	4.49
1935	4.20	68.0	103.6	84.1	0.6	4.00
1936	4.78	65.3	105.9	81.4	0.7	3.60
1937	5.03	62.6	105.4	79.7	0.6	3.24
1938	4.77	66.1	99.7	85.2	0.6	3.26
1939	5.18	66.5	108.2	85.4	0.8	3.19
1940	5.62	66.3	111.4	86.9	0.8	3.01
1941	6.34	59.0	121.0	78.9	1.2	2.84
1942	7.16	50.7	128.1	68.2	1.0	2.77
1943	8.10	53.3	133.2	76.5	1.1	2.83
1944	8.69	55.5	138.3	79.5	1.4	2.73
1945	8.54	65.3	132.3	92.1	1.2	2.72
1946	5.98	64.2	122.5	98.3	1.1	2.62
1947	5.93	57.3	104.7	56.5	1.0	2.53
1948	5.36	57.5	108.1	87.5	1.9	2.61
1949	5.37	53.7	107.3	87.3	1.7	2.82
1950	5.13	49.0	113.1	81.8	1.7	2.66
1951	5.48	49.0	109.3	76.8	1.7	2.62
1952	5.64	48.8	111.5	77.5	1.7	2.86
1953	5.90	47.5	113.7	76.3	1.7	2.96
1954	5.81	49.5	107.9	77.3	1.7	3.20
1955	5.81	46.5	114.9	75.7	1.8	2.90
1956	5.92	45.0	112.1	72.9	1.8	3.06
1957	6.00	43.8	111.2	71.1	1.8	3.36
1958	5.93	46.2	100.8	72.2	1.8	3.89
1959	6.31	43.2	107.6	71.2	1.7	3.79
1960	6.47	42.5	106.6	68.6	1.6	4.38
1961	6.60	43.9	108.0	70.4	1.7	4.41
1962	6.67	43.8	107.8	61.4	1.6	4.35
1963	6.68	44.9	107.3	63.3	1.6	4.33

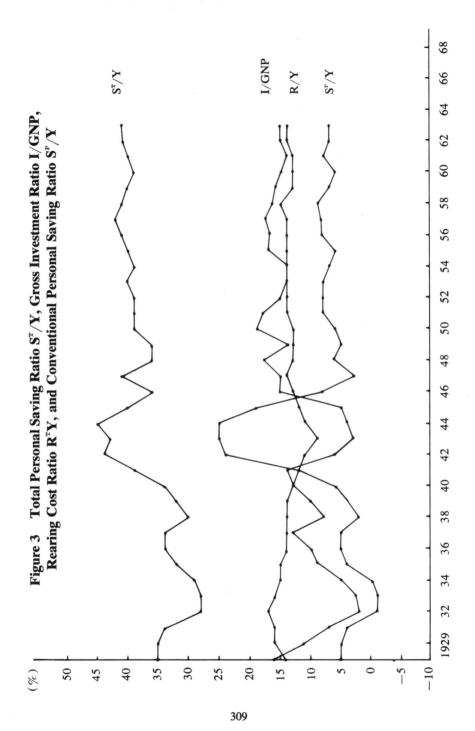

Figure 3   Total Personal Saving Ratio S^T/Y, Gross Investment Ratio I/GNP, Rearing Cost Ratio $R^T Y$, and Conventional Personal Saving Ratio S^F/Y

309

we note that the conventional personal saving ratio surged upward during the war years. This was apparently due to the government wartime policies of encouraging saving in financial assets and discouraging expenditures on goods and services.[14]

Secondly, we note that the conventional personal saving ratio and the gross investment ratio show greater fluctuations than the total personal saving ratio. Thirdly, during the post World War II period, the conventional personal saving ratio and the gross investment ratio do not show any long-run rising trend, but the total personal saving ratio shows a slightly rising trend. This rising trend may have resulted from increasing expenditures on the consumer durable goods, medical and educational expenditures.[15]

To see if the fluctuations in the newly defined total personal saving ratio can be explained by some of the conventional variables, the following models are tested:

$$\frac{S^P}{Y} = F_1\left(\frac{Y_t}{C_0} , \frac{M}{Y} , \left(\frac{\Delta N}{N}\right)_{t-1}, i_{t-1}, e_1\right)$$

$$\frac{S^T}{Y} = F_2\left(\frac{Y_t}{C_0} , \frac{M}{Y} , \left(\frac{\Delta N}{N}\right)_{t-1}, i_{t-1}, e_2\right)$$

---

[14]The slight dip was not caused by decreasing birth rates. The average annual birth rate was 18.9 per 1,000 population during 1936-40, and 21.36 during 1945. The average annual rate of growth in population was 0.8% during 1936-40, and 1.16% during 1941-45. (U.S. Department of Commerce, *Historical Statistics of the United States, Colonial Times to 1957*, 1960, p. 23). During World War II in order to check the inflationary pressures, price control and rationing policies were adopted.

[15]The total personal saving ratio increased from 34.6% in 1929 to 40.6% in 1963. The medical expenditures ratio increased from 3.5% to 5.9%, and the educational expenditure ratio increased from 0.80% to 1.41% during the same period. The expenditure ratio on the consumer durable goods increased from 11.1% to 12.9%. But the rearing cost ratio decreased from 14.19% to 13.61%. See Table 5.

$$\frac{I}{GNP} = F_3\left(\frac{GNP}{I_0}, \frac{M}{GNP}, \left(\frac{\Delta N}{N}\right)_{t-1}, i_{t-1}, e_3\right)$$

where

$S^P/Y =$ the conventional personal saving ratio to the disposable income[16]

$S^T/Y =$ the total personal saving ratio to the disposable income

$I/GNP =$ the conventional gross domestic private investment ratio to GNP

$Y_t/C_0 =$ the current income ratio to the past peak consumption

$M/Y =$ the total money supply ratio to the disposable income (supply of money plus time deposits)

$(\Delta N/N)_{t-1} =$ the rate of increase in population with one year of time lag

$i =$ Yield on AAA corporate bonds

$GNP/I_0 =$ the GNP ratio to past peak investment

$M/GNP =$ the total money supply ratio to GNP

Before we present the empirical results, we may briefly discuss the expected signs of the regression coefficients. First,

---

[16]The implicit personal saving function is,

$$S = a_1 Y + b_1\left(\frac{Y_t^2}{C_0}\right) + c_1\left(\frac{M}{Y}\right)Y + d_1\left(\frac{\Delta N}{N}\right)_{t-1}Y + m_1 i_{t-1}Y$$

and the marginal propensity to save is

$$\frac{dS}{dY} = a_1 + 2b_1\left(\frac{Y_t}{C_0}\right) + d_1\left(\frac{\Delta N}{N}\right)_{t-1} + m_1 i_{t-1}$$

as to the "theoretical" personal saving ratio, that is, if the Keynesian or the Classical definitions are used, it is rather easy to predict the signs of the independent variabls, since the question the consumer has to make is whether to spend on goods and services or not to spend, or whether to purchase now or in the future. Under these alternatives, we expect that the income-peak consumption ratio (Y_t/C_0) will have a positive sign according to the relative consumption hypothesis.[17] The money-income ratio (M/Y) will have a negative sign according to the money asset or real money balance hypothesis.[18] The rate of interest (i) will have a positive sign according to the classical saving theory.[19]

---

[17]According to the Duesenberry's (1949) relative income hypotheses, the ratio of current income to the past peak income (Y_t/Y_0) should be used. By the analogy, Y_t/C_0 represents the relative consumption hypothesis. For the permanent income hypothesis a weighted average of the past incomes may be used (Friedman, 1957). For the Koyck distributed lag model, previous year's consumption will be used. In this paper the consumption function is given by

$$C_t = a \ Y_t + bC_0$$

$$\text{then } C_t/Y_t = a + bC_0/Y_t \quad \text{or} \quad S_t/Y_t = c + dY_t/C_0$$

If $C_0 = C_{t-1}$ the relative consumption hypothesis, the permanent income hypothesis, and the Koyck distributed lag model become equal.

[18]Tobin's (1951) money-asset hypothesis states that when the nominal money stock increases, consumption will rise. Pigou's (1943) real money balance effect states that when the level of prices and wage rate fall in the same proportion, consumption will still rise due to an increase in real money balance (M/P), where M is constant.

[19]As an opposite view (Weber, 1970), when the rate of interest rises, consumers will have an opportunity to reach the same amount of savings with less saving presently. Consequently they will increase current consumption in response to the increase in the rate of interest.

If some consumers wish to save more as a result of an increase in the rate of interest, while others wish to consume more, the two forces can balance out and the effect of a change in the rate of interest can be insignificant.

The rate of increase in population ($\Delta N/N$) will have a negative sign since a larger increase in population will increase demand for residential houses as well as conventional consumer goods and services.[20]

However, when the "conventional" personal saving includes expenditures on new residential houses in addition to the purchases of financial assets, the prediction of the signs is not so easy. When population increases, for example, the demand for new residential houses and conventional consumer goods and services will rise.

Similarly, the effect of the rate of interest on the conventional personal saving ratio is uncertain. Assume that the demand for new residential houses and the consumer durable goods is negatively correlated with the rate of interest. When the rate of interest rises the demand for financial assets will rise, but the demand for new residential houses and the consumer durable goods will fall. Since expenditures on new residential houses are included in the conventional personal saving, when the rate of interest rises, the conventional personal saving ratio will decrease, as far as the effect on new residential houses is concerned. However, if an increase in the demand for financial assets outweighs the decreases in the expenditures on new residential houses and consumer durable goods, then the newly defined conventional personal saving ratio will rise.

The prediction of the signs of the regression coefficients for the total personal saving ratio is more complicated than for

---

[20]Recall that under the Keynesian or the Classical definition, the expenditures on new residential houses are included in consumption. We have allowed one year of time lag for the rate of interest and the rate of growth in population. For monetary lags, see Hamburger (1967), Karen and Solow (1965).

the conventional personal saving ratio. Under the new classification, the consumer's portfolio is more diversified. The total personal saving consists of expenditures on financial assets, residential houses, consumer durable goods, medical expenditures, educational expenditures and the rearing cost. When the income-peak consumption ratio (Y_t/C_0) or the money-income ratio (M/Y) increases, expenditures on financial assets may fall on the one hand, but if expenditures on new residential houses, consumer durable goods, medical and educational services and rearing children rise on the other hand, the total personal saving ratio will rise or fall depending upon the net effect of the two counteracting forces.

Similarly, when the rate of interest rises, expenditures on financial assets may rise, and the expenditures on new residential houses, consumer durable goods, education, medical care, and rearing children may fall. Whether the total saving ratio will fall or rise will depend upon the net balance of the increase and decrease in the expenditures. The same reasoning applies to the effect of an increase in the rate of growth in population on the total personal saving ratio. When the rate of growth in population increases, the expenditures on financial assets may fall, but expenditures on residential houses, consumer durable goods, education, medical care, and rearing children may rise. The net effect will depend upon the net balance of the decreases and increases.

Now we turn to the expected signs for the conventional gross investment ratio. By analogy with the income-peak consumption ratio (Y_t/C_0) for the conventional personal saving ratio, we have included the GNP-peak investment ratio (GNP/I_0) for the gross investment ratio, and we expect that it will have a positive sign.[21] The money-GNP ratio (M/GNP) will also have

---

[21]Let $I_t = aY_t - bI_0$

a positive sign, since the firm will wish to invest more when the money asset increases, just as the consumer will wish to spend more on consumption, decreasing the personal saving ratio, when the money asset increases. However, we recall that the conventional gross investment includes household expenditures on new residential houses. If the consumer increases conventional consumption expenditures when the money asset increases, and reduces the expenditures on new residential houses, then the gross investment ratio will also fall.

The rate of increase in population ($\Delta N/N$) is expected to increase the gross investment ratio, since the demand for residential houses will increase. The rate of interest (i) is expected to have a negative sign according to the marginal efficiency of investment hypothesis.[22]

The statistical results obtained from the ordinary least squares multiple regression are summarized for the two types of personal saving ratios and the gross investment ratio in Table 8.[23]

First, for the conventional personal saving ratio, we note that the income-peak consumption ratio and the rate of growth in population are both significant at the 5% level, and both have positive signs. The Durbin-Watson statistic indicates no serial correlation.

---

then

$$I_t/Y_t = a - bI_0/Y_t \quad \text{or} \quad I_t/Y_t = c + dY_t/I_0$$

It is assumed that the higher the past peak level of investment, the smaller will be the current level of net investment.

[22]For a review of other empirical investment functions, see Evans (1969, pp. 73-149).

[23]The basic statistical data are obtained from U.S. Department of Commerce, *The Statistical Abstract of the U.S.* and *Survey of Current Business.* See Tables 4 and 6. Note that the period 1941-46 is excluded from the regressions.

Table 7. Statistical Results (1929-63: Excl. 1941-46)

Dep. Vari.	Intercept	Y_t/C_o (%)	M/Y (%)	$\Delta N/N_{t-1}$ (%)	i_{t-1} (%)	$\bar{R}$	$\bar{R}^2$	S	D.W.	d.f.
SP/Y(%)	−23.9824	0.2322	−0.0093	2.0419	0.8221	0.926	0.858	1.010	1.860	24
(S.E.)		(0.0381)	(0.0274)	(0.5052)	(0.3756)					
(T.R.)		(6.090)**	(−0.341)	(4.042)**	(2.189)*					
(5.21) (M.V.)		(104.41)	(77.18)	(1.31)	(3.62)					
S^T/Y(%)	44.0149	0.0675	−0.2311	4.6328	−0.8019	0.976	0.952	0.943	1.428	24
(S.E.)		(0.0356)	(0.0256)	(0.4717)	(0.3507)					
(T.R.)		(1.897)*	(−9.046)**	(9.822)**	(−2.286)**					
(36.58) (M.V.)		(104.51)	(77.18)	(1.31)	(3.62)					

Dep. Vari.	Intercept	GNP/I_o (ratio)	M/GNP (%)	$\Delta N/N_{t-1}$ (%)	i_{t-1} (%)	$\bar{R}$	$\bar{R}^2$	S	D.W.	d.f.
I/GNP(%)	38.0100	0.0752	−0.3064	−0.2507	−2.2947	0.900	0.810	1.929	1.346	24
(S.E.)		(0.9320)	(0.1114)	(1.6545)	(0.5213)					
(T.R.)		(0.081)	(−2.752)**	(−0.152)	(−4.402)**					
(12.78) (M.V.)		(5.35)	(55.44)	(1.31)	(3.62)					

*Significant at the 5% level. **Significant at the 1% level. S = Standard error of the estimate. S.E. = Standard error of the regression coefficient. T.R. = T-ratio. M.V. = Mean value.

Secondly, for the total personal saving ratio, all the independent variables are significant at the 5% level or less. The money-income ratio and the rate of interest have negative signs; and the income-peak consumption ratio and the rate of growth in population have positive signs. We note that the rate of interest is positive for the conventional saving ratio, but is negative for the total personal saving ratio. This result is due to the fact that the newly defined total personal saving includes the consumer durable goods and other expenditures that are negatively elastic to the rate of interest. The Durbin-Watson statistic indicates that the serial correlation is inconclusive.

Thirdly, as to the conventional gross investment ratio, the money-income ratio and the rate of interest have negative signs and significant at the 5% level. The GNP/I_0 ratio and $(\Delta N/N)_{t-1}$ are not significant. The Durbin-Watson statistic is inconclusive.

An overall review of the three regression models shows that the total personal saving ratio has the largest adjusted multiple coefficient of determination, $\overline{R}^2 = 0.952$, and the smallest standard error of estimate, $S = 0.943$, compared with $\overline{R}^2 = 0.858$ and $S = 1.1010$ for the conventional personal saving ratio and $\overline{R}^2 = 0.810$ and $S = 1.929$ for the conventional gross investment ratio.

V. Summary and Conclusions

We have estimated that the percentage of the rearing cost in disposable personal income ranged between 9-16% during 1929-63, the average being 14%. If the total personal saving is defined as the sum of the rearing cost, medical and educational expenditures, expenditures on consumer durable goods as well as the conventional expenditures on financial assets and new residential houses, the percentage of the total personal saving to disposable personal income ranged between 28-44%, the average being 38% of the disposable personal income.

To see if the fluctuations in the total personal saving ratio can be explained by the conventional factors influencing the conventional personal saving ratio, multiple regression equations were calculated with four independent variables, namely, the income-peak consumption ratio, the money-income ratio, the rate of growth in population, and the rate of interest. The model explains about 95% of the total variation in the total personal saving ratio during 1929-63 excluding 1941-46. The money-income ratio, the rate of growth in population and the rate of interest and the income-peak consumption ratio were significant at the 5% level or less. The statistical results suggest that increases in the money-income ratio and the rate of interest will decrease the total personal saving ratio, and increases in the rate of growth in population and the income-peak consumption ratio will increase the total personal saving ratio.

The implications and the usefulness of the newly defined total personal saving are as yet to be developed. One application is in the investment theory. Total gross private domestic investment could be redefined to include not only the conventional business expenditures on fixed capital facilities and residential houses, but also household expenditures on consumer durable goods, medical and educational expenditures, and the rearing cost.[24] This implies that the increases in productivities of labor and capital should be partly explained by the increased educational and medical expenditures and rearing cost. However, for this purpose, a more refined statistical definition of the total personal saving would be necessary to exclude certain types of expenditures on consumer durable goods, medical and educational expenditures, and the rearing cost which are not directly related to the capital stock or the productivity of the economy.

---

[24]Government investment expenditures should be included in the total national investment.

Another application is the reconstruction of the empirical models of income determination by recalculating some of the aggregate economic functions such as consumption, saving and investment functions. However, if the usefulness of a model depends upon its predictability, the usefulness of the new approach will depend upon the statistical results of the recalculated empirical functions. We have seen that the empirical total personal saving ratio showed a higher coefficient of determination than the conventional personal saving ratio. Thus, for instance, the newly defined total personal saving function could be preferred to the conventional personal saving function as far as predictability is concerned. However, the empirical results are not conclusive and these applications are suggested only for the purpose of illustration.[25] The newly defined saving, consumption and investment functions would need more compehensive new economic theories.[26]

---

[25]The usefulness of a model may depend upon its pedictability, but a model may predict well without a logical consistency and realism of the assumptions. Also for the evaluation of the new and old approaches, the entire empirical macroeconomic models should be compared.

[26]Personal saving and total investment can be defined in various measures with serialized names:

S_1 = Household expenditures on financial assets and hoarding

$S_2 = S_1$ + expenditures on new residential houses

$S_3 = S_2$ + consumer durable goods

$S_4 = S_3$ + educational expenditures

$S_5 = S_4$ + medical expenditures

$S_6 = S_5$ + rearing cost

I_1 = Business expenditures on fixed capital assets (private domestic gross)

$I_2 = I_1$ + household expenditures on new residential houses

$I_3 = I_2$ + consumer durable goods

$I_4 = I_3$ + educational and research expenditures.

$I_5 = I_4$ + medical expenditures

$I_6 = I_5$ + rearing cost

The government building expenditures may be added to I_2.

REFERENCES

David, P.A., and Scadding, J.L., "Private Savings: Ultrarationality, Aggrega-
tion, and Denison's Law," *Journal of Political Economy*, March/April,
1974, pp. 225-249.

Denison, E.F., *The Sources of Economic Growth in the United States and the
Alternatives before Us*, Committee for Economic Development, 1962.

Duesenberry, J.S., *Income, Saving and the Theory of Consumer Behavior*,
1949.

Evans, M.K., *Macroeconomic Activity*, 1969.

Friedman, M., *A Theory of the Consumption Function*, 1957.

Friend, I., and Schors, S., "Who Saves?," *Review of Economics and
Statistics*, May 1959, pp. 213-248.

Hamburger, M., "Interest Rates and the Demand for Consumer Durable
Goods," *American Economic Review*, Dec. 1967, pp. 1131-1153.

Hollingsworth, H., M.C. Klem, and A.M. Brady, *Social Security Administrative Medical Care and Costs in Relation to Family Income, A Statistical
Source Book*, Federal Security Agency, Bureau Memorandum, No. 51, May
1947, p. 177.

Kendrick, J.W., *Total Investment in the United States*, 1965 (mimeographed).

Kendrick, J.W., *Economic Accounts and Their Uses*, 1972.

Karen, J. and R.M. Solow, "Lags in Monetary Policy: A Summary," in
Smith, W.C., R.L. Teigen, eds., *Readings in Money, National Income and
Stabilization Policy*, 1965, pp. 76-80.

Keynes, J.M., *The General Theory of Employment, Interest, and Money*, 1936.

Marshall, A., *Principles of Economics*, 1890, 8 ed., 1920, reset and rep. 1962.

Pigou, A.C., "The Classical Stationary State," *Economic Journal*, Dec. 1943,
pp. 343-351.

Ruggles, R., and Ruggles, N., *National Income Accounts and Income Analysis*, 1956.

Schultz, T.W., ed., "Investment in Human Beings," *Journal of Political
Economy*, Supplement, October 1962, No. 5, Part 2, pp. 1-157.

Senior, N.W., *An Outline of the Science of Political Economy*, 1836, rep. 1951.

Shapiro, E., *Macroeconomics*, 1966, pp. 317-321.

Tarver, J.D., "Costs of Rearing and Educating Farm Children," *Journal of
Consumer Purchase Study*, Misc. Pub. No. 465, U.S. Department of Agriculture, 1941, pp. 182-193.

Tobin, J., "Relative Income, Absolute Income, and Saving," in *Money,
Trade, and Economic Growth, Essays in Honor of John H. Williams*, 1951,
pp. 135-56.

U.S. Department of Commerce, "Personal Consumption Expenditures by
Types of Product," *Survey of Current Business*, July 1964, p. 16.

Weber, W.E., "The Effect of Interest Rates on Aggregate Consumption,"
American Economic Review, Sept. 1970, pp. 591-600.

Chapter 12

Home Ownership
and Apartment Renting:
The Comparative Cost Advantage

I. Introduction

A number of studies have been published on the determinants of home ownership. Maisel (1966), Kain-Quigley (1972), Morgan (1965), Carliner (1974), and Struyk-Marshall (1975) showed empirical evidence that the probability or the rate of home ownership depends upon many factors such as income, family size, age, education, sex, marital status, race, occupation, etc. However, these studies ignored the cost factor of the home ownership. Other conditions being equal, if home ownership costs less than apartment renting, the rate of home ownership will increase.

However, very few studies are available on the specific monetary cost advantage of home ownership and apartment renting.[1]

---

[1]Most good textbooks on personal finance discuss the general advantages and disadvantages of home ownership and apartment renting, and explain in detail technical aspects of home purchase. For instance, see Cohen, J.B., and

Shelton (1968) calculated the annual apartment rent that should be charged by the apartment owner, and the annual home ownership and operation cost that is to be incurred by the home owner, in percentage terms of a house value. His conclusion is that home ownership is less expensive if the home is occupied for 3.5 years or longer. Very similar conclusions are reached by Lindberg (1969). He compared the net revenue to be gained when a home is purchased and sold after a certain period of occupancy, and the net revenue to be gained when the cash not tied up in operating a home is invested in an alternative investment. He concluded that home ownership is profitable after 2 years of occupancy, if the house value increases 2% per year; after 3 years, if the value stays the same; after 7 years, if the value decreases 2% a year.

In this paper, we wish to illustrate a general model of evaluating the comparative monetary cost advantages for home ownership and apartment renting. The model is formulated in section II, and a basic numerical example is given in section III. Alternative numerical examples are given in Section IV under the title of uncertainty and the sensitivity analysis. The policy implications of the sensitivity analysis is discussed in section V, and a summary is presented in the final section VI.

A.W. Hanson, *Personal Finance*, 3. ed., 1972. In this paper, by home we refer to an owner-occupied and by apartment a renter occupied residential dwelling. Thus, a home or an apartment may be part of a multi-family housing residential structure or a single family residence.

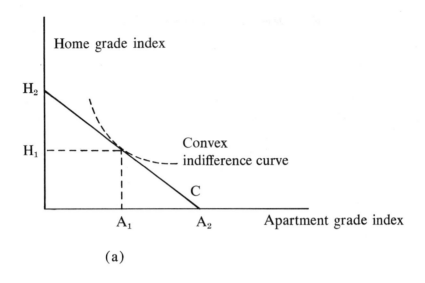

(a)

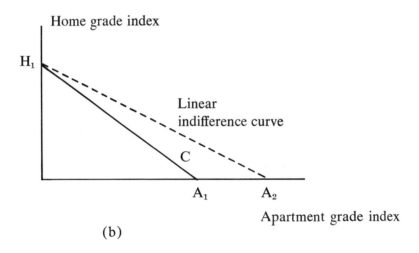

(b)

Figure 1   Two Indifference Curves

II. The Model

The problem of choice between home purchase and apartment renting may be explained by the general theory of choice, that is, in terms of utility maximization, cost minimization, or the indifference curve analysis. Assume that a consumer is indifferent between a specific grade of home and a specific grade of apartment. Then the consumer will choose the home or the apartment whichever costs less, given the planned period of occupancy. The choice problem may be stated as a cost minimization problem:

$$\text{Minimize } C = P_H \cdot H + P_A \cdot A \tag{1}$$

$$\text{subject to } U = F(H, A) \tag{2}$$

$$\text{and} \quad \text{If } H > 0, \ A = 0; \text{ if } A > 0, \ H = 0 \tag{3}$$

$$\text{or,} \quad A + H > 0 \quad \text{and } A \cdot H = 0$$

where

H = a home of a certain grade, which may be expressed in terms of a composite index of quantity and quality. See Kain-Quigley (1970) and Morris (1972)

A = an apartment of a certain grade, which may be also expressed by a composite index.

P_H = price of a home per unit of the grade index.

P_A = apartment rent per unit of the grade index.

It should be noted that this problem setting is different from the ordinary indifference curve problem formulation in that equation (3) is added as an additional constraint. In an ordinary indifference curve formulation, the difference curve is smooth and convex, as in Figure 1(a). So the solution will be where the budget line is tangent to the convex indifference curve, implying that the consumer's utility is maximized in general both with home ownership and apartment renting. Such a situation exists when a consumer has an apartment in a city and a country house in the suburbs for weekends, vacation, and retirement.

However, in this paper we deal with a more ordinary case where the consumer must choose one or another. Constraint (3) forces the solution at a corner. Thus the indifference curve may be drawn as a straight line which has a different slope than that of the budget line as in Figure 1(b), or a convex, or a concave curve which must touch the two axes, and must intersect with the indifference curve only at a corner.

Now the question is how to calculate the costs of home ownership and apartment renting at each corner of the indifference curve.

A. Home Ownership Cost (cumulative total cost at time T)

The following may be the major components of the total revenue (+) and expenditures (−) in home purchase, operation and resale at the end of a certain number of years of occupancy.

(1) $+ H_0 e^{gT}$

H_0 is the initial house value that grows at an annual rate of g. T stands for the terminal year of occupancy. $t = 1,2..T \leq n$. n is the maturity year of amortization of loan balance. The subscript $_0$ stands for the time of purchase.

(2) $- (D_0 + C_0) e^{iT}$

D_0 is the down payment, C_0 is the closing cost. If these amounts are invested, they will grow at an annual rate of i.

(3) $- \int_0^T (P_0 + M_0 + E_0)\ e^{gt} dt$

P_0 is the property tax, M_0 is the maintenance cost, E_0 is the insurance cost. These initial costs rise at an annual rate of g. The cumulative total cost is the cumulative sum of these annual costs.

(4) $-\int_0^T K\, dt$

K is the constant annual mortgage payment which includes the interest cost and amortization payments. The cumulative mortgage payment is the cumulative sum of the annual mortgage payments.[2]

(5) $+\int_0^T [R(t)+P(t)]a\, dt$

R is the annual interest payment in year t, and P is the annual property tax payment, and a is the marginal tax rate of the home buyer. Thus $(R+P)a$ represents the federal income tax saving in year t, and the cumulative sum is the total federal income tax saving during the years of occupancy.

(6) $-L(T)$

If the home buyer resells the home before the completion of amortization, the loan balance to be paid is L.

(7) $-b\, H_0\, e^{gt}$

The home seller must pay b% of the sale value of the house as selling cost to the broker. The selling cost may include the renovation cost for the sale.

---

[2]The annual mortgage payment K satisfies:

$$L_0 = K \left[\frac{1}{(1+i)} + \ldots + \frac{1}{(1+i)^n} \right] = K \left[\frac{1-(1+i)^{-n}}{i} \right]$$

$$K = L_0\, \frac{i}{1-(1+i)^{-n}}$$

where L_0 is the initial loan balance. The interest payment in year T is $R(T) = mL(T)$ where m is the mortgage rate. The loan balance in year T is $L(T) = L_0 - \int_0^T [K-R(t)]\, dt$. The property tax in year T is $P(T) = P_0\, e^{gT}$. The subscript o indicates the initial time of home purchase.

We multiply each of these items by e^{-iT} to convert into the present value, and sum up all the items to obtain the "home ownership cost":

$$C(H) - H_0 e^{gT} \cdot e^{-iT} - (D_0 + C_0) e^{iT} \cdot e^{-iT}$$

$$- \int_0^T (P_0 + M_0 + E_0) e^{gt} \cdot e^{-it} \, dt$$

$$- \int_0^T K \, e^{-it} \, dt + \int_0^T [R(t) + P(t)] \, a \, e^{-it} \, dt$$

$$- L(T) \, e^{-iT} - b H_0 e^{gT} \cdot e^{-iT}$$

$$= H_0 \, e^{(g-i)T} - (D_0 + C_0)$$

$$- \int_0^T (P_0 + M_0 + E_0) \, e^{(g-i)t} \, dt - \int_0^T K \, e^{-it} \, dt$$

$$+ \int_0^T [R(t) + P(t)] \, a \, e^{-it} \, dt$$

$$- L(T) \, e^{-iT} - b \, H_0 \, e^{(g-i)T} \tag{4}$$

B. Apartment Cost (cumulative total cost at time T)

The following items are the major expenditures ($-$) and revenues ($+$) involved in apartment renting:

(1) $+ (D_0 + C_0)\, e^{iT}$

>Instead of using the cash for down payment and closing cost to buy a home, a consumer could invest it and the value could grow at an annual rate of i.

(2) $-\int_0^T A_0 e^{gt} dt$

>A_0 is the initial annual apartment rent, which increases at an annual rate of g. The sum is the total cumulative rent.

(3) $\dfrac{-A_0}{12}\, e^{iT} + \dfrac{A_0}{12} = \dfrac{A_0}{12}(1 - e^{iT})$

>One-month-equivalent apartment rent is paid as a security deposit, but it will be returned to the renter when he leaves the apartment. The security deposit could earn interest, but it is not paid to the renter. So he loses the opportunity interest income. (But under a state law, interest may be paid to the renter annually or may be applied toward rent. The landlord is entitled to 1% of the deposited money to cover the administration expenses. Also if the renter leaves the apartment before the agreed period of occupancy he may lose the deposit.)

(4) $+\int_0^T (K - A_0\, e^{gT})\, e^{i(T-t)} dt$

>For a given year t, $K - A_0 e^{gt}$ represents the difference between the constant mortgage payment for the home ownership and the apartment rent. If this

difference is positive, the apartment renter can invest for an annual rate of return i%. If the difference is negative, it represents home buyer's saving, which can be invested. The sum represents the cumulative net saving of the apartment renter or home buyer. T is the total number of years of occupancy.

We multiply each of these items by e^{-iT} to convert into the present value, and then sum up all the items to obtain the "apartment cost":

$$C(A) = (D_0 + C_0) e^{iT} \cdot e^{-iT} - \int_0^T (A_0 e^{gt}) e^{-it} dt$$

$$+ (A_0/12) (1 - e^{iT}) e^{-iT}$$

$$+ \int_0^T (K - A_0 e^{gt}) e^{i(T-t)} \cdot e^{-iT} dt$$

$$= (D_0 + C_0) - \int_0^T A_0 e^{(g-i)t} dt + (A_0/12) (e^{-iT} - 1)$$

$$+ \int_0^T [Ke^{-it} - A_0 e^{(g-i)t}] dt \qquad (5)$$

The comparative cost advantage of home ownership is defined as home ownership cost minus apartment cost:[3]

---

[3]In the above cost items of the basic numerical example, we have omitted the capital gain tax to avoid further complications since the capital gain tax depends upon various situations. However, we have shown the effect of the

$$C(NH) = C(H) - C(A) \qquad\qquad (6)$$

The decision rule for the potential home buyer who wishes to minimize the housing cost is then,

If $C(H) < C(A)$, buy home

If $C(H) > C(A)$, rent apartment

---

capital gain tax in Table 3. We note that the introduction of the capital gain tax does not change the payoff period of the basic numerical example.

If the consumer does not plan to buy another house after he sells his old residence, the amount of capital gain tax should be added as item 8 of the home ownership cost:

$$- (H_0\, e^{gT} - H_0 - C_0 - bH_0 e^{gT} - F)\, 0.25 \cdot e^{-iT} \qquad (8)$$

or

$$- (H_0\, e^{gT} - H_0 - C_0 - bH_0 e^{gT} - F)\, 0.5 \cdot a \cdot e^{-iT} \qquad (8)'$$

where

H_0 = the initial house value
C_0 = the initial closing cost
F = the fix up cost.
$bH_0 e^{gT}$ = the selling cost including the broker's fee, legal fee, transfer tax, advertising cost and other selling expenses.

In Equation (8), 25% of the capital gain is the capital gain tax. In Equation (8)', 50% of the capital gain is added to the ordinary income, and taxed at the effective marginal tax rate a %. If a < 0.5, then Equation (8)' minimizes the capital gain tax. If the home seller incurs a capital loss, it is not deductible.

If the house is sold and if the consumer plans to buy another house, the capital gain tax is:

$$- (H_0\, e^{gT} - C_0 - bH_0 e^{gT} - F - H_1 - C_1)\, 0.5 \cdot a \cdot e^{-iT}$$
$$(8)''$$

where

H_1 = the new house value.
C_1 = the closing cost for the new house

The total rate of return on investment in home ownership is defined as the comparative cost advantage at the terminal year divided by the home ownership cost at the same year:

In Equation (8)″, 50% of the capital gain is added to the ordinary income to be taxed at a %. Also the cost basis of the new house will be decreased by the amount of non-taxed capital gain.

Also it should be noted that if the home seller is above 65 years of age, there will be no capital gain tax or there may be a partial capital gain tax depending upon other qualifications.

In the case of apartment renting, the taxes will vary with the type of investment. If the renter invested the extra available fund in the security market, he will pay the capital gain tax on items 1 and 4, and the annual ordinary income taxes on the dividend (with $100 exclusion) and the interest income. However, if he purchased the State and municipal bonds at the original issue discount price less than the face value, and if he held them until maturity, he will not pay any capital gain tax nor the ordinary income tax on the interest income.

Thus the omission of the extra tax items implies the assumption that the consumer will buy an equally or a more expensive house than the house he sold, and that the renter has invested the available fund in a long-term tax free bond.

Also equations 4 and 5 are not necessarily positive. That is, the expenditures may be greater than revenues for home ownership and apartment renting. If both equations are negative, and if equation 6 is also negative, the negative comparative cost advantage indicates that home ownership costs less than the apartment renting. If both equations 4 and 5 are negative and if equation 6 is positive, the positive comparative cost advantage indicates that the apartment renting costs more than the home ownership. If equations 4 and 5 are positive and if equation 6 is also positive, it indicates that home ownership is more profitable than apartment renting is.

For numerical calculations, descrete equations are used instead of continuous equations (4) and (5).

$$r(t) = \frac{C(H) - C(A)}{C(H)} \tag{7}$$

The average annual rate of return on investment in home owner-ship is obtained by dividing the total rate of return by the number of years of occupancy:[4]

$$r(a) = \frac{r(t)}{t} = \frac{C(H) - C(A)}{C(H) \cdot t} \tag{8}$$

III. The Basic Numerical Example

In this section, we shall see only one "representative" example, which may be called the basic reference model. The basic assumptions for the parameters are summarized in Table 1.[5]

For instance, the basic reference model assumes that the house value is $50,000, the closing cost is $1,000 (2% of the house value), the down payment is $10,000 (20%), and the loan balance is $40,000 (80%). The mortgage interest rate is

---

[4]The conventional rate of return on investment in home ownership is measured by: (sale value of the house−purchase value)/total cost (not relative cost). The total cost may include purchase price, maintenance, renovation, insurance costs, property taxes, and federal income tax saving (−). But this measure will underestimate the rate of return since it does not deduct the imputed rent for owner-occupied home from the total cost. Or the imputed rent could be added to the numerator instead of deducting it from the denominator.

[5]The prcentage parametric assumptions are very close to the values esti-mated by Shelton (1968) and Lindberg (1969). Certain exceptions include the mortgage rates ·which were lower in their good old times.

Table 1. Parameter Values for the Basic Reference Model

	Initial values	Growth path (current value or opportunity cost)	% of house value
1. House value (H)	$50,000	$H(t)=50,000\,(1+0.03)^t$	
2. Down payment (D)	$10,000	$D(t)=10,000\,(1+0.03)^t$	20%
3. Closing cost (C)	$1,000	$C(t)=1,000\,(1+0.03)^t$	2%
4. Mortgage rate (m)	8.5%		
5. Discount rate (i)	6.5%		
6. Amortization period (n)	25 years		
7. Annual mortgage payment (K)	$3,908.8		7.8%
8. Maintenance, insurance costs (M+E)	$750	$M(t)+E(t)=750\,(1+0.03)^t$	1.5%
9. Property tax (P)	$1,000	$P(t)=1,000\,(1+0.03)^t$	2%
10. Income tax rate (a)	25%		
11. Sales fee (b) (% of house sale value)	8%		8%
12. Annual apartment rent (A)	$5,000	$A(t)=5,000\,(1+0.03)^t$	10%
13. One month apartment rent security deposit (A/12=S)	$416.7	$S(t)=416.7\,(1+0.03)^t$	
14. The rate of inflation (g)	3%		

Note: (1) The house value, maintenance-insurance costs, property tax, apartment rent are all assumed to increase at 3% per year. The 3% of inflation will double all the costs in 25 years, and the house value will increase to $104,689 at the end of the 25th year.

(2) The sum of mortgage payments (7.8% of the house value), maintenance-insurance costs (1.5%) and property tax (2%) is equal to 11.3% of the initial house value. If the down payment, closing cost and the resale fee are averaged over 25 years, and added to the annual housing cost, it increases to 12.2% of the house value.

333

Table 2. Comparative Cost Advantage of Home Ownership: Basic Reference Model

Years of occupancy	(1) C(H)	(2) C(A)	(3) C(H) — C(A) = C(NH)	(4) H(t)	(5) L(t)	(6) r(t)	(7) r(t)/t = r(a)
1	− 7915	4973	−12889	51500	39491	−162.8	−162.84
2	−10737	− 958	− 9779	53045	38939	− 91.1	− 45.54
3	−13468	− 6790	− 6677	54636	38340	− 49.6	− 16.53
4	−16110	−12522	− 3588	56275	37690	− 22.3	− 5.58
5	−18668	−18150	− 518	57964	36985	− 2.8	− 0.56
6	−21143	−23673	2530	59703	36220	12.0	2.00
7	−23538	−29089	5552	61494	35390	23.6	3.37
8	−25856	−34398	8543	63339	34489	33.0	4.13
9	−28099	−39599	11500	65239	33512	40.9	4.54
10	−30269	−44690	14421	67196	32452	47.6	4.76
11	−32370	−49672	17303	69212	31302	53.5	4.86
12	−34403	−54546	20143	71288	30053	58.6	4.88*
13	−36370	−59310	22940	73427	28699	63.1	4.85
14	−38274	−63967	25693	75630	27230	67.1	4.79
15	−40116	−68515	28399	77898	25635	70.8	4.72

	C(H)	C(A)	C(NH)	H(t)	L(t)	r(t)	r(a)
16	-41899	-72957	31058	80235	23906	74.1	4.63
17	-43624	-77292	33668	82642	22029	77.2	4.54
18	-45294	-81523	36228	85122	19993	80.0	4.44
19	-46910	-85649	38739	87675	17783	82.6	4.35
20	-48474	-89673	41200	90306	15386	85.0	4.25
21	-49987	-93596	43609	93015	12785	87.2	4.15
22	-51452	-97419	45968	95805	9963	89.3	4.06
23	-52869	-101144	48275	98679	6901	91.3	3.97
24	-54241	-104772	50531	101640	3578	93.2	3.88
25	-55568	-108305	52737	104689	- 26	94.9	3.80

Note:

(1) C(H)   : Home ownership cost (cumulative present value, $)
(2) C(A)   : Apartment renting cost (cumulative present value, $)
(3) C(NH) : Comparative cost advantage of home ownership=C(H)-C(A)
(4) H(t)   : House value (current value, $) at time t
(5) L(t)   : Loan balance (current value, $) at time t
(6) r(t)   : The total rate of return on home investment at time t, C(NH)/C(H) in %
(7) r(a)   : The average annual rate of return on home investment at time t, r(t)/t (%)

The signs of the rate of return are changed. The positive sign indicates advantages of home ownership and the negative sign indicates the advantages of apartment renting.

*We note that the average annual rate of return is highest in the 12th year.

8.5%. The amortization period is 25 years. Thus the annual mortgage payment is $3,908.8 (7.8%). Maintenance, insurance, and other costs at the time of purchase is $750 (1.5%). The property tax is $1,000 (2%). So at the beginning of the year, the annual home ownership cost excluding the down payment and the closing cost is $5,658.8 (11.3%). The selling cost after a certain period of occupancy is assumed to be 8% of the sale value of the house.[6]

Alternatively, the consumer can rent an apartment for $5,000 (10% of the house value) for the base year and one month security deposit, $416.7. Also it is assumed that he can invest the cash not tied up in down payment $10,000 and the closing cost of $1,000 for the annual rate of return 6.5% which is lower than the mortgage rate by 2 percentage points. Also it is assumed that the house value, maintenance, insurance costs, property taxes, and apartment rent all increase at an annual rate of 3%.

Substituting these parameter values in the discrete versions of equations (4) and (5), using a simple computer program, we have calculated the home ownership cost and the apartment cost. The results are summarized in Table 2. A brief explanation may be useful to read the table.

First, the present values of home ownership and apartment renting are listed in columns 2 and 3, and the comparative cost

---

[6]When the down payment (20%), closing cost (2%) and the selling cost (8%) are averaged over 25 years, the average annual cost is about 0.9% of the house value. Adding to this, the annual home ownership cost $5,658.8 (11.3%), we obtain the average annual home ownership cost, 12.2% of the initial house value. Leeuw (1971) showed that the percentage of annual housing cost to the house value decreases from 15.2% to 10.5% as the average house value increases from $7,153 to $32,701. The average percentage is 12.2%.

advantages are listed in column 4. We note that home ownership costs more than apartment renting through the 5th year in
which the comparative cost advantage is $-518. However, in
the 6th year, home ownership costs less than apartment renting
by $2,530.[7] By the end of the 25th year, the comparative cost
advantage of home ownership reaches $52,737 in present value.

Second, the total rate of return on investment in home
ownership is listed in column 6. In the 5th year, the rate of
return is -2.8 ($-518/-18,668=0.028$). The negative sign is
added to indicate a negative rate of return. In the 25th year, the
total rate of return reaches $+94.9\%$.

Third, the annual average rate of return is listed in column
7. In the 5th year, it is -0.56% ($-2.8\%/5=-0.56\%$). We
note that the total rate of return increases continuously from
year 1 to year 25. However, the average rate of return increases
gradually and reaches the peak 4.88% in the 12th year and falls

---

[7]It should be noted that in this paper we are using the "payoff period"
and the "break-even year" in different senses: the payoff period is the number of years in which the home ownership cost is greater than the apartment
cost. The "break-even year" is the year in which the home ownership cost
just begins to be smaller than the apartment cost. The conventional definition
of "payoff period" or "payback period" refers to the time when the cost is
exactly equal to the revenue.

In this paper, the payoff period is five years in which the home ownership cost is greater than the apartment cost, and the break-even year is the
6th year in which the home ownership cost just turns to be smaller than the
apartment cost. The payback period in which the home ownership cost is
exactly equal to the apartment cost is 5 years and 2 months: $[518/(2530-
(-518))]+5$ years$=5.17$ years$=5$ years and 2 months.

The payoff period 5 years obtained in this paper is a little longer than
those obtained by Shelton (1968) and Lindberg (1969). The difference is
partly due to lower mortgage rates in their studies. Shelton used 6%, and
Lindberg used 7.5%. In the basic reference model in this paper 8.5% is used.
For results obtained with alternative mortgage rates, see Appendix Table 1.

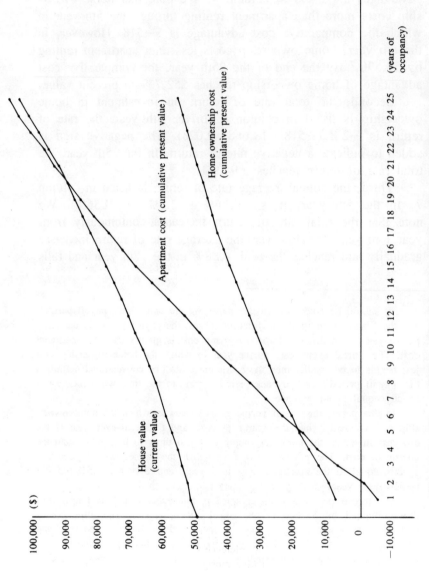

Figure 2   Home Ownership Cost, Apartment Cost, and House Value

Table 3. Comparative Cost Advantage of Home Ownership
(With Capital Gain Tax)

Years of occupancy	(1) G	(2) C'(NH)	(3) $\frac{C'(NH)}{C(H)} = r'(t)$	(4) $\frac{C'(NH)/C(H)}{t} = r'(a)$
1	(−425)	−12889	−162.84	−162.84
2	(−242)	− 9779	− 91.08	− 45.54
3	(− 76)	− 6677	− 49.58	− 16.53
4	75	− 3663	− 22.74	− 5.69
5	212	− 730	− 3.91	− 0.78
6	336	2194	10.38	1.73
7	448	5104	21.68	3.10
8	549	7994	30.92	3.87
9	640	10951	38.97	4.33
10	721	13701	45.26	4.53
11	793	16510	51.00	4.64
12	856	19350	56.25	4.69*
13	912	22028	60.57	4.66
14	962	24731	64.62	4.62
15	1004	27395	68.29	4.55
16	1041	30017	71.64	4.48
17	1072	32598	74.72	4.40
18	1099	35129	77.56	4.31
19	1121	37618	80.19	4.22
20	1138	40062	82.65	4.13
21	1152	42457	84.94	4.04
22	1162	44806	87.08	3.96
23	1168	47107	89.10	3.87
24	1172	49359	91.00	3.79
25	1173	51564	92.79	3.71

(1) G: The capital gain tax on home sale (present value, $)

(2) C' (NH): The comparative cost advantage of home ownership net of the capital gain tax = C(NH) − G = C(H) − C(A) − G. (present value, $)

(3) r'(t): The total rate of return on home ownership net of capital gain tax = C'(NH)/C(H) in %.

(4) r'(a): The average annual rate of return on home ownership net of capital gain tax = r'(t)/t = C'(NH)/C(H)·t.

The numbers in parentheses are capital losses on the home sale, and so the capital gain tax is zero since a capital loss on a residential home sale is not deductible for income tax.

339

back to 3.8% in the 25th year. This suggests that the optimal period of home occupancy is 12 years in our example.

In order to see the effect of the capital gain tax on the comparative cost advantage of home ownership, the following capital gain tax is added as another cost item of home ownership:

$$(-)G = (H_0 e^{gT} - H_0 - C_0 - bH_0 e^{gT})\, 0.5 \cdot a\, e^{-iT} \qquad (9)$$

where

G = the capital gain tax in the present value
H_0 = the initial house value, \$50,000,
C_0 = the initial closing cost, \$1,000,
$b\, H_0 e^{gT}$ = the selling cost, 8% of the selling price,
a = the effective marginal tax rate of the home seller, 25%.

Under the current tax law, the home seller can add 50% of the long term capital gain to the ordinary income. So the home seller will pay 12.5% (0.50×0.25) of the long term capital gain as tax when he sells the house. e^{-iT} is multiplied to obtain the present value of the capital gain tax, where $i=0.065$. (See Footnote 3).

The present values of the capital gain tax, the comparative cost advantage net of the capital gain tax, the total rate of return and the average rate of return net of the capital gain tax are listed in columns 1-4 of Table 3. We note the following points:

First, through the third year, there will be no capital gain tax since the home seller will incur a capital loss, and the capital loss is not deductible for the income tax. Second, the comparative cost advantages are reduced by the amount of the capital gain tax, ranging from \$75 in present value in the 4th year to \$1,173 in the 25th year. However, the payoff period of 5 years remains the same. Third, the total and the average rates of return are also reduced slightly. For instance, the total rate of return is decreased from 12% to 10.38%, and the average rate of return is decreased from 2% to 1.73% in the 6th year. However, the optimal number of years of home occupancy remains the same at 12 years, in which the average rate of return is the highest.

In summary, the basic reference model indicates that home ownership costs less than apartment renting if the home is occupied for 6 years or longer, and that the optimal period of home occupancy is 12 years in which the annual average rate of return is the highest. These results are not affected by the introduction of the capital gain tax. The growth paths of home ownership cost, apartment cost, and the current house value are depicted in Figure 2.

IV. Uncertainty and the Sensitivity Analysis

The above model of calculating the comparative cost advantage is determined by the following parameters: (1) mortgage rate, (2) discount rate, or the rate of return on alternative investment, (3) amortization period, (4) down payment or loan balance, (5) closing cost, (6) property tax, (7) income tax rate, (8) maintenance and insurance costs, (9) house value, (10) apartment rent, (11) resale fee, (12) growth rate or the growth path of the house value, and (13) inflation rates of other costs such as maintenance, insurance costs and property taxes.

In the above basic numerical example, we have assumed that the parameter values are given. However, in reality, many of the parameter values are uncertain. For instance, the rate of return on alternative investments, property tax rate, maintenance-insurance costs, growth rate of the house value, and the inflation rate are all uncertain future events.

Thus it is apparent that different combinations of parameter values will yield different results. To see the sensitivity of the model or the effects of changes in these parameter values, about 80 examples were computed. Since it is impossible to present all the results in the same form as Table 2 due to space limitation, the results are summarized in Appendix Tables 1-4, which are designed not only to save space but also help an easy comparison of effects of changes in parameter values.

In Appendix Tables 1-4, we have shown the following statistical results: (1) The payoff period and the comparative cost advantage, in column 1. (2) The break-even year and the comparative cost advantage, in column 2. (3) The comparative cost advantage in the 6th year, in column 3. (4) The total rate of return on home investment in the 25th year or the maturity year, in column 5. (5) The average annual rate of return on home investment, in column 6. Also we have shown two concepts of elasticity, namely, (6) the elasticity with respect to the comparative cost advantage, in column 4, and (7) the elasticity with respect to the total rate of return, in column 7.

The formula for the elasticity with respect to the comparative cost advantage is given by:

$$\frac{(\% \text{ change in the comparative cost advantage in the 6th year})}{(\% \text{ change in the parameter value})} = E(C) \qquad (10)$$

For instance, in the basic reference model, when the mortgage rate is 8.5%, the break-even period is 6 years, and the comparative cost advantage is $2,530. However, when the mortgage rate decreases to 8%, holding all other parameters constant except that the discount rate is also reduced to 6%, the comparative cost advantage increases to $4,597 in the 6th year. In other words, as a result of a decrease in the mortgage rate by 5.88%, the comparative cost advantage has increased by 81.7%. Dividing 81.7% by −5.88%, we obtain the elasticity value −13.89, as listed in Appendix Table 1, column 4, Example No. 5. No. 5.

The elasticity with respect to the total rate of return is given by:

$$\frac{(\% \text{ change in the total rate of return in the 25th year or the maturity year})}{(\% \text{ change in the parameter value})} = E(T) \qquad (11)$$

For instance, in the basic reference model, when the mortgage rate is 8.5%, the total rate of return in the 25th year is 94.9%. When the mortgage rate decreases to 8%, by 5.88%, the total rate of return in the 25th year increases to 113.4%, or by 19.49%. Dividing 19.49% by −5.88%, we obtain the elasticity value −3.32, which is listed in Appendix Table 1, column 7.

Of these two measures of elasticity, we note that the elasticity with respect to the comparative cost advantage produced most conspicuous results. In terms of this elasticity measure, all parameters except one, closing cost, have the absolute value of elasticity greater than one. Thus we may conclude that the model is highly sensitive with respect to mortgage rate, discount rate, amortization period, down payment, apartment rent relative to house value, sales fee, property tax, income tax rate, maintenance-insurance costs, the rate of inflation, and the growth path of house value.

Some policy implications of the above analysis of payoff period, elasticity, and the rate of return are discussed in the following section.

V. Policy Implications

In the above sections, we have shown a model of calculating the comparative cost advantages of home ownership and apartment renting, and some numerical examples with alternative parameter values. We have calculated the payoff period; the total and average annual rates of return on home investment; and the elasticities with respect to the total rate of return and the comparative cost advantages, as shown in Table 2 and Appendix Tables 1-4. This type of information may be useful not only for the potential home buyers in their decision making between home purchase and apartment renting, but also for some public policy formulation and evaluation.

As an example of public policy implications, a group of economists, including Goode (1960), White and White (1965), and Laidler (1969), pointed out that home owners are much favorably treated than renters in that imputed rental income is not taxed, and that interest payments on mortgage loans and local property taxes are deducted from the federal income taxation. For fairness of taxation, if the imputed rental income is to be taxed, and if the deduction system is to be abolished, the comparative cost advantage of home ownership will be further reduced. Our analysis indicates that if the federal income tax deduction system of the property tax and interest payments is abolished, the payoff period will increase from 5 years to 7 years, and the average annual rate of return on home investment will decrease from 3.8% to 2.4%. (See Appendix Table 3, Example No. 36.) How much this will discourage home ownership will depend upon an empirical investigation. However, for the sake of fairness of taxation between home owners and apartment renters, if taxation on imputed rental income is to be adopted, and/or if the deduction system for property tax and interest payments is to be abolished, such policies may be applied to individual home owners only after the payoff period has passed, since the home ownership cost is greater than the apartment cost during the payoff period.

Another group of economists, such as Morton (1955), Heilbrun (1969) and Eisenmenger and others (1975), advocated lower property taxes to encourage housing construction and rehabilitation of owner-occupied homes and apartmental dwellings as well as business structures. In Appendix Table 3, Example No. 34, we note that if the property tax rate decreases from 2% to 1%, the payoff period decreases from 5 years to 4 years, and the average annual rate of return increases from 3.8% to 4.8%. (The elasticity with respect to the comparative cost advantage is −1.26). If the property tax is completely eliminated, the payoff period will be 4 years and the average annual rate of return increases from 3.8% to 6.1%. These results suggest that manipulation of property tax rate may be very much effective to encourage housing construction, rehabilitation and home ownership.

However, the above two policy suggestions are apparently in conflict. The first argument advocates an increase in taxes for home owners, while the second advocates a decrease in taxes for home owners. These two apparently conflicting proposals may be reconciled in the light of payoff period analysis as presented in this paper, that is, by adopting a flexible tax program. For instance, during the payoff period a lower property tax rate may be adopted or property tax may be eliminated during the early years of payoff period, and a higher property tax rate may be applied after the payoff period is passed. Such a policy has two objectives: one, to shorten the payoff period to encourage the home ownership, and two, to maintain the fair taxation principle between home owners and apartment renters.

As to the mortgage policies, Appendix Table 1 indicates the following results:(1) If the mortgage rate decreases from 8.5% to 7.5%, the payoff period decreases from 5 years to 4 years, and the average annual rate of return increases from 3.8% to 4.5%. (The elasticity with respect to the comparative cost advantage is −9.90). (2) If the amortizaton period is increased from 25 years to 30 years, the payoff period decreases from 5 years to 4 years, and the average annual rate of return falls from 3.8% to 3.6%. (The elasticity with respect to the comparative cost advantages is 1.79). (3) If the down payment is reduced from 20% to 10% of the house value, the payoff period decreases from 5 years to 4 years, and the average annual rate of return decreases from 3.8% to 3.7%. If the down payment is completely abolished, the payoff period decreases from 5 years to 2 years, and the average rate of return decreases from 3.8% to 3.7%. We note that the payoff period and the average annual rate of return do not necessarily move in the same direction in favor of a longer amortization period and a smaller down payment. However, if the consumers are more sensitive to the payoff period than to the rate of return, the public policy should be directed toward a decrease in the amount of down payment and a longer amortization period. These policies will certainly increase the rate of home ownership especially among the low income consumers.

Another public policy suggestion is concerned with the home purchasing and selling practices. As Appendix Table 2, Example No. 30, indicates, if the sales fee decreases from 8% to 6%, the payoff period decreases from 5 years to 4 years, and the average annual rate of return increases from 3.8% to 3.86%. (The elasticity with respect to the comparative cost advantage is −1.29). Thus a decrease in the sales fee will encourage home ownership. Furthermore, the "snowball effect" of sales cost on the house value should be noted.[8] Even if the home seller wishes to recover only his initial purchase price, he has to charge a higher price than his initial purchase price to cover the sales cost. The high sales cost relative to house value will not only push up the house value in general in the area, but also will prolong the period of idle home occupancy.

One possible method of reducing the sales fee, the rate and period of idle occupancy, and most of all the hardship which new residents as well as old residents face in search for a new

---

[8]Assume that a first consumer bought a home at $50,000, and he wishes to resell the home without any capital gain, but at his initial purchase price. To cover the 8% of the selling commission charge, he will have to charge $54,347.826. If the second buyer wishes to resell the home, he will have to charge $59,073.723. The third buyer will have to charge $64,210.568...These increases in the value of the house are purely due to selling commission fee and it is neither for any improvement to the house nor for the general inflation. In the above example, the house value will rise by 8.7% at every transaction.

residence is to establish a government or community sponsored "home clearing and exchange center," or simply what may be called a "home clearing center" in every area all over the country, just as there are employment service offices all over the nation. By such a local home clearing center, not only the excessive inflationary sales costs can be reduced, but also two consumers may be able to "exchange" homes in two locations without appreciating the house values excessively, when the two consumers are switching their locations of residence and employment. Home exchange may be necessary between two consumers not only in two different locations, but also between the "growing family" and the "retiring family" in the same area.

The significance and the usefulness of an employment service agency as a clearing center for the labor market is widely recognized, and yet a clearing center for the housing market does not seem to have been proposed elsewhere in spite of the significance of residential homes and apartments. If a higher rate of home ownership is a desirable policy objective, the rate of home ownership will be also increased by a decrease in hardship in search for a new residence through such a home clearing center. The labor mobility will also increase due to the easiness of home search and home sale.

VI. Summary

As a final summary, in this paper we have demonstrated the following; (1) In a general situation, home ownership costs more than apartment renting during the first 5 years of home occupancy. (2) However, if some public policies are wisely adopted, the payoff period may be further reduced, and the rate of return on home investment may be increased, increasing the rate of home ownership. Such public policies may include: (1) Easy mortgage policies concerning down payment, amortization period, as well as a lower mortgage rate. (2) Flexible property tax programs which would require a lower property tax rate during the payoff period and a higher property tax rate after the payoff period. (3) A home clearing center to reduce the inflationary pressure due to high sales costs, to reduce the hardship involved in home search, and to reduce the rate and the period of idle home occupancy. The sensitivity of such policies was tested in Section IV in terms of sensitivity analysis, and the results are summarized in Appendix Tables 1-4.

Appendix Table 1. Mortgage Terms

Example number and Parameter values	(1) Payoff period year (and amount, $)	(2) Break-even year (and amount, $)	(3) 6th year comparative cost advantage	(4) Elasticity (cost advantage)	(5) Total return at maturity (%)	(6) Average annual return (%)	(7) Elasticity (total return)
I. Mortgage rate (m)							
(2) 0.0%($1600.0=K)	2(−1024)	3(5929)	24893		283.7	11.3	
(3) 7.0%($3432.8)	4(−453)	5(3270)	6924		122.1	4.9	
(4) 7.5%($3588.8)	4(−1487)	5(2021)	5476		112.7	4.5	
(5) 8.0%($3747.2)	4(−2227)	5(1194)	4597	−13.89	113.4	4.5	−3.32
* 8.5%($3908.8)	5(−518)	6(2530)	2530		94.9	3.8	
(6) 9.0%($4072.4)	5(−2192)	6(517)	517	−13.53	78.5	3.1	−2.94
(7) 9.5%($4238.4)	6(−475)	7(2158)	−475		78.3	3.1	
(8)10.0%($4406.8)	6(2099)	7(323)	−2099		70.2	2.8	

(K = annual mortgage payments: Discount rate i varies with m: i = m−2%)

	(1)	(2)	(3)	(4)	(5)	(6)	(7)
II. Discount rate (i)							
* 6.5%	5(−518)	6(2530)	2530		94.9	3.8	
(9) 8.5	5(−2077)	6(454)	454	−2.67	65.2	2.6	−1.01
(10)10.5	6(−1391)	7(579)	−1391		43.3	1.7	

(Mortgage rate m is held constant at 8.5%.)

III. Amortization maturity period (n)

(11) 0 years, no mortgage	9(−2797)	10(2184)	−18781		106.9	4.3	
(12) 20 ($4227.2)	5(−1844)	6(984)	984	+3.06	77.6	3.9	+0.91
* 25 ($3908.8)	5(− 518)	6(2530)	2530		94.9	3.8	
(13) 30 ($3722.4)	4(−2949)	5(259)	3436	+1.79	196.5	3.6	+0.61
(14) 35 ($3607.6)	4(−2555)	5(737)	3993		114.7	4.6	

IV. Down payment (D)

(15) $ 0 (0%, $4886)	2(−1536)	3(767)	7858		91.9	3.7	
(16) 5,000 (10%, $4397.4)	4(−1322)	5(2226)	5720	+2.52	93.4	3.7	+0.03
* 10,000 (20%, $3908.8)	5(− 518)	6(2530)	2530		94.9	3.8	
(17) 15,000 (30%, $3420.2)	6(− 134)	7(3198)	−134	+2.11	96.4	3.9	+0.03
# 50,000 (100%)	9(−2797)	10(2184)	−18781		106.9	4.3	

Note: The parameter values with asterisk * are those assumed in the basic reference model to which model number 1 is assigned. See Tables 1 and 2. Unless specified, all other values are held constant as in the basic reference model. # No mortgage, the same as No. 11.

350

Appendix Table 2. House Value, Apartment Rent, Closing and Sales Costs

Example number and Parameter values	(1) Payoff period year (and amount, $)	(2) Break-even year (and amount, $)	(3) 6th year comparative cost advantage	(4) Elasticity (cost advantage)	(5) Total return at maturity (%)	(6) Average annual return (%)	(7) Elasticity (total return)
IV. House Value (H)							
(18) $20,000	5(− 207)	6(1012)	1012		94.9	3.8	
(19) $30,000	5(− 311)	6(1518)	1518		94.9	3.8	
(20) $40,000	5(− 414)	6(2024)	2024		94.9	3.8	
* $50,000	5(− 518)	6(2530)	2530		94.9	3.8	
(21) $60,000	5(− 207)	6(3036)	3036		94.9	3.8	

(Apartment rent also varies with the house value as 10% of the house value.)

Example number and Parameter values	(1) Payoff period year (and amount, $)	(2) Break-even year (and amount, $)	(3) 6th year comparative cost advantage	(4) Elasticity (cost advantage)	(5) Total return at maturity (%)	(6) Average annual return (%)	(7) Elasticity (total return)
V. Apartment Rent (A)							
(22) $4,000 (8%)	11(− 843)	12(656)	−8189	+21.18	34.8	1.4	+3.17
* $5,000 (10%)	5(− 518)	6(2530)	2530		94.9	3.8	
(23) $6,000 (12%)	3(−1049)	4(3794)	13250	+21.19	155.0	6.2	+3.17
(24) $7,000 (14%)	2(−2150)	3(4580)	23969		215.1	8.6	

(House value stays the same at $50,000.)

VI. Closing Cost (C)

(25) $ 0 (0%)							
(26) $ 500 (1%)	4(2588)	5(482)	3530	−0.79	97.6	3.9	−0.06
* $1000 (2%)	5(− 518)	6(2530)	2530	−0.79	94.9	3.8	
(27) $1500 (3%)	5(−1517)	6(1530)	1530	−0.79	92.3	3.7	−0.05

VII. Sales Fee (b)

(28) 0.0%	4(− 89)	5(2867)	8717		101.2	4.05	
(29) 4.0	4(−1839)	5(1175)	4167		98.0	3.92	
(30) 6.0	4(−2714)	5(328)	3349		96.4	3.86	
(31) 7.0	5(− 94)	6(2940)	2940	−1.30	95.7	3.83	−0.07
* 8.0	5(− 518)	6(2530)	2530		94.9	3.80	
(32) 10.0	5(−1364)	6(1712)	1712	−1.29	93.4	3.74	−0.06

352

Appendix Table 3. Property Tax, Income Tax Rate, Maintenance-Insurance Costs and the Rate of Inflation

Example number and Parameter values	(1) Payoff period year (and amount,$)	(2) Break-even year (and amount,$)	(3) 6th year comparative cost advantage ($)	(4) Elasticity (cost advantage)	(5) Total return at maturity (%)	(6) Average annual return (%)	(7) Elasticity (total return)
VIII. Property Tax (P)							
(33) $ 0 (0%)	4(− 527)	5(2879)	6540		151.5	6.1	
(34) 500 (1%)	4(−2208)	5(1180)	4535	−1.58	119.6	4.8	−0.52
* 1000 (2%)	5(− 518)	6(2530)	2530		94.9	3.8	
(35) 1500 (3%)	5(−2215)	6(525)	525	−1.58	75.2	3.0	−0.42
IX. Income Tax Rate (a)							
(36) 0 (%)	7(− 458)	8(1888)	−2786		59.5	2.4	
(37) 20	5(−1432)	6(1467)	1467	+2.10	86.6	3.5	+0.44
* 25	5(− 518)	6(2530)	2530		94.9	3.8	
(38) 30	4(−2833)	5(397)	3594	+2.10	103.9	4.2	
(39) 35	4(−2078)	5(1311)	4657		113.4	4.5	
(40) 40	4(−1322)	5(2226)	5720		124.8	5.0	+0.47

X. Maintenance-Insurance Costs (M+E)

(41) $ 500 (1%)	4(−2668)	5(614)	3867	−1.59	110.7	4.4	−0.50
* 750 (1.5%)	5(− 518)	6(2530)	2530		94.9	3.8	
(42) 1000 (2%)	5(−1650)	6(1194)	1194	−1.58	81.3	3.3	−0.43

XI. The Rate of Inflation (g)

(43) −1 (%)		25(−7335)	−11072		−12.3	−0.5	
(44) 0	15(− 270)	16(336)	−7883		7.3	0.3	
(45) 1	8(−1286)	9(256)	−4557		30.7	1.2	
(46) 2	6(−1088)	7(1227)	−1088	+4.29	59.2	2.4	+1.13
* 3	5(− 518)	6(2530)	2530		94.9	3.8	
(47) 4	4(−1249)	5(2519)	6302	+4.47	141.1	5.6	+1.46
(48) 5	3(−3278)	4(1152)	10234		203.7	8.1	
(49) 6	3(−1533)	4(3615)	14331		293.9	11.8	
(50) 7	2(−5423)	3(241)	18598		436.4	17.5	
(51) 8	2(−4311)	3(2046)	23043		697.5	27.9	
(52) 9	2(−3188)	3(3882)	27672		1338.5	53.5	
(53) 10	2(−2056)	3(5749)	32490		5498.9	220.0	

(House value, maintenance-insurance costs and all other costs increase at the same rate.)

Appendix Table 4. House Value Growth Path

Example number and Parameter values	(1) Payoff period year (and amount,$)	(2) Break-even year (and amount,$)	(3) 6th year comparative cost advantage($)	(4) Elasticity (cost advantage)	(5) Total return at maturity (%)	(6) Average annual return (%)	(7) Elasticity (total return)
XII. House Value Growth Path $H=H_0(1+g)^t$							
(54) −2 (%)	23(− 375)	24(104)	−11482		0.89	0.004	
(55) −1	19(− 479)	20(29)	−9728		3.6	0.1	
(56) 0	15(− 270)	16(336)	−7883		7.3	0.3	
(57) 1	11(− 462)	12(400)	−5944		12.4	0.5	
(58) 2	8(−1025)	9(244)	−3906		19.6	0.8	
(59) 3	7(− 2)	8(1619)	−1766		30.0	1.2	
(60) 4	5(−1757)	6(481)	481		47.0	1.9	
(61) 5	4(−2548)	5(245)	2838		74.0	3.0	
(62) 6	4(− 868)	5(2325)	5311		127.9	5.12	
(63) 7	3(−2987)	4(859)	7902		272.0	10.88	
(64) 8	3(−1667)	4(2686)	10618		1686.1	67.44	
(65) 9	3(− 322)	4(4463)	13463		576.8	23.07	
(66) 10	2(−4428)	3(1048)	16440		284.0	11.39	
* 3%	5(− 518)	6(2530)	2530		94.9	3.8	

(Only house value grows; other costs, tax and rent remain constant at the initial values.)

XIII. House Value Growth Path

(67) $H = 110{,}000 - 6{,}000$ $(0.92)^t$	$3(-\ 95)$	$4(4093)$	11305	93.5	3.7
(68) $H = 50{,}000 + 4{,}000t$ $-160t^2$	$3(-2166)$	$4(1535)$	7913	64.1	2.6
(69) $H = 50{,}000 + 8{,}000t$ $-320t^2$	$2(-\ 309)$	$3(5877)$	19414	64.1	2.6
(70) $H = 50{,}000 + 1{,}000t$ $-80t^2$	$6(-1620)$	$7(\ 571)$	-1620	53.1	2.1
(71) $H = 50{,}000 + 2{,}000t$ $-160t^2$	$5(-1836)$	$6(\ 347)$	347	43.3	1.7
* $H = 50{,}000$ $\cdot (1+0.03)^t$	$5(-\ 518)$	$6(2530)$	2530	94.9	3.8

(All other costs increase at the rate of 3% per year.)

XIV. House Value Growth Path

(72) $H = 110{,}000 - 6{,}000$ $\cdot (0.92)^t$	$3(-1443)$	$4(1915)$	7008	29.0	1.2
(73) $H = 50{,}000 + 4{,}000t$ $-160t^2$	$4(-\ 642)$	$5(1713)$	3617	7.3	0.3
(74) $H = 50{,}000 + 8{,}000t$ $-320t^2$	$2(-1005)$	$3(4529)$	15117	7.3	0.3
(75) $H = 50{,}000 + 1{,}000t$ $-80t^2$	$...\#$	$25(-423)$	-5916	-0.7	-0.003
(76) $H = 50{,}000 + 2{,}000t$ $-160t^2$	$...\#$	$25(-5187)$	-3949	-7.5	-0.3
* $H = 50{,}000$ $(1 + 0.03)^t$	$5(-\ 518)$	$6(2530)$	2530	94.9	3.8

(Only house value changes, all other costs, and tax remain constant at the initial values.)

356

XV. House Value Growth Path

(77)	$H = 110{,}000 - 6{,}000 \cdot (0.92)^t$	2(−3370)	3(1195)	12013	87.6	3.5
(78)	$H = 50{,}000 + 4{,}000t - 160t^2$	3(− 804)	4(2797)	8926	70.4	2.8
(79)	$H = 50{,}000 + 8{,}000t - 320t^2$	1(−6099)	2(1019)	19273	56.5	2.3
(80)	$H = 50{,}000 + 1{,}000t - 80t^2$	5(−2062)	6(306)	306	74.0	3.0
(81)	$H = 50{,}000 + 2{,}000t - 160t^2$	5(− 227)	6(2033)	2033	62.6	2.5
*	$H = 50{,}000 \cdot (1 + 0.03)^t$	5(− 518)	6(2530)	2530	94.9	3.8

(Property tax, maintenance-insurance costs follow the house value growth path, i.e., P(t)=0.02 H(t), M(t)+E(t)=0.015 H(t).

Note: # indicates that there is no payoff period during the amortization period. The house value growth paths are depicted in Appendix Figure 1 to show that the house value can take various growth paths, and that the total rate of return measured at the maturity year can be misleading.

357

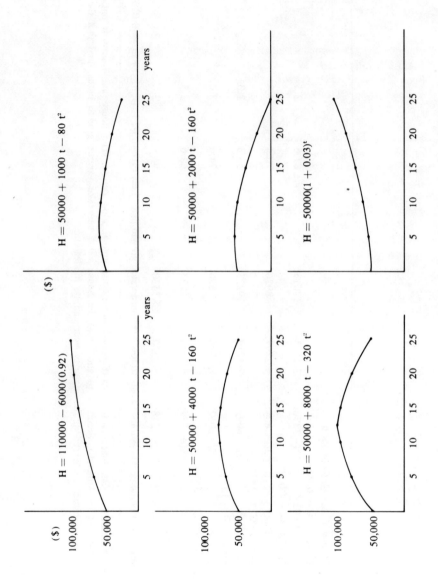

$H = 110000 - 6000(0.92)$

$H = 50000 + 4000\,t - 160\,t^2$

$H = 50000 + 8000\,t - 320\,t^2$

$H = 50000 + 1000\,t - 80\,t^2$

$H = 50000 + 2000\,t - 160\,t^2$

$H = 50000(1 + 0.03)^t$

Appendix Figure 1   Possible Growth Paths of House Value

REFERENCES

Carliner, G., "Determinants of Home Ownership," *Land Economics*, May, 1974, pp. 109-119.

Curry, C.F., and D.H. Gensch, "Feasibility of Rent Tax Incentives for Renovation in Older Residential Neighborhoods," *Management Science*, April 1975, pp. 883-896.

Eisenmenger, R.W., and Others, "Needed: A New Tax Structure for Massachusetts," *New England Economic Journal*, Federal Reserve Bank of Boston, May/June, 1975, pp. 3-24.

Goode, R., "Imputed Rent of Owner Occupied Dwellings Under the Income Tax," *Journal of Finance*, Dec. 1960, pp. 504-530.

Heilbrun, J., "Reforming the Real Estate Tax to Encourage Housing Maintenance and Rehabilitation," in A.P. Becker, ed., *Land and Building Taxes: Their Effect on Economic Development*, 1969, ch. 3.

Kain, J.F., and J.M. Quigley, "Measuring the Value of Housing Quality," *Journal of the American Statistical Association*, June 1970, pp. 532-548.

Laidler, D., "Income Tax Incentives for Owner Occupied Housing," in A. Harberger, ed., *Taxation of Income from Capital*, 1969, pp. 50-76.

Leeuw, F. de, "The Demand for Housing: A Review of Cross-Section Evidence," *Review of Economics and Statistics*, Feb. 1971, pp. 1-10.

Lindberg, P. "Is Home Still A Good Investment?" *Better Homes and Gardens*, Sept. 1969, pp. 46-54.

Maisel, S., "Rates of Home Ownership, Mobility and Purchase," in *Essays in Urban Land Economics, in Honor of Sixty Five Birthday of Leo Grebler*, 1966, pp. 76-108.

Morgan, J.N., "Housing and Ability to Pay," *Econometrica*, April, 1965, pp. 289-306.

Morris, E.W., M.E. Woods, and A.L., Jacobson, "The Measurement of Housing Quality," *Land Economics*, Nov. 1972, pp. 583-587.

Morton, W.A., *Housing Taxation*, 1955.

Shelton, J.P., "The Cost of Renting Versus Owning a Home," *Land Economics*, Feb. 1968, pp. 59-72.

Struyk, R., and S.A. Marshall, "Income and Urban Home Ownership," *Review of Economics and Statistics*, Feb. 1975, pp. 19-26.

White, M. and A. White, "Horizontal Inequality in the Federal Income Tax Treatment of Homeowners and Tenants," *National Tax Journal*, Sept. 1965, pp. 225-239.

Index

361

Eisenmenger, R.W., 344
Elasticity
    comparative cost advantage of
        home ownership, 342
    in economic policy, 194
    price expectation, 73
Emulation effect
    consumption, 119
    investment, 119
Evans, M., 315, 320
Excess demand for labor theory,
    7-9
Expectation hypothesis of
    inflation, 135
Expected rate of inflation,
    4, 73, 136
Expected stock price, 44

Financial assets, 274
Fisher, I., 141
Fisher effect, 40
Friedlander, A.F., 230, 233
Friedman, M., 5, 130, 141,
    173, 197, 312
Friend, I., 244, 254, 274

Game theory, 259
Generalized inflation theory,
    10-18
Generalized statement of quantity
    theory, 13
Gensch, D.H., 252

Gibson, W.E., 74, 91
Goode, R., 252, 254, 344, 359
Grebler, L., 244, 254
Growth-inflation hypothesis,
    10-18
Grunewald, A.E., 259
Growing family, 347
Gurley, J., 75, 91

Hamburger, M.J., 37, 66,
    313,320
Hanson, A.W., 322
Harrod, R.F., 115, 125
Haugen, R.A., 252, 254
Hester, D.D., 173, 197
Heilbrun, J., 344
Heins, A.J., 252
Hicks, J.R., 9
Higgins, B., 118
High powered money, 156
Hinrichs, H.H., 94
Hirschman, A.O., 124
Holt, C.C., 9, 34
Homa, K.E., 37, 66
Home Clearing and Exchange
    Center, 347
Home investment
    average annual rate of return,
        337, 343
    total rate of return, 337, 343
Home ownership cost, 321, 325
    advantage over apartment
        renting, 334
    with capital gain tax, 339